The Liberation of Sovereign Peoples

THE FRENCH FOREIGN POLICY OF 1848

La Sainte Alliance des Peuples, bas-relief executed by Carpeaux, Musée de Valenciennes.

The Liberation of Sovereign Peoples

THE FRENCH FOREIGN POLICY OF 1848

James Chastain

OHIO UNIVERSITY PRESS □ ATHENS

Library of Congress Cataloging-in-Publication Data

Chastain, James.
   The liberation of sovereign people: the French foreign policy of 1848 /
James Chastain.
        p.   cm.
   Bibliography: p.
   Includes index.
   ISBN 0-8214-0888-7 :
   1. France—History—Second Republic, 1848–1852. 2. France—Foreign
relations—1848–1870. 3. France—Foreign relations—Europe. 4. Europe—
Foreign relations—France. 5. Lamartine, Alphonse de, 1790–1869—
Influence. I. Title.
DC273.6.C47 1988
944.07—dc19   88-1240
                                                                     CIP

TABLE OF CONTENTS

ILLUSTRATIONS

frontispiece La Sainte Alliance des Peuples, bas-relief executed by Carpeaux, Musée de Valenciennes.

p. 23 Departure of the Poles at Mairie of IIeme Arrondissement: "These brave then after having shed their blood on the barricades for liberty and France, thought that the hour of deliverance of their country had arrived. Whilst trusting in our promises, they proceed to face their oppressors, shall we permit the world to think that the French forgot them? (the 30th March)," lithograph by V. Adam and J. Arnout, Bibliothèque Nationale (Paris).

p. 58 Alexandre Bixio, French Envoy in Turin, by Honoré Daumier, Bibliothèque Nationale (Paris).

p. 84 Jules Bastide, French Minister of Foreign Affairs, by Honoré Daumier, Bibliothèque Nationale (Paris).

p. 112 The Uprising by Honoré Daumier, The Phillips Collection (Washington, D.C.).

p. 134 General Eugene Cavaignac (1802–57), painting by Ary Scheffer, Musée de Versailles.

p. 176 Charles Ludwig Bernays, French Secret Agent and Secretary to Legation in Vienna, photograph, Missouri Historical Society.

p. 216 Emmanuel Arago, French Envoy in Berlin, by Honoré Daumier, Bibliothèque Nationale (Paris).

ACKNOWLEDGMENTS

Research was supported by grants from the Ohio University Research Institute, American Philosophical Society (Penrose Fund), German Academic Exchange Service, and the Fulbright Commission.

The Liberation of Sovereign Peoples

THE FRENCH FOREIGN POLICY OF 1848

Prologue
New Personnel for the Republic

*T*HE FALL OF THE FRENCH KING Louis Philippe in the February Revolution of 1848 overturned an old order and reverberated throughout Europe. Memories of the wars of the great French Revolution struck terror in the chancelleries of the major powers, especially in Austria and Russia; for this was an age of idealism, of unbounded faith in the potency of ideas, of the belief that idea and action followed in a direct relationship like lightning and thunder. And while no one expected an immediate reappearance of French legions on the horizon, the great powers feared an advance guard of propagandists, followed by subversives bent on undermining the foundations of the existing power structures.

The best-known figure of the new French regime was Alphonse de Lamartine, the literary and political embodiment of revolt. Recent author of a popular history of the French Revolution, poet, orator, and rabble rouser, Lamartine took command of a Provisional Government which included Louis Blanc and Alexandre Martin (known as Albert), the first self-declared socialists to sit in a European government; Ledru-Rollin and Flocon, radicals associated with the newspaper *La Réforme*; as well as seven moderates. Four years earlier, when Karl Marx and Arnold Ruge had journeyed to Paris to establish a cooperative forum that would combine the best in German and French revolutionary thought, one of the first potential collaborators they identified was Deputy Lamartine, already the best-known opponent of the repression of free thought.

Lamartine epitomized the political dilemma of modern French history: the endeavor to bridge the gap between the several French revolutionary traditions. Having popularized the use of the term "Girondins," Lamartine both recognized the failings of this group and strove to avoid their mistakes. As moderate revolutionaries, the Girondins' fatal error had been to arouse the mistrust of the Mountain, which divided the revolutionary left. Thus the historically conscious Lamartine included representatives of all the major anti-monarchist revolutionary factions in the Provisional Government of 1848. Not only did the Provisional Government embrace the successors to the moderate Girondists of the Year I (1792), but it hoped to ally itself with the extremist sympathizers of Robespierre and even Babeuf.

Representative of this extremist faction was Lamartine's chief assistant in directing French foreign affairs, the implacable zealot Jules Bastide, who combined ideological purity and honesty with the steel nerves required for action under stressful exigencies. The leader of the charge on the Tuileries Palace in the July revolution of 1830, this intrepid street fighter and Carbonarist conspirator had been arrested during an insurrection in Grenoble during 1832, but had been acquitted by a jury. Condemned to death in absentia for his participation in a Paris uprising on June 5, 1831, Bastide escaped to London. In 1834 he returned to Paris, where he once more was acquitted by a jury. For the next few years the devout Bastide worked as a journalist associated with the extreme Roman Catholic socialist left. Bastide saw both Robespierre and Christ as defenders of the common man. In 1848, he joined a cabinet that was primarily composed of other radical journalists.[1]

The issue in 1848 was whether or not Lamartine could reformulate Doumouriez's contradictory diplomatic system of 1792. The system was based both on the Declaration of the Rights of Man and Citizen, and on the decree of May 22, 1790, which had promised that France would never fight a war of conquest, yet, somehow would free all mankind from "oppression." It remained to be seen whether Lamartine would be any more successful than Doumouriez in making diplomacy frank, open, and pacific without inciting a hostile coalition to declare war on the republic. In order to accomplish this, he would have to fulfill the Girondist promise to liberate the "oppressed," while avoiding the blatant interference in the internal affairs of France's neighbors that Doumouriez had exercised. Above all, Lamartine could not allow Parisian radicals to take control in their impatience to immediately liberate all Europe from "oppression." The radicals of 1848 seemed determined to repeat the ill-advised actions of the Jacobins of the National Convention; that is, they might attempt to reissue some variant of the historic decree of December 15, 1792, which had set Europe on fire in a revolutionary war by promising to end the oppression of "peoples" by the privileged castes. Lamartine realized that the fate of the Second Republic hinged on two negative calculations: not rousing the fears of hostile powers, and not allowing extremist elements in Paris to launch a brash military crusade against the crowned heads of Europe. The joint command of Lamartine and Bastide hoped to fuse the two major revolutionary currents, the Girondin and the Jacobin, in order to circumvent such a misfortune. Bastide represented the radical Christian socialist-Jacobin element peculiar to the 1848 revolution who glorified equally Robespierre and Jesus as revolutionists, and Lamartine, author of a *History of the Girondins*, stood for moderation.

Publicly, both Lamartine and Bastide emphasized the positive aspect of the diplomatic programs of the Girondins and the Mountain, particularly the pacific pledge of open and frank relations. From the outset, however, Lamartine and Bastide secretly embraced a foreign policy which was revolutionary in both means and ends. Thus, a tension existed between revolutionary public rhetoric and the moderate language used in diplomatic discourse.[2]

Lamartine and Bastide faced a problem common to all revolutionary governments—that of being forced to carry on diplomatic relations at several levels. Secretly, they maintained links to members of the traditional diplomatic corps, whom they attempted to convince that France meant no harm to governments of other European states. This entailed persuading the diplomats that Lamartine was doing everything humanly possible to hold back the hotheads within his own cabinet. Simultaneously, Lamartine made public promises that he would lend support to sister republics that might spring up across the continent.

The diplomatic agents of the major powers generally reported to their home governments that Lamartine was a "moderate" who was "for the moment" the only person capable of taming the whirlwind. The *gros mots* that were reported in the press, Lamartine assured them, were added by his more extremist colleagues in the Provisional Government. Thus, the reports of the accredited representatives of the great powers were couched in almost identical words. Count Heinrich von Arnim of Prussia, Count Anton Apponyi of Austria (the most skeptical about Lamartine's honesty), Count Paul Kiselev of Russia, and especially Constantine Henry Phipps, Lord Normanby, the British Ambassador, were all, to some degree, taken in by Lamartine's assurances that he meant no harm to their governments. Presenting himself as the sane voice of moderation, the French leader begged for time to tame the brutal forces unleashed by the upheaval in France.

At the same time, the former editor of the radical journal *La Réforme*, Ferdinand Flocon, one of the self-styled socialists in the Provisional Government, was just as assiduously reassuring foreign extremists like Frederick Engels that France would remain the arsenal for revolution, supplying weapons and moral support for insurrections against the old order. These revolutionary leaders left Paris with a public promise, delivered by Lamartine himself in his "Manifesto to Europe," that France would never allow any power to re-establish the old order in a sister republic that had overthrown its monarch. Such a public statement was a direct challenge to the entire diplomatic system of Prince Clemens von Metternich of Austria, who, ever since the Congress of Vienna, had repressed revolutions in Italy, Spain, and Poland through the united congress system.

Since Bastide and Lamartine had little direct knowledge of conditions in east central Europe, they were heavily dependent on the advice of Prince Adam Czartoryski, the exiled "King of Poland" living in France, and of his well-organized network of secret agents throughout the Balkans.[3] More importantly, Czartoryski provided France with a program for her actions, joining a principle of nationalism and federalism into a sort of universal cure to guarantee a future balance. What Czartoryski envisaged was a Danubian federation stretching from Vienna to the Black Sea; an Italy of federated states, and a federated Germany (which would necessarily raise the matter of Poland); as well as a transformed relationship between Paris and Vienna. Such a configuration might checkmate Russia's domination of the nations on her European borders.[4]

Soon after the February Revolution of 1848, Adam Czartoryski proposed to Lamartine that they attempt to reorganize east central Europe. With the collapse of Metternich's regime, France could act as midwife for a new system to replace Austria's control of central Europe. France, urged Czartoryski, should assume the mission of transforming east central Europe by establishing a federation of Danubian peoples.

While France continued official contacts with the diplomats of the great powers, her foreign policy was animated by a new revolutionary spirit. According to the personnel records at the Quai d'Orsay, following the February Revolution, the Provisional Government recalled France's diplomatic personnel to Paris and asked for a personal oath of loyalty. Those who gave such an oath were reassigned to new posts and given oral instructions; so Lamartine claimed in his history of 1848. He also indicated that in addition to the traditional corps of diplomats, the Provisional Government sent out another group of emissaries, secret agents accredited to the underworld of revolutionary leaders. Through Bastide's *chef de cabinet*, Jules Hetzel, as well as through Czartoryski's network, the French foreign ministers had direct links to the violent foreign revolutionaries.

Jules Hetzel's correspondence, until now unexamined by historians, utterly belies Lamartine's professed pacific intent. Indeed, Hetzel's office was an instrument of subversion touching all Europe. The notorious Russian anarchist Mikhail Bakunin, co-conspirator with Marx in the First International, was one of the French agents sent into central Europe to "make revolution."[5] Another former associate of Marx was the French subversive Carl Ludwig Bernays, who was so close to him in spirit that a Prussian police spy believed that the two individuals were the same person, reporting to his superior in Berlin that "the name Bernays is Marx."[6]

Not only did France have two sorts of representatives abroad, one accredited to the legitimate governments and the other to the revolutionary underground, they spoke diametrically opposed languages. At the very time that France's regular diplomats conveyed the accommodating notion of "live and let live" to the European despots, her secret agents sought to overthrow them. This meant that French policy existed on three levels: a publicly proclaimed sympathy for "oppressed peoples"; a private disavowal of interference in the affairs of foreign states; and, finally, a top secret subversive contact with popular leaders planning the overthrow of the rulers of these states.

The roster of men selected by Lamartine to serve as secret agents reflects the new spirit in French diplomacy that emerged as Lamartine and his assistant, Bastide, set to work to transform the structure of the French diplomatic apparatus. Lamartine's first alterations in operations were made in Paris. He called together the employees of the ministry to inform them of his willingness to "leave them inactively at their posts or employed in works of simple formality." He would reserve for his private cabinet or for himself "all ideas *(esprit)*, all the secrets, and all the conduct of the diplomacy of the republic." The heads of the four departments of

6 The Liberation of Sovereign Peoples

the foreign ministry were retained to carry out the technical functions of their bureaus. The policy-making and secrets of diplomacy fell to Lamartine's personally chosen staff in the ministry of foreign affairs.[7]

The new "private cabinet" created in the foreign ministry to deal with the secrets of the republic's diplomacy was "gathered in the streets," apparently drawn entirely from outside the ranks of the professional diplomats. It was largely made up of intellectuals and newspapermen. One of the new men was Ernest Sain de Boislecomte, like Bastide, a Christian Socialist. He had earlier collaborated with Bastide in editing the second edition of Buchez and Roux's *l'Histoire parlementaire de la révolution française* and was a fellow editor of the *Révue nationale*. After the February Revolution, Boislecomte was chosen as the principal private secretary (*chef de cabinet*) to the foreign minister, then sent as minister to Naples on May 24, 1848. Lamartine's personal private secretary was an academic intellectual, the brilliant young botanist Jean Baptiste Payer, whom Lamartine described as "active, honest, intrepid, and devoted."

Another of the intellectuals typical of the new group was Bastide's *chef de cabinet*, Jules Hetzel, a man of letters and a well-known editor and publisher, whose friends and clients included Victor Hugo, Georges Sand, Proudhon, and Lamartine. He, too, had earlier been employed with Bastide, as an editor on the *National*. After a confidential mission in Belgium early in 1848, Hetzel was appointed as the *chef de cabinet* to the foreign minister. After the June Days, Bastide would promote Hetzel to under-secretary of state. Lt. Colonel Charras, acting head of the war ministry, had worked with most of the members of the group on the *National*. All of the intellectuals were firmly committed republicans in 1848, without compromising bonds to earlier monarchs.[8]

Lamartine then set about making equally drastic changes in the French embassies. He "recalled successively all the ambassadors and nearly all the ministers plenipotentiary" from their posts. The diplomats from the days of the July Monarchy who were retained were mostly reassigned to new posts. Lamartine explained that "these ambassadors were in general politicians, former ministers personally attached by their sentiments and by their loyalties to the fallen royalty." He placed in the consulates "a number of his friends or partisans of the republic."[9]

During the first week in March, Bastide personally drew up

a list for "*Lettres de Revocation*" for Hetzel's action; those in Paris were called in for personal interviews to measure their devotion to the new regime, and an oral resignation was apparently accepted on the spot if their devotion was in question, since letters of resignation are missing from personnel files in these cases.[10]

A recent claim that "diplomatic ranks were not really republicanized or greatly altered" ignores the fact that loyalty to the republican government was the test diplomats had to pass in order to be retained, and that all important matters were handled by secret agents. In some cases, the first and second secretaries of legations were also recalled in a search for devoted servants of the republic.[11]

In addition to rejuvenating the republic's diplomatic corps, Lamartine opened up new lines of information through a group of confidential envoys, whose activities have largely escaped the notice of historians. Not only were the old diplomats in official posts replaced by younger men, but their importance as sources of information was reduced. "Secret or confidential agents" who were chosen "among men of republican opinions or those without ties to the former dynasty" took on a new significance. These deputies of the foreign minister did not usually take command of the old embassies. Secret emissaries could more easily gather information outside of established diplomatic channels, indeed, even among foreign revolutionaries.

The archives contain interesting traces of the secret agents' activities. The case of Hetzel indicates a new diplomatic style. Hetzel, apparently an important framer of policy within Lamartine's secret cabinet at the foreign ministry, joined the artist Tony Johannot on a confidential mission to Belgium where they contacted the republican revolutionary movement.[12]

Carl Ludwig Bernays, one of Karl Marx and Frederick Engels' most intimate associates in Paris before 1848, was used throughout 1848 as a special diplomatic envoy in Germany and Austria. A close friend of Bastide on the *National*, a man who signed his dispatches "Klein," was sent on a fact-finding mission by Lamartine on March 10 to Karlsruhe, Stuttgart, Darmstadt, Kassel, and other cities in southern Germany. He carried with him letters of recommendation addressed to "nearly all of the [German] democratic notabilities." On March 27, 1848, Alexandre Rey, a colleague of the utopian socialist Louis Blanc on the *Revue de Progrès*, was also sent to Germany on a confidential assignment to gather information.

The most industrious envoy, however, was Dr. Kraetzer-Rasserts, on loan from the ministry of war, who went first to Strasbourg and then, incognito, to the Rhineland. Lamartine had instructed him to make "observations on the political state of Germany" and to collect information on the movement of troops in the vicinity of France.[13]

After July 1, Heinrich Börnstein (a former editor with Marx, Engels, Bernays, and Bakunin on the radical newspaper *Vorwärts*) wrote a daily "Bulletin of news from Germany." Located in Paris, he extracted information from German newspapers and from letters of German friends. According to Börnstein's memoirs, Bastide "often expressed verbally and in writing his thanks for this service." There is even evidence suggesting that Mikhail Bakunin, the Russian anarchist, was one of Lamartine's secret agents in Germany.[14]

Most of these confidential envoys seem to have been sufficiently skillful to escape detection, but exceptions give us an insight into the workings of the new diplomacy and of the dangers it posed. One case in point was a mission to Belgium. Lamartine determined that Belgium was important because "at no price did he wish to give the English aristocracy a pretext to force the English cabinet into a crusade against the republic." Thus, he believed that the Provisional Government had to resist with an "inflexible energy" any pressure to overthrow the regime in Brussels. He claimed to have rejected all contacts with the Belgian republicans who worked with the "French republicans of the old school," noting that he "sent to Brussels several confidential agents with the order to observe the true state of opinion and to dampen rather than to excite the demagogic nucleus *(foyer)*" there.[15]

Meanwhile, the radical republican Etienne Arago recommended Bakunin to Hetzel:

> This is to introduce M. Bakunin, precisely the man whom I indicated to you yesterday as the most capable to guide you in the choice of Brussels patriots with whom you ought to confer. The arrival of M. Bakunin in Paris is good fortune for you. Take one of his almanacs and you can find out who can bring rain and fair weather there.[16]

Hetzel secured from Bastide a letter of introduction to the official French diplomatic representative in Brussels, Count Louis de Sérurier, acting chargé, who was to receive Hetzel and give him full confidence. Hetzel's mission was to explain to the Belgians that the "French policy presented in Lamartine's Manifesto had no hidden ulterior motives on our part." Bastide went on to inform Hetzel, "Lamartine asks you to remain in Belgium as a simple observer," and to relate that "the republic is definitive." Hetzel did not take command of the official French diplomacy and Sérurier continued to be the only Frenchman in contact with the Belgian government.

Accompanied by Johannot, Hetzel traveled to Bruges and other Belgian towns, visiting political meetings and clubs and contacting Bakunin's friends. Hetzel's accounts of conditions in Belgium were not sent to the foreign minister, but to his friends Bastide or Boislecomte. Bastide read Hetzel's reports to Lamartine, who was "astonished *(frappé)*" by his observations. Lamartine was very satisfied with Hetzel's activities, Bastide wrote. "I have no objections to what you write and how you speak of the Belgian question and the sense that you indicate is certainly true. I read your letter to M. Lamartine who completely agrees with you."[17]

The Belgian authorities were less pleased with Hetzel's activities. M. Hody, the administrator of the Belgian *Sureté publique*, reported that Hetzel had entered Belgium on March 13, accompanied by the lithographer Tony Johannot. Hody related that the two "got in touch with all the persons known for their demagogic principles and traveled to different towns where they hoped to proselytize. Hetzel had printed in Brussels an apology for the republic, signed P. J. Stahl, entitled *Lettre d'un Français en voyage à ses compatriotes de Paris et des départements.*"

By March 21, C. d'Hoffschmidt de Resteigne, the Belgian foreign minister, complained to the Belgian ambassador in Paris, the Prince de Ligne, of the activities of Hetzel and Tony Johannot, and only intervention by Sérurier prevented their immediate expulsion from Belgium.[18]

The French and Belgian governments differed in their interpretations of Hetzel's mission. Hoffschmidt was disturbed by the presence of a French diplomat sent secretly to "contact the men most hostile to the [Belgian] government and having political relations" with the radicals. Lamartine explained that Hetzel was "a man of ardor but inexperienced in diplomacy, who was suspected in Brussels."[19] Hetzel's mission indicated the new method of French diplomacy: he contacted the revolutionary movements while Sérurier maintained normal relations with the ruling government.

Thus, Lamartine used revolutionary or Jacobin agents to assist in the Girondist's universal war against oppression. At the same

time, his spirit of domestic reconciliation was typified by his retention of those diplomats who, having served Louis Philippe, now
adjusted to new conditions; the old personnel was allowed to oversee
only routine operations. The actual animators of the French diplomatic staff were an energetic coterie of intellectuals. Under Bastide, and not a little inexperienced and presumptuous, Lamartine's
confidential subordinates were experienced in public relations, having worked as publicists before the uprising that overthrew the
king. Immature and idealistic, the youthful journalists, now turned
neophyte diplomats, gave full devotion to the Girondist-Jacobin
cause. The young revolutionaries' approach to day-to-day operations differed as much in procedures as in the objectives themselves.
Not limiting themselves to the standard routines of accepted diplomatic practice, they moved freely in the underworld of radical
street agitators, as well as contacting heads of opposition movements
and the present wielders of governmental power. Thus, France's
new diplomatic leadership surrounded itself with a circle of ideologically committed republicans.

The result of the changes in diplomatic practices was the
transfer of power to Paris and its simultaneous removal from the
old officials in the ministry. All diplomacy was thus centralized in
the hands of the foreign minister. The French historian Charles
Pouthas concluded that:

> [the] concentration of affairs in Paris reduced the [official dip-
> lomatic] agents to a purely informational role. Business was
> transacted more between the minister and foreign ambassadors
> than between our agents and the governments to which they
> were accredited.[20]

Behind a facade of business as usual created by the retention
of much of the old diplomatic personnel, far-reaching changes were
being made in France's role in Europe. These changes combined
complementary traditions of French diplomacy and indicate that
1848 was the revolution of intellectuals.

Lamartine and his successor, Bastide, returned to Richelieu's
insistence that the house of Habsburg was France's primary enemy.
Jules Bastide, author of a history of the religious wars, was conscious
that France's primary objective was to prevent the emergence of a
universal monarchy ruled by the house of Austria.

This fundamental principle was given revolutionary sanction
by the Girondist declaration of war in 1792. The French revolu-

tionaries recognized the Pillnitz Declaration as the Habsburgs' attempt to rescue their brother-in-law, Louis XVI, by organizing a reactionary coalition that would turn back the clock in France and reinstate the *ancien régime*. Thus, the myth persisted that the Viennese were originators of francophobic alliances.

In order to defend her very existence, France sought client states in Germany. That strategy of Richelieu's confidential emissary, the grey eminence Père Joseph, was effectively used against the Habsburgs during the Thirty Year's War. Likewise, in subsequent wars France sought allies among the German princes. Thus, two themes that spanned three centuries had been a permanent enmity separating Paris and Vienna, and the French attempt to counter the Habsburgs by championing the "liberty" of the German princes.

With the advent of the "age of democratic revolutions" (R. R. Palmer) the old French-Austrian strife assumed an ideological aspect. If the governments of Paris and Vienna were polar opposites of nineteenth-century European politics, there were several competing doctrines on the left. The political left of Europe was united in its regard of the Austrian Habsburgs as an enemy. This broad coalition of potential allies for republican France ranged across the political spectrum. Thus, in 1848 the Parisian government hoped to mobilize Austria's ideological and territorial enemies. Throughout the year the French would seek to rally revolutionary forces both within the Austrian Empire and beyond her borders. Lamartine and his successors supported German unity, Italian liberation, reconstitution of a Polish state, and autonomy for Hungary, while protecting the identity of the south Slavic peoples. That is, the French offered encouragement to all peoples who might cause embarrassment for the house of Habsburg. As the year 1848 progressed, French preoccupation with an Austrian menace spread from an initial concern for Polish and Italian freedom to an increasing preoccupation with the lower Danubian basin. Thus, the locus of France's revolutionary agitation shifted eastward as revolutionary passions rose with the temperature during the summer of 1848. But at the outset let us consider Lamartine's critical definition of his strategy to isolate the Habsburgs in his Manifesto to Europe of March 4.

NOTES

1. Alphonse de Lamartine, *Histoire de la révolution de 1848* (Paris, 1849) 2 vols.; *Mémoires politiques*, vol. 39 of *Oeuvres complètes* (Paris, 1863), p. 244 and *passim*.

2. For a discussion of the principles of Girondist foreign policy see Patricia Chastain Howe, "Charles-François Doumouriez and the Revolutionizing of French Foreign Affairs in 1792," *French Historical Studies* XIV (1986), 367–90.

3. See Marceli Handelsman, *Adam Czartoryski* (Warsaw, 1948–50); Marian Kukiel, *Czartoryski and European Unity, 1770–1861* (Princeton, N.J., 1955); the superb dissertation of Robert Allen Berry, "Czartoryski and Balkan Policies of the Hotel Lambert," (Ph.D. diss., University of Indiana, 1974); and Hans Henning Hahn, *Aussenpolitik in der Emigration: Die Exil-Diplomatie Adam Jerzy Czartoryski, 1830–1840* (Munich and Vienna, 1978).

4. Marceli Handelsman, *Czartoryski, Nicolas Ier et la question du proche orient* (Paris, 1934).

5. On Hetzel, see Antoine Parmenie and Catherine Bonnier de la Chapelle, *Histoire d'un éditeur et de ses auteurs, J.-P. Hetzel* (Paris, 1953); Bibliothèque Nationale (Paris), Fonds Hetzel (hereafter BN).

6. Dr. Foelix to Bülow (Prussian Minister of Interior), Paris, March 3 and 8, 1844, Zentrales Staatsarchiv-Historische Abteilung II Merseburg, Rep 77, Tit 343A, fo. 107, 117 (hereafter ZSA).

7. Lamartine, *Histoire*, II, 27–28; Adolphe de Circourt, *Souvenirs d'une mission à Berlin en 1848* (Paris, 1908–09), I, 95–96.

8. Lamartine, *Histoire*, II, 7–9; Parmenie and Bonnier de la Chapelle, *Histoire d'un éditeur, passim.*; Charles H. Pouthas (ed.) *Documents diplomatiques du gouvernement provisoire et de la commission du pouvoir exécutif* (Paris, 1953–54), introduction, I, p. viii (hereafter DDF); Heinrich Börnstein, *Fünfundsiebzig Jahre in den neuen und alten Welt: Memoiren eines unbedeutenden* (Leipzig, 1884), I, 437.

9. Lamartine, *Histoire*, II, 28–29; Charles H. Pouthas, "La politique étrangère de la France sous la seconde République et le Second Empire" *Cours de la Sorbonne* (Paris, 1949), p. 20; Pouthas, introduction, DDF, pp. x–xi; all translations from French and German are my own.

10. BN, Fonds Hetzel, fz. 35, fo. 44ff.; Bastide to Hetzel, Paris, n.d., fz. 3, fo. 150, and *passim*.

11. Lawrence C. Jennings, *France and Europe in 1848: A Study of French Foreign Affairs in a Time of Crisis* (Oxford, 1973), p. 26.

12. Lamartine to Hetzel, Paris, March 7, 1848, BN, Mss. N. F. Fonds Hetzel, fz. 35, fo. 44ff.; Bastide to Hetzel, Paris, n. d., fz. 3, fo. 150 and *passim*.

13. Ewerbeck to Karl Marx, Paris, May 21, 1848, Hedwig Föder ed. *Der Bund der Kommunisten: Dokumente und Materialien* (Berlin, 1970), I, 788; Bernays to Engels, Paris, March 31, 1848, Internationaal Instituut voor Sociale Geschiedenis (Amsterdam), L. 436; Bernays to Lamartine, Strasbourg and Karlsruhe, April 29, 1848, Archives des Affaires Etrangères (Paris), Mémoires et Documents, Allemagne, fz. 170, fo. 21 and 24 (hereafter AEF and MD); Lefebvre to Lamartine, Karlsruhe, April 29, 1848, DDF, I, 1088; Klein to Lamartine, Frankfurt and Strasbourg, April 24 and May 10, 1848, DDF, I, 1004–05 and II, 150–52; Klein to Bastide, Munich, August 3, September 6, and October 13, 1848, AEF, MD, Allemagne 170, fo. 14–44; Lamartine to Alexandre Rey, Paris, March 27, 1848, Instructions, AEF, MD, Allemagne 171, fo. 175; Lamartine to Dr. Kraetzer-Rasserts, Paris, May 4, 1848, Instructions, AEF, MD, Allemagne 129, fo. 4.

14. Heinrich Börnstein, *Fünfundsiebzig Jahre*, I, 438–39; Henri Boernstein, "Bulletin de nouvelles de l'Allemagne," July 1, 1848 to November 1848, AEF, MD, Allemagne 129, fo. 230, No. 123; July 17, 1848, fo. 42 notes, "Bakunin, chargé d'une mission en Allemagne par le gouvernement provisoire, proteste dans la Gazette rhénane de Cologne contre l'accusation de plusieurs journaux, qui la dénonçaient comme agent russe." (underlined by Bastide).

15. Lamartine, *Histoire*, II, 164–65; Brison D. Gooch, *Belgium and the February Revolution* (The Hague, 1963), p. 81; Lamartine told the Belgian chargé, the Prince de Ligne, in early March that he could not send an official diplomatic representative until the republic had been "definitely constituted." Ligne guessed that Hetzel would be Lamartine's choice to be sent to Brussels as chargé, Ligne to Hoffschmidt, Paris, March 10, 1848, Alfred de Ridder, ed. *La crise de la neutralité belge en 1848: le dossier diplomatique* (Brussels, 1928), I, 177.

16. Etienne Arago to "Mon cher Hetzel," Paris, Cabinet du Directeur général des Postes, Paris, n. d., BN, Fonds Hetzel, fz. I, fo. 325; Parmenie and Bonnier de la Chapelle, *Histoire d'un éditeur*, p. 94; E. H. Carr, *Michael Bakunin* (New York, 1937, reprinted 1961), pp. 152–57; after Guizot expelled him from Paris, Bakunin spent from December 1847 to the end of February 1848 in Brussels, where his acquaintances included Jottand, Karl Marx, and Lelewel, the president and vice-president of the Democratic Federation, and other revolutionaries.

17. Bastide to Hetzel, Paris, n. d., BN, Fonds Hetzel, fz. 3, fo. 150; Bastide to Sérrurier, Paris, n. d. *Ibid.*, fo. 151–52; Parmenie and Bonnier de la Chapelle, *Histoire*, pp. 94–95.

18. Ridder, I, pp. xi–xii and II, 130–131; Hoffschmidt to Ligne, Brussels, March 21, 1848, Ridder, I, 235–36.

19. Lamartine, *Histoire*, II, 65.

20. Pouthas, introduction to DDF, I, p. xi; Lamartine, *Histoire*, II, 29; the position of a French diplomat in foreign capitals was painful; the Prussian cabinet was often better informed of French policy than the French chargé; previous writers have neglected the role played by informal gatherers of information outside diplomatic ranks and have failed to appreciate that diplomats were thought of as mere gatherers of information, not framers of policy; this study, therefore, relies heavily as a primary source on the lengthy reports of frequent conversations between the French foreign ministers and foreign agents in Paris, especially the Prussian chargé, to whom the "almost unlimited confidence" was given by Bastide, who succeeded Lamartine on May 12, 1848; Hatzfeldt to Foreign Minister, Paris, December 27, 1848, GSA, Frankreich, fz. 862, fo. 83; note that Bastide continued the practices, promising Normanby to "send a secret agent to Madrid whom he could trust" when the English complained of intrigue in the Spanish capital, Normanby to Palmerston, Paris, November 11, 1848, Public Record Office, F. O. 27/815, fo. 86 (hereafter PRO).

Introduction
The Manifesto of
March Four and Secret Agents

*T*HE FEBRUARY REVOLUTION INITIATED a new era in French history, one in which external affairs developed largely independent of domestic politics. During the first phase, which lasted through the spring months, Lamartine struggled against disruptive radicals until a military victory over the lower classes in the June Days, when General Cavaignac instituted a conservative republic. The extremists were definitely a factor to be reckoned with, and these Parisian radicals did press Lamartine to act immediately on freeing Poland and Italy from the oppression of the Habsburgs and Romanovs. Above all, Lamartine sought to divide the three northern courts by encouraging Prussian ambitions in Germany. All other initiatives were subordinate to the objective of finding a firm ally for France in overthrowing Habsburg-Romanov tyranny in Italy and Poland.

A second phase of foreign affairs opened with Lamartine's replacement by his former assistant, Jules Bastide, in mid-May. Bastide's major initiative, requesting an alliance with the Frankfurt parliament in order to enfranchise Italy and Poland, was offered as a unanimous resolution of the French assembly. Simultaneously, the Polish Prince Adam Czartoryski argued that the way to Warsaw (and presumably Rome) lay through Budapest; that France should counter the Habsburg-Romanov menace to Poland and Italy by fostering dissension in the Balkans, creating a "Danubian Confederation" and extending France's zone of interest into east central Europe.

The final phase in French foreign affairs began in late July, when the Frankfurt assembly seemed to be siding with the oppressing Habsburgs against the "oppressed peoples." The new

French revolutionary regime hoped to "enfranchise" not only the Germans, Italians, and Poles, but the Magyars, Rumanians, and various Slavic peoples of east central and southern Europe. Bastide responded with two major initiatives: he continued alliance discussions with Prussia initiated by Lamartine, and renewed interest in Czartoryski's proposed Danubian Confederation to counter the threat posed by the Habsburgs, now reinforced by a belligerent German parliament. This three-phase scenario minimized the influence of domestic events on French foreign affairs, emphasized continuities in French policy, and countered head-on the frequently repeated claim that French policy during 1848 was essentially conservative.

AFTER THE FEBRUARY REVOLUTION of 1848 the new Provisional Government faced a seemingly impossible task. To carry out an effective policy it had to satisfy the population of Paris on the one hand and to prevent the formation of a coalition of anti-revolutionary powers against France on the other. Lamartine changed this apparent liability into an asset by using the Paris mob to create alarm among foreign statesmen.

Paris was filled with political refugees from various parts of Europe, including Italians, Poles, Germans, and a medley of others, split between advocates of immediate action and those advising a policy of waiting for events in their home countries to evolve naturally. Both sides had their French supporters, and Lamartine's public pronouncements gave hope to all.

Addressing the great powers, Lamartine promised peace if they allowed the "oppressed peoples" to develop freely. France would only intervene, he asserted, if the great powers interfered to crush popular revolts. This did not satisfy some of the Parisian radicals, who feared that Lamartine might let the crucial moment pass. This group would continue to agitate in the streets calling for the overthrow of the Provisional Government whenever the radicals saw Lamartine as failing to keep his promise to support revolution abroad.

In addition to the internal tension between Lamartine and the domestic proponents of a more active policy, Lamartine had to consider the possibility of a European coalition by the reactionary powers bent on destroying the French republican government. Lamartine therefore immediately set about reassuring the corps of foreign diplomats in Paris that the new government did not harbor

the expansionary designs of the first French republic. His enunci-
ations were taken largely at face value, and Lamartine impressed
the members of the diplomatic community in Paris as the most
capable member of the Provisional Government, the man of peace
and order.

On February 29, the Prussian ambassador (and later foreign
minister in Berlin) Baron Heinrich von Arnim-Suckow praised the
Provisional Government's measures as most "energetic" and "most
appropriate to the circumstances." The new authorities seemed to
be showing intelligence as well as force, he noted:

> The greatest part of this praise returns to M. de Lamartine.
> During the first days when the government had no material
> force at its disposal, he, by his moral force alone and the
> prestige of his word, contained the popular wave which
> menaced overflowing. One can say that he saved Paris from
> pillage and conflagration at the peril of his life. It is he who
> is the soul of the government and the man of the people.[1]

Arnim emphasized the precarious character of the revolutionary regime. "He exercises for the moment the sovereignty of genius,
but this cannot suffice for long; all governments need material force
to maintain themselves." The new regime in Paris was increasing
the strength of the National Guard with workers and students.
No one yet knew whether there might be a future competition
between the revolutionary directors and the army.[2]

On February 28, Arnim cautioned the Prussian government
against any hint of armed intervention in France. In a ciphered
message he warned that the republican regime of France might be
forced to desperate expedients to keep its unruly population busy.
To avoid social reform, the French government might encourage
its population to pursue foreign conquests. He therefore advised
Frederick William IV against a hostile alliance or a reinforcement
of troops along the frontier which would only mean *"la guerre sur
le Rhin."*[3]

Arnim understood from the beginning the chief focus of French
policy in 1848. The prime concern of the French republicans was
neither the Rhine nor Prussia but Italy and Austria. France might
send armies to the Rhine, but only because it was easier to reach
than the Adige. Its actual goal was Italy and the destruction of
the treaties of 1815.

Metternich too was advised not to intervene in French affairs.
King Louis Philippe, in exile in London, told the Belgian minister,

Sylvain Van de Weyer, that the powers for the moment should "maintain peace and avoid any action which could produce against them an irritation in France."[4]

The well-informed Belgian minister in Berlin, Baron Jean-Baptiste de Nothomb, learned from the Prussian minister of foreign affairs on March 2 that Prussia would leave France to constitute its government as it wished.

> Prussia had no wish to repeat the mistake of 1792. Prussia refuses all aggression against France, understanding that it, on its side, abstains from all aggression against not only the German states, but all states constituted by existing treaties.[5]

Only Russia showed interest in actively opposing the French republic, but it received little encouragement from Prussia. On February 29, Baron Peter von Meyendorff met with the Austrian ambassador, Count Joseph von Trauttmansdorff, at the home of the Prussian foreign minister, Baron Karl von Canitz und Dallwitz. Meyendorff feared a precipitous recognition by Prussia of the new French government and told Canitz that the tsar would never recognize the republic. If Prussia did, it could never again count on Russian aid. He reminded Canitz of the 1830 agreement among the three northern courts, Austria, Prussia, and Russia, forever excluding the recognition of a republican regime in France. "Recall what I tell you today," he warned, "in two years you will have a war on the Rhine, and be certain that 200,000 Russians will be more useful to you than the English fleet."[6] Although Meyendorff cautioned that the danger of French aggression necessitated an immediate entente, Canitz, attempting to calm the Russian envoy, reminded him that the present condition of France was highly provisional. There would soon be another change in government, "the republic being, in the long run, impossible in that country."[7]

The diplomatic representatives of the great powers in Paris were understandably apprehensive after Lamartine's early statements, since he presented himself simultaneously as a moderate and as the leader of the European revolution. This contradiction was reflected in the report to Vienna by Austrian ambassador Count Anton Rudolf Apponyi concerning Lamartine's first interview with a foreign diplomat, Lord Normanby, the British ambassador. Normanby had been impressed by Lamartine's moderation and peaceful demeanor. Lamartine had told him that no French regime could openly speak of the maintenance of the hated treaties of 1815, but that the change of government had not altered the policies of the French authorities. "France," Lamartine said, "sincerely desires to conserve peace and not to attack anyone unless it was to repel an armed intervention directed against the peoples who wish to defend their independence and their liberty."

Apponyi, however, seemed less reassured than Normanby by Lamartine's language; he conjectured:

> This explanation, far from offering some guarantee for the conservation of peace seems to announce on the contrary that it cannot be maintained for long, and that the irresistible force of circumstances will soon lead to a general war. In reflecting on conditions in Italy, Switzerland, and part of Germany it is hardly possible to form any other opinion.[8]

Lamartine made his policies public in his flamboyant "Manifesto to Europe," published in the *Moniteur* on March 4. He later claimed that the statement was intended first of all to reassure the cabinets of Europe that the republic of 1848 should not be confused with the republic of 1792, "France is peaceful."

Lamartine assured the Prussian ambassador that both he and the masses were only interested in "industry and commerce, therefore wishing peace, because war would destroy both." The Manifesto, he asserted, was directed at Frenchmen, "far from being a declaration of war against all of monarchical Europe, [it] addresses itself rather to France to prove to it that as a republic it can and ought to remain at peace with the entire world." War might threaten liberty itself in France by causing the rise of a Caesar or a Napoleon.[9] The first interest of France was peace.

On the eve of the Manifesto's publication, Lamartine minimized its revolutionary import and blamed his colleagues, who found the language too diplomatic, for adding a few *gros mots*. In conversation with Arnim, Lamartine divulged the most important parts of the Manifesto, especially a passage concerning the treaties of 1815. As reported by Arnim, Lamartine asserted that:

> France does not recognize in right the treaties of 1815; but it admits them as facts, as a base of territorial circumscription and as a point of departure to arrive *peacefully* and with *common accord* at modification.[10]

Lamartine pledged that France would make no "secret or incendiary propaganda among her neighbors," because "durable liberties were only created on their own soil."[11] A revolutionary movement brought in from the outside, without deep roots among the people, would inevitably fail. "Nations, like individuals," Lamartine continued, "have different ages." He went on to say:

> Principles rule the successive phases. Monarchical, aristocratic, constitutional, and republican governments are the expression of different degrees of maturity in a nation's genius. They demand more liberty as they are capable of supporting it. . . . It is a question of time. A people is lost in advancing before maturity, as it is dishonored in allowing the moment to escape them.[12]

Noting that change would only come where nations were prepared to forward their own progress, Lamartine indicated that France's role would be to prevent outside pressure by the reactionary powers to crush a successful rebellion.

Lamartine's simultaneous promises of peace and liberation were inherently inconsistent. He announced an end to the era of the "Holy Alliance"; France would no longer allow the "Three Northern Courts" to interfere in the internal politics of European states where the liberals were struggling against reactionary forces. France declared herself the protector of liberal Europe. The Manifesto, Lamartine cautioned, promised "peace if you [European rulers] are just, war if you are the oppressors of nations."[13] Lamartine resolved the contradiction between peace and war in his policy only to the extent that he promised that France would not be an aggressor; she would defend herself and the other struggling nations. France declared "peace to territories," "sympathies for peoples," and "moderation to governments."[14]

This "policy of peace" is among the most misunderstood of Lamartine's slogans. It represented a commitment to the spread of liberal ideas rather than to the expansion of France's frontiers, and since Lamartine shared the belief—widespread in 1848—that the pen was mightier than the sword, he assumed that it was the strength of the French ideas of liberty, equality, and fraternity that would ultimately bring freedom to the oppressed nationalities rather than military intervention.

Lamartine expanded on his idealistic interpretation of revolutionary dynamics in a speech to the Constituent Assembly on May 8. He distinguished between two sorts of revolutions: revolutions of "territory" and revolutions of "ideas." For the former war was necessary, while the latter depended on peace. French ideals would ultimately triumph, since "a law of nature makes these truths contagious, and ideas tend to find their level like water."[15]

Lamartine's Manifesto of March 4 confused everyone. The European diplomats hoped for peace, but expected war. The best they could do was to wait and see how France would act. Most feared that the explosion would be in Italy. Britain's Lord Palmerston openly supported Lamartine's promised "policy of peace"[16] leaving Austria isolated.[17] Prussia was ready to allow France complete freedom in managing her internal affairs as long as she honored her promise to live peacefully with her neighbors.[18] The diplomatic community in Paris generally saw Lamartine's position as insecure. At any moment another revolution might bring down the Provisional Government, "among pikes and revolutionary tribunal." Lamartine, they believed, was the most conservative leader available at the time. The next revolutionary wave might well bring to power the most violent extremists led by Auguste Blanqui, who was bent on undermining the Provisional Government.[19]

Given this fear, the great powers had no choice but to follow the advice of their envoys in Paris to give Lamartine a chance to restore order in Paris without further inflaming the volatile passions of the populace. Thus Lamartine received the tacit recognition as the real head of the government and directed foreign policy with little interference until May 1848, because all factions were committed to a revolutionary extension of France's ambitions to free its neighbors from Habsburg domination. He carried out this difficult assignment by operating as a conciliator among the different factions, and he did so as leader of the moderate majority in the council.

By taking this ambiguous position Lamartine puzzled his contemporaries as well as posterity. In May 1848, Gustav Ölsner-Monmerqué, a journalist and secret agent sent to Paris by the Frankfurt Assembly, noted that Lamartine "had no convictions, instead he was prepared to please everyone." In practice this meant that Lamartine raised inconsistency to the level of an institution.[20]

The apparent gap between Lamartine's promises of peace and Bastide-Flocon's policy of liberation suggests an irreconcilable conflict in the inner circles of the French government during the crucial events of March-November 1848. It appears that while Lamartine promised aid for the oppressed peoples of Europe he failed to honor that pledge; indeed, he apparently refused to do anything that would weaken the traditional enemy, Austria. More than a half-century ago, A. J. P. Taylor argued that this was proof that the French were more interested in maintaining a "live and let live" policy than in revolutionizing Europe. Lawrence C. Jennings's more recent study of French diplomacy concluded that her diplomatic practice remained within the general parameters of her traditional interests and that the revolutionary regime "pursue[d] a cautious, basically conservative foreign policy."[21] In spite of widespread public support among Frenchmen for the revolutionary cause in central and eastern Europe,[22] the republican regime reportedly turned its back on revolution and allowed these peoples to be conquered by the Austrians.

The pursuit of a cautious policy which supposedly sacrificed the hopes of European peoples for freedom fails to mesh with the high-minded idealism of both Lamartine and his assistant Bastide. And Lamartine never limited his operations to grandiose pronouncements calculated to set Europe on fire. His secret agents spread across Europe, stirring up insurrectionary-minded trouble-makers and causing discord. Within a matter of days Prussian border stations reported the presence of these revolutionary French emissaries.[23] Proclaiming the contentious credo of resistance to the jurisdiction of the old order, the roving agents of disorder sought to spread the spirit of revolt from the borders of France eastward. And although Lamartine remained a cipher,[24] his assistant and then his successor as a foreign minister throughout the year 1848 was Jules Bastide, a professional revolutionary conspirator, widely respected for his integrity. Even in his self-serving account Lamartine declared that he chose Bastide because "under the eyes of Bastide no treason to the Republic was to be feared."[25] Yet the standard accounts maintain that Bastide underwent a radical change of character and rejected every ideal to which he had devoted his life when power was briefly thrust into his hands.

Some of the mystery in the apparent contradiction between the promises made in Lamartine's Manifesto of March 4 to liberate peoples from tyranny and lack of evidence of French direct involvement in foreign revolutions recedes when placed in a wider context of French policies during the first half of the nineteenth century. For freedom to maneuver would depend to a great degree on the weight of the past: for the line up of friends and foes of the new republic would to a great extent be predetermined by an historical consciousness which characterized the French as heroes or villains.

The new French Provisional Government was overwhelmed with expectations and by apprehensions. Both the Great Powers and the forces who had brought the overthrow of the French July

Departure of the Poles at Mairie of IIeme Arrondissement: "These brave then after having shed their blood on the barricades for liberty and France, thought that the hour of deliverance of their country had arrived. Whilst trusting in our promises, they proceed to face their oppressors, shall we permit the world to think that the French forgot them? (the 30th March)," lithograph by V. Adam and J. Arnout, Bibliothèque Nationale (Paris).

Monarchy expected great things of the new Parisian government. There was first of all the widespread anticipation that the new republic would not allow the territorial settlement of 1815 to stand unaltered. Generally, ,Frenchmen resented the ignominy of the dictated peace of 1815. The French sense of humiliation was directed against the territorial concerns highlighted by Talleyrand in his instructions for the Congress of Vienna. Talleyrand saw Poland and Italy as primary areas of French interest. French preoccupation with these two issues would cause Poland and Italy to be the polar stars around which French policies would revolve in 1848. States which the French perceived as enemies of Italy and Poland were to be considered the primary adversaries of the French republic. This placed Austria and then secondarily Russia in the roles of France's major opponents. But Prussia's position was ambiguous, depending on whether liberal or conservative forces gained the upper hand in Berlin. Prussia could either stand in a solid line of conservative monarchs or, if liberals seized control, side with the French and English, the liberal states.

The touchstone of France's attitude toward Germany was the twin issues of Italy and Poland. Any Germans who blocked the reconstitution of Poland and the unification of Italy could expect France's hostility. By the same note, France's primary aspiration was to bring Prussia into a close alliance, if this meant freedom for Poland and Italy. The changes in that Paris-Berlin axis during 1848 turned on perceptions of Prussia's willingness to liberate Poland and to oppose Austria's control over northern Italy. Likewise, French relations with the revolutionary German parliament in Frankfurt am Main first warmed and then cooled as the French first believed that the German parliamentarians would join with France to free Poland and Italy and later learned that the parliament would not stand by France after all. Thus, as long as a united German state seemed to be a possible ally for France and was prepared to aid the French in freeing Poland and Italy, the French revolutionary regime favored German national consolidation.

Occasional French expressions of doubt concerning a united Germany only emerged when it appeared that a strong German nation might impede Polish and Italian freedom.

Among Anglo-Saxons the least appreciated area of French concern was east central Europe. Superb works of historical analysis by Marceli Handelsman (Poland), István Hajnal (Hungary), and Cornelia Bodea (Rumania) force us to reexamine French interest in the east of Europe. During 1848 the Budapest revolution increasingly concerned policy makers in Paris. The primary anxiety remained in Italy and Poland, which could be directly affected if Hungary were to break away from Viennese control to set up an independent power center. Hajnal has shown that such hopes were more than idle speculation on the part of the French, since there was indeed some inclination in Budapest to break out from patterns of obedience to Vienna. The cabinet in Budapest did seek British and French diplomatic recognition as a free and independent Hungarian state. Thus an initial preoccupation with Italy and Poland expanded as the French searched for new cohorts in the lower Danube valley, until by the autumn of 1848 the fate of the revolution in Budapest had become a cause of anxiety as well.

The fundamental nature of revolutionary dynamics drew in an ever widening circle of states to the vortex of upheaval. Beginning in February, as the leaders of revolt in France were apprehensive for the safety of their own situation, they progressively expanded contacts with revolutionists across Europe. The process caused that expansion to areas which in the early months of the year were remote to the primary impulse. Yet by the fateful month of Vendémiaire (late September in the revolutionary calendar), what a short time before had seemed removed now appeared essential. The outcome of the entire revolutionary process—even France itself—depended on developments within these territories on the borderlands of western European civilization.

Unfortunately for the fate of the revolutions generally, like other social movements during 1848, they relied on diplomatic activity and political developments. The Magyar army and other insurrectionaries would succumb without help from France. But for reasons other than a lack of interest; our primary objective is to explain why the French would fail to hold back the reactionary course of events. The old powers would eventually regroup their forces as the year of revolutions closed to overcome armed rebellion in the decisive centers of revolt, particularly in northern Italy, Hungary, Vienna, and the German states. But this outcome could not be foreseen at the beginning of a year which began with such exalted prospects.

Accepted wisdom maintains that even though France was the traditional center of liberation struggle, it did nothing to stop that resurgence of the forces of reaction. Indeed, the French themselves by crushing the June Days revolt of 1848 set an example for the reactionary powers who used soldiers to reestablish order in the streets. Thus the history of France during 1848 has usually been depicted as a dichotomy between an early radical phase followed by a conservative republic. The French military victory over the popular forces in the June Days revolt was supposedly the moment when reaction set in and the tide of revolution in France began to recede.

Yet let us defy accepted historical wisdom for a moment and invert the negative question to ask how France could have intervened in foreign revolutions. The French second republic inherited a very dubious legacy of extreme distrust founded on strong memories of French meddling in the politics of neighboring states during the first republic. During the Revolution friends of the French republic had established republics from the North Sea to the Adriatic. The names of the Batavian Republic, the Helvetian Republic, the Ilyrian Republic, etc., are reminders from an earlier era of past French assistance to foreign republicans. These short-lived sister republics all too often were preludes to outright annexation by the French first republic. Thus the French second republic had to overcome extremely negative historic recollections. Above all, the French and their latter day sympathizers in 1848 had to avoid any reminder of casualities resulting from conscription into the French army or of service under national banners when a united European army chased the Corsican from the homeland of various European peoples. Hence Lamartine's constantly reiterated promise that the new French republic would liberate peoples peacefully. Still, this begs the question of how Lamartine's republic would operate if it chose to intervene abroad to encourage the founding of sister republics. The intermediaries between the French government and their foreign friends would be necessarily clandestine; any hint of direct French involvement would be a public relations disaster for their chosen partners in arms. Territorially, these foreign associates were vital in the various states of disunited Germany. Yet nowhere was the distrust of French intentions greater. Such reminders as the annexations of the Rhineland, the shame of conquest and occupation, these were an embarrassment to possible collaboration in 1848. Thus all contacts between the French and their new confederates had to be clandestine. There would necessarily not be a single sort of secret agent. The mission of a confidential operator varied to coincide with circumstances: gathering intelligence, making direct contacts to the revolutionary foreign underground, rabble rousing in the streets, carrying on delicate discussions with a foreign government considering a secret military alliance with the French, and the overthrowing of these same cabinets. All of these were the usual activities of a European revolutionary underground sympathetic to the French.

The clandestine agents' optimistic tone colored the French foreign minister's dispatches. The rose-colored spectacles of ideologically convinced republicans distorted descriptions of the conditions abroad and utterly misconstrued matters. Thus the French minister of foreign affairs in Vendémiaire mistakenly presumed himself in command of a phantom army of like-minded brothers in arms who would arise at a moment's notice to support the French government. The agents then were not mere auxiliaries of French policy but were an essential element shaping perceptions in Paris. But the optimism was a factor in a rout of these various revolutions, because erroneous analyses accorded a false sense of complacency, an assumption that momentarily the French might create a new system of satellite republics.

During the early weeks following the Parisian February Revolution, Lamartine and his assistant Jules Bastide believed that their real authority rested on a sympathy that France enjoyed abroad. Thus the French operatives were far more than mere conduits of information but also a potentially active instrument in the hands of the French government. Lamartine and Bastide presumed that their agents were a secret link to a potential reserve army of peoples in the event of war. And to underscore the importance of France's secret agents we turn to the example of the mission of Adolphe de Circourt to Berlin where he concluded a top secret military alliance between the French and Prussian cabinets. The French initiative depended on a wave of revolt that spread across all central Europe.

NOTES

1. Arnim to Foreign Minister, Paris, February 29, 1848, Germany, Stiftung Preussischer Kulturbesitz, Geheimes Staatsarchiv (Berlin), III. Hauptabteilung, fz. 855, fo. 54 (hereafter GSA); Lord Normanby, *Une année de révolution d'après un journal tenu à Paris en 1848* (3d. ed., Paris, 1860), I, 165; for fears of French aggression see Gooch, *Belgium and the February Revolution*.

2. Arnim to Foreign Minister, Paris, February 29, 1848, GSA, fz. 855, fo. 54; for the role of the national guard see Louis Girard, *La Garde nationale, 1814–1871* (Paris, 1964), p. 287ff; Apponyi to Metternich, Paris, March 1, 1848, Austria, Haus-, Hof- und Staatsarchiv (Vienna), Politisches Archiv (PA), IX Frankreich, Kart. 29, III, fo. 212 (hereafter HHSA); Arnim to Foreign Minister, March 1, 1848, GSA, fz. 855, fo. 57.

3. Arnim to Foreign Minister, Paris, February 28, 1848, GSA, fz. 855, fo. 51.

4. Similarly the former French minister, François Guizot, told the Austrian ambassador on March 4 that the powers would abstain from any measures which would stir up or isolate France, Count Moriz von Dietrichstein-Proskau-Leslie (Austrian Ambassador) to Metternich, London, March 6, 1848, copy, GSA, fz. 691, fo. 91.

5. Nothomb to Hoffschmidt, Berlin, March 2, 1848, Belgium, Archives des Affaires Etrangères, correspondance politique, Légations, Prusse IX, 35 (hereafter AEB); Baron Eugène de Meneval to Lamartine, Dresden, March 13, 1848, in Helmut Kretzschmar and Horst Schlechte, eds. *Französische und Sächsische Gesandtschaftsberichte aus Dresden und Paris, 1848–1849* (Berlin, 1956), p. 51; Bernstorff reported that Germans were more hostile to Russia than to France, Graf Bernstorff to King Frederick William IV, Munich, February 29, March 2 and 6, 1848, in Anton Choust, ed. *Gesandtschaftsberichte aus München, 1814–1848: III. Abteilung, Die Berichte der preussischen Gesandten* (Munich, 1951), IV, 398–400, 415; Bourgoing to Lamartine, Munich, March 4, 1848, DDF, I, 31; Billing to Lamartine, Frankfurt, March 2, 1848, DDF, I, 13; Veit Valentin, *Geschichte der deutschen Revolution 1848–49* (Berlin, 1930–31), I, 378; Possible Prussian political motivation in not aiding Austria in Italy: Nothomb to Hoffschmidt, Berlin, March 2, 1848, AEB, Prusse IX, 35.

6. Trauttmansdorff to Metternich, Berlin, February 29, 1848, HHSA, III Preussen, Kart. 31.

7. *Ibid.*

8. Apponyi to Metternich, Paris, February 29, 1848, HHSA, IX Frankreich, fo. 206–09.

9. For Lamartine's motives and the editing of the manifesto see Normanby, *Une année*, I, 192 and Arnim to Frederick William IV, Paris, March 2, 1848, GSA, fz. 859, fo. 30–38; Alphonse de Lamartine, *Le passé, le présent et l'avenir de la République* (Brussels, 1850), p. 63.

10. Arnim to Foreign Minister, Paris, March 3, 1848, GSA, fz. 855, fo. 62–63, underlined in Berlin; private letter March 2, 1848, fz. 859, fo. 35ff.; *Moniteur*, May 7, 1848; Lamartine, *Histoire*, II, 39.

11. Lamartine, *Histoire*, II, 40.

12. *Ibid.*, II, 35; *Moniteur*, May 24, 1848.

13. Lamartine, *Le passé*, pp. 63–64.

14. *Moniteur*, May 7, 1848.

15. *Moniteur*, May 9, 1848; Lamartine, *Le passé*, pp. 63–64; Lamartine, *Histoire*, II, 40.

16. Van de Weyer to Hoffschmidt (Belgian Foreign Minister), London, March 2, 7, and 16, 1848, in Ridder, *La crise de la neutralité belge*, I, 47–49, 143–44, and 213.

17. Metternich called Lamartine's Manifesto "a poor apology for a republic." He was "hardly reassured by the passage concerning the observation of treaties." Its only significance, Metternich believed, was that "France would respect the treaties until strong enough to declare them void." Heinrich Friedrich von Arnim-Werberlow to Canitz, Vienna, March 12, 1848, GSA, fz. 691, fo. 86; Manifest impérial, March 10, 1848 in Metternich, *Mémoires, documents et écrits divers laissés par le Prince de Metternich* (Paris, 1883), VII, 601; Metternich to Lebzeltern (Austrian Ambassador in St. Petersburg), Vienna, March 7, 1848, *Ibid.*, VII, 599.

18. Westmorland to Palmerston, Berlin, March 9, 1848, PRO, FO 64/282; Canitz to Arnim, Berlin, March 9, 1848, GSA, fz. 691, fo. 81–82; Canitz to Senkendorff, Berlin, March 5 and 9, 1848, GSA, fz. 804, fo. 77 and 90; Van de Weyer to Hoffschmidt, London, March 4, 1848, Ridder, I, 77; The Belgian ambassador in Berlin reported: "It seems to be believed that France will be absorbed for a long time with her internal reorganization; what is feared is not a regular war but a system of propaganda aided by emissaries and affiliations." Nothomb to Hoffschmidt, Berlin, March 4, 1848, Ridder, I, 86.

19. Ligne to Hoffschmidt, Paris, February 29, 1848, Ridder, I, 26; Canitz to Hatzfeldt (Prussian chargé in Arnim's absence), Berlin, March 12, 1848, GSA, fz. 855, fo. 80; Hatzfeldt to Canitz, Paris, March 13, 1848, GSA, fz. 855, fo. 93–97; Normanby, *Une année*, I, 199.

20. Gustav Ölsner-Monmerqué, *Drei Missionen: Politische Skizzen aus Paris* (Bremen, 1850), p. 8.

21. Jennings, *France and Europe*, pp. 20–23, 58–60, 67–70, 76–81; For a more balanced picture of general sincerity of Lamartine's attitude toward Germans and other peoples seeking self-determination see Robert J. Hahn, "The Attitude of the French Revolutionary Government toward German Unification in 1848," (Ph.D. diss., Ohio State University, 1955).

22. Emile Tersen, *Le Gouvernement provisoire et l'Europe* (Paris, 1948), pp. 14–15.

23. Prussian Military Attaché to Canitz, Frankfurt am Main, March 4, 1848, ZSA, Rep 77 Tit. 343A Nr. 72 I, fo. 108; Oberpräsident Raumer to Bodelschwingh, Cologne, *ibid.*, fo. 59; Bodelschwingh to the Königlichen Regierungs-Präsident zu Erfurt and the Polizei-Präsident zu Breslau, Berlin, March 2, 1848, *ibid.* Bl. 13; Regierungs-Präsident to Bodelschwingh, Bromberg, March 17, 1848, *ibid.*, fo. 200–01; cf. similar reports on the activities of the French Provisional Government's emissaries: internal memorandum of the Prussian Minister of Interior, dated Berlin, April 27, 1848, ZSA, 2.4.1. 8048, fo. 96–104.

24. Alvin Calman, *Ledru-Rollin and the Second French Republic* (New York, 1922), pp. 73–82; Lamartine, *Histoire*, II *passim.*; Louis Garnier-Pagès, *Histoire de la révolution de 1848* (Paris, 1861–72) 10 vols.; Henri Guillemin, *Lamartine en 1848* (Paris, 1948); Charles Samaran's introduction to Rudolf Apponyi, *De la Révolution au coup d'état, 1848–1851* (2d. ed.; Geneva, 1948), p. x; Louis Bertrand, *Lamartine* (Paris, 1940); for the view that Lamartine was an unrealistic dreamer see William F. Griese, "Lamartine: A Portrait," *University of Wisconsin Studies in Language and Literature*, XX (1924), pp. 182–83, 193, 209 and *passim* and Jean Knight, "Lamartine, Ministre des affaires étrangères," *Revue d'histoire diplomatique*, XX (1906), 260–84; cf. Alexis de Tocqueville, *The Recollections of Alexis de Tocqueville* (New York, 1946), p. 118; A. J. P. Taylor, *The Struggle for Mastery in Europe, 1848–1918* (London, 1957), p. 15; Taylor, *The Italian Problem in European Diplomacy, 1847–1849* (Manchester, 1934); the following analysis was suggested by Marius-François Guyard, the stimulating commentaries to his paper by Paul Bastide and Jean Pommier, and Guyard's response, "Les idées politiques de Lamartine," *Revue des travaux de l'academie des sciences morales et politiques*, pt. 2 (1966), 1–16; Gordon Wright, "A Poet in Politics: Lamartine and the Revolution of 1848," *History Today*, VIII (1958), 616–27, implied that the interpretations of the Provisional Government are mutually exclusive, rather than complementary, each describing one aspect of the government's policy; Lamartine himself was responsible for the confusion by his rejection of his revolutionary past after his fall from power; Henri Guillemin's study of earlier drafts of the *History of the Girondins* and other unedited documents indicate that Lamartine on the eve of the revolution was a sincere and fervent true believer in the republic; Lamartine's memoir accounts expressly minimized his radical convictions of 1848, and these published accounts must therefore be used with extreme caution. Henri Guillemin, *Lamartine et la question sociale (Documents inédits)* (Paris, 1946).

25. Lamartine, *Histoire*, II, 8–9.

Part One

THE RICHELIEU-GIRONDIST POLICY

Chapter One
The Revolutionary Situation and French Response
FEBRUARY-MARCH 1848

*D*URING THE INITIAL WEEKS that followed the February Revolution, the old order in Europe came under attack from all sides. With the announcement of each outbreak of violence in another corner of Europe, Lamartine's heart soared ever higher. He became increasingly confident that the potency of France was strengthened by the dynamics of the new revolutionary situation. The future of a republican government in France rested on the support she might expect from the formerly oppressed lower orders, who were now seizing control in one state after another. Lamartine believed that if this evolutionary process continued, France would be invincible. An ideological bond of republicanism that could stretch from the Baltic to the Black Sea linked her to new sister republics. Ideas were more important than armies, the pen mightier than the sword, and no nation would dare approach France in arms if that might lead to an uprising among its own people in support of France. Above all, Lamartine, like most Frenchmen, expected that the major objective of the revolution in France was to secure the liberation of Poland and Italy from Habsburg oppression. He surely realized, as well, that the historic buttress of Habsburg power was formed by the francophobic German princes. Thus, the spread of revolution to the German states was an immediate concern. With the German people as allies against the Habsburg emperor, he was invincible; without the backing of the Germans, Lamartine could never hope to free Poland and Italy. With this in mind, Lamartine would send a number of confidential agents into Germany to report on the situation and to explore every possibility of linking up with those Germans who were restless under the historic tutelage of the Habsburgs. The list of potential allies included not only German liberals but Prussian patriots anxious to push King Frederick William IV into the role of founder of a new German Empire, free of Habsburg domination. In order to win over these German liberals and Prussian patriots, Lamartine had first to overcome their unfortunate memories of past French invasions and occupations. His policy of peace was vital to the fusion of the potentially mighty coalition of all those with a grudge against the Habsburgs.

AN UPRISING IN JANUARY IN PALERMO against Ferdinand, the Bourbon King of the Two Sicilies, heralded the political unrest that would manifest itself on much of the continent that year. The death of King Christian VII of Denmark at the same time spelled trouble in the north, where that country was embroiled in a dispute with the German states over the fate of the border duchies of Schleswig and Holstein, then under the Danish crown.

Ferdinand responded to the uprising by granting a constitution on February 10. Similarly beset, the Duke of Tuscany granted a constitution in Florence. On February 22, violence broke out in Paris; within two days King Louis Philippe had abdicated and was replaced by a Provisional Government.

Even as the *Communist Manifesto* went to press in London, the first government to include openly avowed socialists took control in France. Their proclamation of the "right to work" guaranteed jobs to every worker through the establishment of National Workshops. The fact that a self-appointed government, dedicated to ending misery for unemployed proletarians, ruled in France was profoundly disturbing to the despots of the three northern courts— Berlin, Vienna, and St. Petersburg.

Violence spread during the first four days of March, with uprisings occurring in Munich, Karlsruhe, and other German cities, and with Prussian police reporting the presence of French emissaries in the Rhineland. On March 4, France, the generally acknowledged voice of all "oppressed peoples," declared her support for the struggles of the downtrodden in a "Manifesto to Europe." The following day, the French Provisional Government announced elections for a National Assembly on the revolutionary basis of universal suffrage.

Also on March 5, in Heidelberg, the traditional center of free thought, liberal Germans called for a "Preparliament" to meet in

Frankfurt am Main to plan elections for a German constituent assembly. And in Turin, King Charles Albert proclaimed a constitution for the Kingdom of Piedmont-Sardinia, the most important Italian state.

The next day, March 6, Berliners were stirred by a series of popular meetings. Within a week, barricades appeared in the streets. A most uncharacteristic spirit of insubordination infected even the usually disciplined Berliners. The Prussians were following the example of their fellow Germans. On March 9, Württemberg and Baden, closest both physically and spiritually to France, installed liberal cabinets. The first of the German "March Ministries" called on hitherto excluded liberals to take charge of states which faced defiant threats from extremists both in the countryside and in urban workshops.

On March 11, a liberal cabinet was appointed in Munich, and on the same day the French Provisional Government issued an "Appeal to the Northern Courts," imploring them to emancipate and reconstitute Poland in order to avoid needless bloodshed. At the same moment, the revolution erupted in Prague, a major Slavic city of the Austrian Empire. All this proved to be merely a prelude to the decisive and simultaneous uprisings of March 13 in both Berlin and Vienna.

Benedetto Croce described the temporary insanity:

> One of those rare moments in which mankind is completely filled with happy confidence in itself and its future, when, growing greater in the purity of this joy, it becomes good, generous, and sees brothers on every hand, and loves them. Thus it was at the beginning of the revolution of 1789, which stirred and thrilled hearts all over the world. Thus it was, and to a higher degree in 1848, when formidable obstacles, which had been assaulted in vain for more than half a century, seemed to dissolve as if by magic, like the walls of Jericho at the sound of trumpets. The tide of enthusiasm enfolded and carried away everybody.[1]

The modern historian Rudolf Stadelmann used the phrase "revolutionary psychosis" to characterize the state of mind of large portions of the population of central and western Europe during these months of revolutionary fervor. Stadelmann noted that at this moment of victory there was no organized, equipped white army standing by to take the field against what appeared to be an invincible tide of revolt. The illusion of invincibility blinded friend and foe of revolution alike. For the moment, Russia, the "Rock of the East," appeared to be the only supporter of the old order not to have succumbed.[2]

The troubles in Vienna encouraged changes elsewhere. On March 14, the moderates at the Hungarian Diet meeting in Bratislava pushed through a program of national reforms that declared Hungary to be separate and independent of Viennese control. On the next day, a more radical group of young leftists sparked a revolt in Budapest. The Habsburg court in Vienna capitulated to the Hungarian Diet and accepted its reforms, which were tantamount to a constitution. Hungary became virtually independent, with allegiance to the crown as its sole bond with the rest of the Habsburg Empire. At the same time, the Croats formed a national committee to secure their own government, separate from the newly created Magyar cabinet.

The existence on Russia's border of a constitutional state with close ties to the Polish revolutionary movement was unacceptable to Tsar Nicholas I. The tsar's fear of insubordination from his Roman Catholic Polish subjects was even greater, however, and the news that on March 14 Pope Pius IX had promulgated a constitution for the Papal States, and had thus given his blessing to the constitutional movement, was a terrible blow.

Meanwhile in Paris, preparations were under way for an armed invasion of Germany by a German Democratic Club under the leadership of Karl Marx's old communist friend, the poet Georg Herwegh. Simultaneously, the French Provisional Government faced demonstrations by upper-class members of the old National Guard elite units, who protested their dissolution and merger into the new regiments formed to bolster the armed might of France. On March 17, workers marched in a counter-demonstration to support the decision of the Provisional Government to democratize the militia. This mood of dissension led the government to postpone elections to the Constituent Assembly.

In view of France's domestic problems, the news of revolution occurring throughout central Europe was reassuring. The danger of a reactionary coalition against the French republic was at an end for the moment. Lamartine was convinced that if France remained patient and peaceful and allowed the revolutions to evolve naturally, France had nothing to fear.

Even before the outbreaks of mid-March, Lamartine had been sanguine about the constellation of powers, *vis-à-vis* France. As he noted, "England, the country where liberty had a voice, where the people were the conscience in Parliament, would neither subsidize nor permit a coalition" against France. Prussia, he thought, "neutral in 1792, would not hesitate to remain more than neutral in 1848." Meanwhile in Germany, he maintained, the secondary powers were "unsympathetic to Austria and would be restrained by the neutrality of Prussia and England." Thus, France had only Austria and Russia to fear.

The events of mid-March improved France's situation considerably. Austria was immobilized by the problems in Italy, Vienna, Hungary, and Bohemia; this left France with only Russia to fear. "But our auxiliaries against Russia included Poland, Hungary, Wallachia and Moldavia, and last, Turkey," Lamartine wrote later. "For Russia to attack France it had to traverse all of Germany. Do you believe that Germany, already agitated and democratized, would not have trembled under the Russian columns and not have given us auxiliaries against the omnipotence of the tsar?"

The Manifesto of the republic, "accepted as the basis of our foreign policy, gave France nothing to fear at any point on our horizon," he noted. The government of the republic did not need a war: "Equilibrium was sufficient." The French policy of "respect for nationalities, served by the sympathies of the peoples of Germany," made France so mighty that a "single gesture" from France "could raise Germany and nationalize Italy."[3]

What separated Lamartine from his radical antagonists was not so much whether or not the old order in Europe should be overthrown, but the pace of this transmutation. Lamartine's grandiose plan to remake the map of Europe and to liberate its peoples from the outmoded regime of monarchy required peace. For his Richelieu-Girondist scheme of French sponsorship of client states in central Europe to succeed, he had to avoid blatant reminders of earlier French meddling in the troubled internal politics of the German states. The peoples, themselves, had to appear to take the initiative. Under no circumstances could memories of the French Revolution, whose generals used agents to found sister republics that merely presaged direct annexation to the French republic, be revived. Thus, it was imperative to Lamartine that changes in neighboring states occur "peacefully," that is, without the intervention of French soldiers. This in turn made it all the more important that Lamartine, through his assistant, the old professional revolutionary street fighter, Jules Bastide, use confidential agents as intermediaries so that all changes seemed to owe nothing to the French. Yet even while Lamartine and Bastide discreetly worked by proxy, the exasperated Parisian radicals, fearing betrayal of the revolution, clamored impatiently for action. Lamartine's and Bastide's policy was endangered by radicals who were necessarily uninitiated into the complexities of their strategy, a situation inherent in the contradictions of Lamartine's practice of working on three separate levels. Revolutionary diplomacy could imperil the domestic situation of Lamartine and Bastide if the impatience of Parisian radicals boiled over into a new outbreak of violence.

Lamartine's instructions to his new diplomats—both his regular and secret agents—reflected his confidence that France had no cause for alarm as long as she remained cautious. Each agent was told to "observe, inform, and give, in your conversations with the sovereign, ministers, and the people, the true sense of the republic. Pacific if you understand it, terrible if you provoke it." Lamartine hardly pleased the most extreme republicans with such language, but he believed that premature French action would be self-defeating, provoking a European coalition and a great deal of bloodshed. Instead, if France were patient, time would take care of the enemies of the republic. "To approach the people in arms in such a situation," Lamartine admonished, "would have been like approaching an electrical storm: The explosion of democracy would have resulted beyond our frontiers."[4]

Still, professional revolutionaries believed that aiding the French cause was necessary to the overthrowing of all foreign tyrants. On March 13, 1848, Mikhail Bakunin published a "manifesto" in Flocon's *La Réforme* in which he justified the external policy of the French Provisional Government in the face of attacks by ultra-radicals, who complained that France was not doing enough to assist revolutions beyond her own borders. Bakunin's article reflected his belief in the French intention to overturn all crowned rulers throughout Europe. At the very moment of the outbreak of revolution in Vienna, Bakunin predicted that the Austrian Empire would crumble, and that German and Italian republics would take her place at the center of Europe. These newly unified German and Italian states in turn would give France the necessary leverage to "save" the Russian people. As a Russian, Bakunin's primary interest was the demise of Nicholas I, which could only be accomplished by a broad coalition of emancipated western peoples allied to France. France was the *"foyer"* (nucleus) for world revolution. Bakunin wrote that France was reluctant to become directly involved in the forthcoming revolutions of the other oppressed peoples—not because she lacked interest, but in public Frenchmen had to retain a "tranquil" attitude toward foreign upheavals out of "respect for the independence of peoples themselves." Bakunin touched on the republic's fear of its illegitimate status among the hostile absolutist states: The victory of the "revolutionary principle" was a "matter of life and death" for the French. The future of the French republic depended necessarily on the progress of other revolutionary movements, which would shield her from the attacks of reactionary princes. Yet Bakunin's prediction belied this pose of a "tranquil attitude": "Today France is free. The Poles, Italians, Swiss, Belgians, Germans will be soon."[5]

Poland posed the first practical test of France's dual policy of peace and the promise of freedom for the oppressed nationalities. Nowhere was the contradiction between Lamartine's actions and words more striking than on this question. He secretly proposed to the Poles on "his word of honor" that if he were still in power after the elections to the Constituent Assembly, "Poland shall be reinstated" among the family of nations.[6] At the same time, he attempted to continue on the best terms possible with the governments of the very states that had divided Poland in the late eighteenth century, and who would now be called upon to sacrifice this territory if a Polish state were reconstituted.

This contradiction has led most writers to conclude that Lamartine was merely deceitful; that he lied to the Poles to buy time while he organized the means to destroy the Parisian radicals who were so closely aligned with the Polish extremists.[7] Lamartine, as Bakunin alleged, may well have believed that the policy of peace offered the best hope to the Poles. Like many Frenchmen, he thought that France, without an ally, could not give Poland effective assistance. Everything depended on Germany. If Germans agreed to aid the Poles, Russia could do little in the face of a united European front. If Germany were unwilling to free the Poles, their cause was hopeless, for as an old Polish saying went, "God is far away, and so are the French." The assumption that proved unfounded was that liberal Germans would do something for the Poles.

Lamartine began his diplomatic offensive on behalf of Poland with another public manifesto to the powers that had divided the country. His statement outlined the conditions under which good relations with France were possible. He followed by sending personal agents to Berlin in order to pave the way for a Franco-Prussian military alliance. To satisfy his critics at home and to keep the fire of revolution alive in Poland, Lamartine, on March 11, published an ambiguously worded circular in the French press. It appeared to be a diplomatic dispatch to the French envoys attached to the "northern governments." In fact, the communiqué seems to have existed only in the press. Lamartine was thus bypassing the traditional diplomatic apparatus to reach the domestic and foreign public via the newly developed periodical press.

Stressing provisions for permanent peaceful coexistence between France and central Europe, the circular in no way encouraged the Poles to revolt immediately. Instead, Lamartine assured them that their salvation would come through "debate" with the three courts in succession. France assured the governments of Prussia, Austria, and Russia that: "We desire peace with you, we shall even investigate an alliance on terms equitable to all." But the price of a rapprochement with France was Polish freedom. "The first condition of solidarity for peace, for the intimacy of an alliance, is that usurped, oppressed Poland . . . not come between us!" France called for the reconstitution of divided Poland "in concert with interested powers." The alternative, Lamartine warned, was a "false, precarious, hostile" situation, and ultimately war. Lasting repose in Europe could only be established when the Poles regained their independence.[8]

The ultimate goal of all French diplomacy was the severing of the solid chain binding the three northern powers. French negotiations over Poland could in theory begin with any one of her three dividing powers—and we shall see later that France did indeed attempt direct negotiations in turn with Prussia, Russia, and Austria over an "alliance." The point where Lamartine might entertain the greatest hope was pressure on the weakest link in that unity of the three northern courts, namely Berlin. Prussia was the "cornerstone of continental equilibrium as in 1791," Lamartine realized. "The knot of European peace or war, the emancipation and the reconstruction of Germany, the pacific regeneration of Poland was at Berlin."[9]

Lamartine sent Count Adolphe de Circourt to Berlin to convince the Prussian government that France's intentions were peaceful. Circourt was a man of letters who had recently written a book on Germany. Like Hetzel, Circourt did not manage the daily affairs of the legation; these continued to be handled by the first secretary, Brunet-Denon. This arrangement enabled Circourt to maintain normal relations with the monarch and foreign minister while staying in close contact with the numerous Polish revolutionaries in Berlin, something that might have embarrassed a traditional diplomat.

Circourt's confidential instructions, however, were "written for the ear of the King of Prussia and for his ministers." These repeated Lamartine's message of peace. Circourt was asked to express verbally the main points of the circular to the northern courts. Lamartine wanted a "tacit alliance," not between France and Prussia, but between France and *Germany*. The basis of this alliance would be a moral unity in Germany created by drawing the small states to Prussia and away from Austrian influence. In addition, France was willing to guarantee the inviolability of territory between France and this new united German state in exchange for the reconstitution of Poland.[10]

The instructions for the French minister attached to the Diet of the German Confederation at Frankfurt, Count de Salignac-Fénélon, similarly conveyed a sympathetic policy toward German unity and liberty. Lamartine referred the minister to the Manifesto of March 4, which he imagined left no doubts concerning French policy:

> Germany, like all of Europe, knows the character and tendencies of the foreign policy of the Government of the French Republic. Peace and fraternity are the sincere expression. The republic only aspires to form with the other states fraternal bonds, . . . which should unite all the members of the great family of peoples. The French Republic, pacific and moderate, pure of all ambition and all spirit of conquest, . . . gives to Germany moral support and example and the power for expansion necessary to claim the liberties which can no longer be denied her. France ought to meet in the great German nation only a friendly people, sympathetic to her institutions and her destinies, confident in elevated liberalism.[11]

Lamartine's policy of an alliance with Prussia hinged on the enigmatic character of the Prussian king, and Frederick William was himself beset by contradictory impulses. Having experienced the wars of liberation against Napoleon, he was deeply influenced by German national sentiment. However, this manifested itself as a deeply religious nostalgia for the Middle Ages. Immersed in dreams of the past, he allowed what possibility existed for German unification to slip by, always asserting that Austria must lead Germany. A most unmilitary Hohenzollern, he preferred the company of artists and intellectuals to generals and men of state. Bismarck saw him as a master of his contemporaries in political insight and far superior to his advisers, but noted in him a lack of energy.[12] In March, Frederick William's romantic conception of a kingdom of loyal subjects was dispelled by the eruption of fierce street battles in his beloved capital.

After two weeks of tension, the first barricades in Berlin were thrown up on the evening of March 13. Clashes between civilians and the military ensued, and on March 18 a crowd assembled in front of the king's palace demanding: "Pull back the troops!" As General Prittwitz attempted to disperse the crowd, shots rang out and a civil war was under way. The next day the fate of the military monarchy was decided. Frederick William capitulated to the demands of his burghers; he withdrew the army from Berlin, turned power over to a citizen guard, and promised to merge Prussia into Germany.[13]

A "revolutionary psychosis" had created a common accord between the high and low people of the German states. They demanded a constitution, a flag, an army, and a powerful ruler. This was the opportunity for the Prussian monarchy to join the will of the people, as all classes in society "were seized by restlessness," a desire to fight somewhere, although no one yet knew against whom. The court chamberlain of the dwarf state of Ballenstedt admitted: "Really I have no other desire than to put a musket on my shoulder and take part in a campaign. A militant spirit is pouring over the entire population."[14]

The king's advisors were overwhelmed by these events.[15] The king's adjutant, Leopold von Gerlach, recorded in his diary on March 11 that the monarch was exhausted and felt isolated.[16] Amidst the irresolution and inner conflicts at the court, Baron Heinrich von Arnim-Suckow, the former Prussian ambassador to France, who had recently arrived back from Paris "very liberal," seemed to have made a strong impression on the king, Gerlach noted.[17] Although Gerlach believed on March 12 that the time for resistance had arrived, the royal family lacked the strength for a struggle, and a torpor reigned in Potsdam.[18] Arnim was the man of the hour in Prussia.

A veteran of 1815, known as the "lame Arnim" because of a foot wound, and as the "crude Arnim" because of his blunt manner, Heinrich von Arnim alone offered Frederick William and Germany a bold program to harness the forces of the Berlin revolution and to solve the problem of German unity. Since his return from Paris in early March, Arnim had expounded his new political faith, rejoicing over the fall of Louis Philippe and Guizot and asserting his belief in the necessity and justice of the French republic. He outlined these beliefs and a new foreign policy for Prussia in a significant pamphlet entitled *The Political Memorandum Concerning the French February Revolution and its Consequences for Germany*, which was published in Brussels to avoid Prussian censorship, but appeared in Berlin on March 20.[19] In this pamphlet, Arnim urged that Prussia should immediately take command and carry out two important changes: the increase of the German military potential and the declaration of German neutrality. Arnim declared that:

> This declaration of neutrality should be in the name of united Germany through Prussia, and it should be sent in a circular dispatch to the four great courts. It must state that Germany in the present situation rejects any alliance with one or more of the four great powers. . . . Also, Prussia can declare that she, in the name of united Germany or in her own, neither directly nor indirectly will take part in Austria's war arising from her non-German provinces. The same rejection is awaited from the other great powers. Lastly, Prussia, for herself, might send at once a secret explanation concerning Poland to the courts of London and Paris.[20]

Arnim seems to have been echoing his recent conversations with Lamartine. Like Lamartine, Arnim saw divided Poland as a menace. To achieve lasting order it was necessary to bring about a change in the Polish situation. "The present condition of Poland is irreconcilable with public opinion and with peace in Europe, as well as with the European balance of power," Arnim argued, and urged his king to begin planning for reconstruction. Surrendering Poland freely was only "common sense." Prussia could thus escape internal difficulties and the danger of a conflict with "France and the armed nationalities." To retain any of Poland would be counter to the "principle of sanctity of nationalities and the general spirit of the times." Small sacrifices prudently made by Prussia could not be compared to immediate rewards: a "peace alliance *(Friedensband)* with England and France and a fortress *(Vormauer)*" of Poland as a buffer state against Russia. "In the interest of peace and the balance of power in Europe," Arnim urged, "Prussia should declare that she desires the restoration of old Poland's independence and autonomy under the condition of her eternal neutrality."[21]

Arnim proposed a diplomatic revolution. In place of the reactionary alliance of the three northern courts, he suggested a liberal league of Great Britain, Prussia, and France: a "peaceful ring" around Russia, the last reactionary power untouched by the revolution in 1848. Most important, Prussia must not oppose the "spirit of the age" *(allgemeine Meinung des Zeitalters)*. Arnim called for a new Prussian diplomacy openly hostile to old allies, Austria and Russia, that would champion the cause of revolution and nationalism. Prussia must promise not only to refuse aid to Austria in Italy and in Hungary, but must expect Russia not to help Austria either.

Arnim's liberalism would guarantee that Austria could not expect assistance from the German Confederation during the imminent war with France in Italy. This new direction of Prussian foreign policy would no longer conflict with the French principle of the sanctity of nationalities, since, by the nature of this new policy, Prussia ceased to infringe on the rights of other nations. Imperial expansion over non-Germans was rejected. The "principle" of nationalities had reached the level of international law in Arnim's vocabulary. He contended that countries had "violated" the rights of man by ruling over subject nations. Nationalism should be at the center of Prussian policy as much as it was at the center of the French. Interestingly, Arnim justified this by resorting to the same principle of "balance of power" that Metternich employed to support legitimacy. Although France was linked with the "armed revolution," a change in policy could save Prussia from the danger of a "fire in her own house" if she acted in time.[22]

Arnim had a wide and immediate response to his policy in Prussia. In Berlin, the leader of the 1846 Polish rising, Ludwik Mieroslawski, and other prisoners in the Moabit prison were released by the amnesty of March 20 and cheered by the people in a triumphant procession through the streets of Berlin. At the moment of the March revolution, even Helmut von Moltke was moved by this generous and realistic sentiment, stating that: If "Europe [is] reconstituted according to nationalities, everything foreign will fall away; we ought to retain everything German, so we would be richly compensated."[23]

On March 23, Frederick William received a deputation from Breslau that included Mieroslawski and to which he promised greater Polish autonomy. He pledged to proceed quickly with the national reorganization of the Grand Duchy of Posen (Poznań) in a manner favorable to the Poles. Such a concession to Polish independence was ensured by a cabinet order of March 24, 1848. On April 6, the Prussian Landtag resolved that Posen would no longer be part of the German Confederation, which was equivalent to recognizing the duchy's autonomy.[24]

French diplomats in Germany reported that sympathy for Polish liberation was sweeping that nation. They also reported that the courts of Vienna and Berlin expected compensation for the loss of their eastern provinces. Count de Salignac-Fénélon, who replaced Bourgoing at Frankfurt, wrote:

> The question of the liberation of Poland has not ceased for an instant to dominate discussion. I have been assured that most ministers of the Diet, influenced by the advice of the permanent committee [of 50] will declare themselves frankly for Poland. They are not motivated merely by the ephemeral passions of the multitude, but by the real and permanent interests of Europe. . . . Without a doubt, it is hard for Prussia to render freedom to the Grand Duchy of Posen, . . . but if in exchange she can force Russia back to the east, if Courland and Livonia, German provinces, were incorporated into Prussia, that country would gain by the change. At the same time, if Austria were compensated in the beautiful Danubian principalities, their possession would be worth that of Lombardy and Galicia together. Those are . . . the general views of the majority of the ministers of the Diet. . . . The universal wish . . . is to remain a friend of France, to maintain relations of national confidence.[25]

In spite of the Prussian king's misgivings, Arnim was ready for a pact achieving the unity of Germany and Poland. He told Lamartine's envoy Circourt of his fear that Prussia's relations with Russia would become precarious because of the Poles who had gathered as an army in Prussian territory in order to liberate Russian Poland. While Prussia "was not prepared to offer German troops to the Poles to attack Russia," Circourt reported to Paris that "they would not impede volunteers, German or others, coming from France or elsewhere, from joining in Posen the banner of national Poland." The only condition that Arnim made was that the "auxiliaries," while crossing the Prussian provinces, not be in obviously armed and organized units. "For the rest," Arnim asserted, "when they fight for the principle of the construction of independent nationalities, *that will be for a just principle, that will be for our present* [German] *principle that they fight!*"[26] Since a clash between the armed Poles, operating from Prussian soil, and the Russians seemed unavoidable, Circourt predicted that if the Polish invasion of the Russian Empire were repulsed by force, Prussia would go to war:

> The Prussian nation will impetuously ask for a declaration of war. If Russians, following their advantage, penetrate in turn on Prussian territory, that declaration of war will positively be required, and the King [of Prussia] will have to fight his brother-in-law, his former ally, to unfurl . . . the banner of Germany in a crusade for the Poles.[27]

In this tense situation, with Prussia and Russia on the verge of war, Arnim linked his pamphlet of March 17 to Lamartine's alliance offer. "The Polish organization in the Grand Duchy of Posen," he informed Circourt, was only a preparation for the "reconstruction of the independent nationality of all of old Poland." He assured Circourt that it was "morally impossible" for the Russian tsar not to see the actions of the Prussian cabinet as "an indirect aggression, a hostility against her principle, an imminent danger to her interests." Under these circumstances, Arnim requested the exact terms of the Franco-Prussian alliance; what would France do if Russia attacked Prussia? Circourt was asked to secure from France:

> First, a declaration of alliance and of political solidarity for the reconstruction of Poland. That would give her [Prussia] a moral support of considerable value. Second, if they asked us, to send a squadron into the Baltic to operate as a diversion. Two ships with our flag would suffice to increase notably the force and confidence of the Polish national party and their German auxiliaries.[28]

Within a month, the Provisional Government of France had evolved from the pariah of Europe to partner in an alliance with the sharpest sword on the continent.

The French were elated by this turn of events. The first news of the revolutions in central Europe had met with rejoicing in Paris, as the forces of reaction fell before the overwhelming power of French ideas of liberty, equality, and fraternity. The Belgian chargé in Paris, Prince de Ligne, reported that the king of Prussia's proclamation was observed by the French government as a prelude to German unification. Equally encouraging to the French was the rising in Vienna, because that implied the "dissolution of the Austrian monarchy." With this, foreign relations would be on a new basis. "France will triumph, because any possibility of a coalition against her will be impossible."[29]

From all sides, Lamartine heard the good news that France supposedly did not depend on the Prussian king's cabinet alone, but upon the German masses. Forces far below the surface had burst forth to endanger the existence of the old princes who had been hostile to France. Salignac had reported on March 26 that the "general spirit" in Germany was democratic and liberal. Although Germans were presently inclined to favor a constitutional monarchy rather than a republic, the violence of the March days had gravely weakened the Prussian and other German monarchs, and the maintenance of royalty in the long term appeared to be threatened.

Lamartine was the beneficiary of what Stadelmann called the "revolutionary psychosis" that temporarily immobilized the traditional line of authority in the old monarchies. The first reaction of the triumphant German burghers was an enthusiastic outpouring of sentiment: "They wished to act at any cost and to participate in the responsibility, they wished to represent the nation by leaving everything behind, they wanted to do something together and did not know any other way than by becoming a soldier."[30]

The strange corollary of the German citizenry's newfound sense of omnipotence was a corresponding weakening of the will to resist among the ruling classes in Berlin and Vienna. This paralysis intensified the tsar's feeling of isolation.

But no less than in St. Petersburg, Lamartine could not afford to wound the sensitivities of the German burghers, who were exhilarated by the novelty of a sense of power. Certainly Lamartine's March 4 Manifesto enabled him to allow matters to develop. Revolutionary diplomacy was a delicate matter. He must not repeat the blunder of 1792. The author of *The History of the Girondins* certainly hoped to profit from his knowledge of the fate of the Girondist war of liberation. The enthusiasm of the Parisian radicals for moral conquests in Italy and Poland had to be held in check long enough for Lamartine to assemble a coalition capable of dealing with the tsar without arousing the suspicions of the British. Lamartine seemed capable of accomplishing all this.

Lamartine's agent Circourt obtained a Prussian offer of an alliance, but revolutionary diplomacy was not the old cabinet diplomacy. Heinrich von Arnim might talk of a military alliance, but his ability to deliver was another matter. Both Arnim and Lamartine ultimately depended on the barricade fighters, whose moment of violence placed them in power. By the same token, they had to fear a new outbreak of street fighting in Paris and Berlin. To forestall that eventuality, Lamartine entertained delegations of foreign agitators in Paris and made bombastic public pronouncements. At the same time, he had to fear the formation of a hostile coalition of foreign powers led by the British and Russians, so he assured accredited diplomats in the French capital that he was insincere in his public statements. In this web of contradictions, with Lamartine saying one thing in public to radicals and the opposite in private to members of the diplomatic corps, his cadre of secret agents carried on a diplomatic campaign at a subterranean level.

NOTES

1. Benedetto Croce, *A History of Europe in the Nineteenth Century*, Henry Furst, trans. (New York, 1933), p. 168.

2. Rudolf Stadelmann, *Social and Political History of the German 1848 Revolution*, James G. Chastain, trans. (Athens, Oh., 1975), ch. 5.

3. Alphonse de Lamartine, *Le passé*, pp. 79–80; Lamartine, *Histoire*, II, 13–26; Garnier-Pagès, *Histoire*, VII, 307–08.

4. Lamartine, *Histoire*, II, 29; Note that these instructions were *verbal*, so our records of their contents are necessarily very fragmentary; furthermore, correspondence was private and often sent not to the foreign minister, but to another person in the French ministry; Lamartine, *Le passé*, p. 65.

5. Included as Annex #7 in Hans-Karl Tannewitz, "M. A. Bakunins publizistische Persönlichkeit dargestellt an seiner politisch-journalistischen Arbeit 1849 in Dresden," (Ph. D. diss., Free University of Berlin, 1962), pp. 185–86.

6. Report of "Florian" (Sigmund Sawiczewski) to Apponyi, Paris, March 14, 1848, HHSA, IX Frankreich, printed in Josef Feldman, *Sprawa Polska w Roku 1848* (Cracow, 1933), 95n–96n.

7. In addition to Feldman, *Sprawa Polska*, cf., Jennings, *France and Europe*; R. A. Marwati Djoened Poesponegoro, "La France devant le problème polonais en 1848–1849" (diss., University of Paris, 1968); Wislawa Knapowska, "La France, la Prusse et la question polonaise en 1848," in *La Pologne au VIᵉ Congrès International des Sciences historiques à Oslo, 1928* (Warsaw, 1930), pp. 147–66.

8. Lamartine aux Agents diplomatiques près des gouvernements du nord, circulaire, March [11], 1848, DDF, I, 145; Knapowska placed great importance on the fact that the proclamation was never sent, since no copy exists in the Paris or Berlin archives. There are actually two good explanations. First, this interestingly illuminates the nature of French diplomacy by propaganda, the use of newspapers of Europe as a forum for diplomatic statements. In Lamartine's diplomatic style, the circular was addressed not only to the present holders of power, but to those the coming revolution would put in their places. Its principal points were included in Circourt's instructions as well as many other official documents; Secondly, Bastide stated another reason that a communication would not have been addressed to a foreign state: This would have implied an answer, and France was not recognized, and had only unofficial diplomatic representation in European capitals.

9. Lamartine, *Histoire*, II, 175–79.

10. *Ibid.*; Circourt, *Souvenirs d'une mission à Berlin* 2 vols., *passim*; Circourt to Lamartine, Berlin, March 12, 1848, DDF, I, 163.

11. Lamartine to Salignac-Fénélon, Paris, March 15, 1848, DDF, I, 214–15; cf. his favorable attitude toward an elected parliament for the German people in his letter to Salignac of April 4, 1848, DDF, I, 610, and sentiment of Germans friendly to France, Billing to Lamartine, Frankfurt, March 10, 1848, DDF, I, 123; Bourgoing to Lamartine, Munich, March 10, 1848, DDF, I, 125–26; Friedrich Ley, "Frankreich und die deutsche Revolution 1848–49" (doc. diss., University of Kiel, 1923) and Robert Hahn, "The attitude of the French Revolutionary Government toward German Unification in 1848" (Ph.D. diss., Ohio State University, 1955) include outstanding discussion of the French periodical press, which was almost entirely friendly to Germany and its unification, to the slight extent that it exhibited any interest in events across the Rhine, cf. Hahn, pp. 81–94, Ley, pp. 38–40, 86–92, and *passim*. Even Alexander Scharff, in his most vocal criticism of French opposition to German unity, admitted that there was not a serious question of widespread popular French hostility to Germans, *Die europäischen Grossmächte und die deutsche Revolution: Deutsche Einheit und europäische Ordnung, 1848–1851* (Leipzig, 1942), pp. 79ff.

12. Frederick William IV was torn between the conflicting advice of his ministers: Valentin, *Geschichte der deutschen Revolution*, I, 28–36; Theodore Hamerow believed that Frederick William was "slow to act on good advice. He was a thinker, a visionary, not a doer," *Restoration, Revolution, Reaction: Economics and Politics in Germany, 1815–1871* (Princeton, 1958), p. 73; Hajo Holborn, *A History of Modern Germany, 1840–1945* (New York, 1969), pp. 30–32, 51ff; His friend Leopold von Ranke speculated, "Perhaps he had more temperament than a state can bear." *Allgemeine deutsche Biographie*, VII, 769–772 (hereafter ADB); Circourt, *Souvenirs*, II, 442–43; the best bibliography is Valentin, I, 624–25.

13. Stadelmann, *Social and Political History*, chapter 4.

14. *Ibid.*, pp. 75–77.

15. Heinrich Alexander Baron von Arnim-Suckow (1798–1861), since 1820 in Prussian diplomatic service; 1840–46 Ambassador in Brussels; 1846–48, Ambassador in Paris. He was foreign minister March 21–June 20, 1848, and should not be confused with either Adolf Heinrich Count von Arnim-Boitzenburg (1803–68), nephew of Baron vom Stein, who held various posts in the Prussian civil service, 1842–45 Minister of Interior, delegate to United Landtag, and from March 18 to 28 Prime Minister of Prussia; nor with a third Arnim, Heinrich Friedrich Count von Arnim-Werberlow (1791–1859), who rose in the diplomatic service to Ambassador in Brussels (1831), Paris (1841), and Vienna (1845), Foreign Minister February 24–May 3, 1849, then returned to a post in Vienna; *Allgemeine deutsche Biographie* (ADB), I, 558–66, 570–74.

16. Ludwig von Gerlach, *Von der Revolution zum Norddeutschen Bund*, I, 82, 86–88; Valentin, *Geschichte der deutschen*, I, 538; Gerlach, *Denkwürdigkeiten*, I, 145.

17. Gerlach, *Denkwürdigkeiten*, I, 131.

18. *Ibid.*

19. [Heinrich von Arnim], *Die politische Denkschrift über die französische Februar-Revolution und ihre Folgen für Deutschland* (Berlin, 1848); Arnim personally gave a copy of this memoir to the French envoy in early April to explain Prussia's policy. Circourt to Lamartine, Berlin, April 9, 1848, Circourt, *Souvenirs*, I, 408–09.

20. Arnim, *Die politische Denkschrift*, pp. 20–21.

21. *Ibid.*, pp. 21–22.

22. *Ibid.*

23. Rudolf Stadelmann, *Moltke und der Staat* (Crefeld, 1948), p. 102; Circourt, *Souvenirs*.

24. Paul Henry, "Le gouvernement provisoire," pp. 206–09; Georg W. F. Hallgarten, *Studien über die deutsche Polenfreundschaft in der Periode der Märzrevolution* (Munich, 1928); Eberhard Maier, *Die aussenpolitischen Ideen der Achtundvierziger* "Historische Studien" vol. 337 (Berlin, 1938).

25. Salignac-Fénélon to Lamartine, Frankfurt, April 6 and March 21, 1848, DDF, I, 654 and 321; Bourgoing to Lamartine, Munich, March 30, 1848, DDF, I, 518–19; Brunet-Denon to Lamartine, Berlin, March 23, 1848, DDF, I, 366.

26. Circourt to Lamartine, Berlin, March 29, 1848, in Circourt, *Souvenirs*, I, 307.

27. *Ibid.*, I, 307–08.

28. Circourt to Lamartine, Berlin, March 31, 1848, *Ibid.*, I, 325–26.

29. Ligne to Hoffschmidt, Paris, March 22, 1848, AEB, XIII France, fo. 96.

30. Stadelmann, *Social and Political History*, pp. 76–77.

Chapter Two
The Call for Revolutionary Action
MARCH-APRIL 1848

THREE OF THE SECRET AGENTS that Lamartine sent to Germany in March epitomized the complexity and complications inherent in his policy. They hoped to exploit the marvelous opportunity offered France by March revolutions in the German states. The German liberals were contacted by Lamartine's three agents, but each in different style. Lamartine's old friend, the monarchist Circourt with his noble Polish wife, presumably could relate well with patriotic circles at the Berlin court who might overcome a natural hostility toward France because of the Junkers' ambition to supplant Austria as the preeminent authority in Germany. Lamartine turned first for advice and now for operations support to the Polish Prince Adam Czartoryski, former minister of Tsar Alexander I and leader of the unsuccessful Polish revolt of 1830–31. From his headquarters in the Hotel Lambert in Paris, Czartoryski controlled his network of Polish secret agents scattered across east central Europe. Czartoryski with his secret agents hoped to rally all of those dissident elements now gravitating toward Berlin, who were anxious to throw off tsarist tutelage. Vanguard of the Franco-Polish offensive against tsarism was to be German liberals, who were generally sympathetic to the cause of Polish freedom. Finally, the aristocratic anarchist Mikhail Bakunin represented a peculiar Russian tradition of patrician revolt,[1] yet at the same time the old associate of Marx could appeal to democratic-radical leaders in Germany. During the next several weeks, the trio of roving ambassadors of revolt would be joined by other agents sent by Lamartine and Bastide. Together their goal would be to collaborate Germany's inclination to cooperate with France in a campaign to terminate the old Habsburg domination of central Europe. Thus, Lamartine and Bastide remained committed to the

Richelieu-Girondist tradition of soliciting German clients against the house of Habsburg, endeavoring to fuse Prussian Junkers, bourgeois German liberals, and democratic artisans. And as disparate elements competed as well for power within Germany, each was contacted in turn by French secret agents. Circourt, Czartoryski, Bakunin, and company had high hopes of precipitating the war against tsarism that would free Poland and Italy, because in the process such a war would unite Germans into a single state. However, Lamartine's chief concern had to be the prevention of this great struggle until his great coalition of foreign and domestic associates was in place.

In Paris, Lamartine and Bastide continued to stay in power through a delicate balancing act: trying to convince the radical clubbists that the presence of socialists like Ledru-Rollin was sufficient proof that Lamartine was loyal to his promises to free the peoples of Europe while simultaneously reassuring the foreign statesmen and domestic notables that Lamartine was a moderating force capable of preventing France from sliding into anarchy. This balance became more difficult to maintain during March, with the news of revolutions in Germany. The liberal March revolutions in the German states increased the volume of the voices calling for Lamartine to modify his peaceful posture: Now, they insisted, was the moment for a show of force. But where? And with whom should France ally herself?

The situation in Germany had become highly complex. Arnim's new Prussian government sought an alliance with Lamartine. Yet Arnim's position was hardly secure. Meanwhile, southern German liberals proposed a national parliament to convene in Frankfurt am Main. And, like Lamartine, Arnim was plagued by the most extremist faction of the Poles, ever impatient and hotheaded.

All Europe seemed divided into two factions: the revolutionary radicals and the moderates. Although both agreed that the old frontiers of Europe must be redrawn along national lines, they disagreed on timing. Yet in a revolutionary situation, timing is everything, and friend and foe are often separated by the single issue of the pace of change. In such a situation, the entire former political spectrum loses its significance: Either one is committed to carrying the revolution forward or else one begins to entertain doubts that there is a need for further progress. And at the point of hesitation, the old revolutionaries merge into an amorphous mass of opponents of change. Thus Danton and Robespierre became mortal enemies at that crucial moment when Danton believed that the radicalization of the revolution needed to be halted, that France must relax the terror. Similarly, in 1848, the key question was the timing of change. The old monarchies eventually were to be transformed into new, national conglomerations. But how soon? The faction of Flocon and Ledru-Rollin within the Provisional Government called for immediate action, while a more moderate stand was taken by all those opposing the hotheads of the moment.

During the final week of March 1848, Lamartine was confronted with a difficult choice. He had to decide whether to grasp the outstretched hand of the new Arnim cabinet in Prussia or whether to wait out the possibility of an even more radical turn in the German revolution. The affair of the German Legion illustrates the complexity of Lamartine's predicament. Immediately following the February Revolution, a small group of German extremists in Paris debated what course to take to hasten their homeland's steps down the road to revolution. Calling itself the German Legion, this group planned armed intervention, despite strong warnings by Karl Marx and Frederick Engels that an armed putsch was doomed to failure under the conditions of the day. Marx and Engels publicly distanced themselves from the enterprise, which went forward under the leadership of the poet Georg Herwegh.

Lamartine's role in the matter was devious. First, he covered himself for the eventuality that Marx's prediction proved correct. Just in case the uprising failed to topple the governments of the various German states, Lamartine left the way open for continued relations with the old rulers by giving them a timely warning of the impending invasion. On March 17, a full month before the armed incursion of Baden, Ferdinand Baron von Schweitzer, the Baden chargé, called on Lamartine and his under-secretary, Bastide. From them the chargé received the confidential information that a German democratic club in Paris had resolved to send a band of 5,000 to 6,000 workers from Paris to invade the Grand Duchy of Baden. This column had made preparations to depart on March 22 or 23. Having made these revelations, Lamartine and Bastide requested that Schweitzer tell no one of their conversation, so that Ledru-Rollin would not hear of Lamartine's betrayal of the German workers.[2]

When Lamartine saw Austrian ambassador Apponyi on the afternoon of March 22, he appeared despondent, claiming that he could not count on a hundred men in the entire National Guard to defend the government. "We have nothing but our naked breasts to oppose our adversaries," he bemoaned, claiming that it was not only possible but even probable that within a few days the Provisional Government would pass under the influence of the National Guard leaders, who were, for the most part, the directors of the democratic clubs. Even if they chose to elect Lamartine premier, it would be only as a hostage. Without the protection of the National Guard, Lamartine drew up the specter of a new revolution of 100,000 to 150,000 workers, led by the chiefs of the clubs. But Lamartine characterized Ledru-Rollin not as the instigator of mischief but solely as the "instrument" of his party. Except for a few nuances of opinion, Lamartine assured Apponyi, there was accord among the members of the Provisional Government.[3] It seems likely that there was an element of truth in Lamartine's claim that he was under pressure from the clubs to increase French support of such foreign adventures.

On March 24, the council of the Provisional Government did appropriate 60,000 francs to allow Flocon to pay the "journey costs" of foreign workers requesting a subsidy for their return to their homelands. In spite of the claims that this money was not to be used for arms, Flocon in fact provided weapons from the French arsenal.[4] Yet within the council of the Provisional Government Lamartine maintained that good relations with Prussia were essential for France. Even as France was underwriting the costs of the military expedition into Germany, Lamartine pressed for circumspection. At least in part a cause of concern was his own domestic situation.[5]

And while Lamartine feigned a lack of interest in any direct military intervention in Germany, he was laying the groundwork for a Franco-Prussian alliance.

On March 25, Lamartine felt a need to respond to Prussia's generous gestures toward the Poles. He used Prince Adam Czartoryski, an aspirant to the crown of reconstituted Poland, as an intermediary to inform the Prussian government that he was ready for an alliance. France would "assist Poland by sea, if the Prussian cabinet decided to give it support on land."[6] Confidentially, Lamartine proposed a military pact to restore Poland's freedom and to unify Germany.

In addition, Lamartine sent two other secret agents into Germany at this juncture. Herwegh's confidant, Mikhail Bakunin, went as an advance scout to explore what possibilities existed for a general uprising in the Rhineland. Crisscrossing the entire region during the next two weeks, Bakunin finally arrived in Cologne, where he had a fateful interview with Marx and Engels. It is likely that Bakunin attempted to convince the fathers of scientific socialism that the moment had arrived to move from theory to action.[7]

The instructions for Lamartine's secret agent Alexandre Rey, a former colleague of Louis Blanc on the *Revue de Progrès* and of Bastide on the *National*, indicated the tenor of the foreign minister's thoughts on March 27. He told Rey to travel secretly to Frankfurt with no official title, but, like Hetzel, to carry credentials "in reserve" until "circumstances permit you to present them, that is to say when the French republic is recognized or if . . . eventualities arise which hasten your revealing them." Lamartine instructed him to "observe from the important vantage of Germany the whole new situation and the great future." Rey was to verify what grass-roots support existed throughout Germany for an alliance with France. He should determine the attitude of the masses toward France, noting the "movement of ideas and of conditions, the more or less democratic tendency of opinion, what disposition exists to ally the destiny of liberal Germany to France by a union founded on common interests of liberty, independence, and civilization." In addition, Rey should explain to Germans that "morality, order, fraternity, and human dignity recommend the French republic to the sympathies of peoples."[8]

A few days later, Lamartine made his assumptions about Germany explicit in a dispatch to his chargé in Frankfurt. The tone of the dispatch was as deterministic as that of his conversation with Apponyi less than a week earlier. "The German Diet," he wrote Salignac-Fénélon, "cannot resist the liberal and national impulse which sweeps across all Germany." So far, "Germany, in general, has only reached the era of constitutional monarchies." But these constitutional monarchs had a limited future, since the German nation "was permeated by the democratic spirit."

While he recognized that Germans might be suspicious of the French, Lamartine refused to believe Salignac's report that they were hostile to the republican government "because of a residual defiance toward France."[9] Lamartine was aware that mistrust of the republic existed among Germans, caused by the "impressions and memories from another epoch, the fear of seeing this revolution become expansionistic and spilling over into the German Confederation."[10]

BIXIO.

– Plus désinteressé encore que les grands hommes de Plutarque, Bixio n'a consenti a passer qu'une semaine dans le palais du Ministère du commerce, – le huitième jour ce nouveau Cincinnatus est retourné arrose ses laitues Romaines.

Alexandre Bixio, French Envoy in Turin, by Honoré Daumier, Bibliothèque Nationale (Paris).

Thus it appears that Lamartine believed in late March that the rebellious circumstances in Germany favored the French and that the inevitable wave of revolution that was sweeping across central Europe would also enhance the French position.[11]

As early as March 25, the same day that he had instructed Czartoryski to inform the Prussian cabinet of his willingness to conclude an alliance to liberate Poland, Lamartine spoke with Ambassador Apponyi of Austria. He anticipated that the events of the past week were the first of many that would lead to a general upheaval that would destroy the old system of government and bring a "completely democratic organization to all the states" of Germany. Lamartine expected that the new German order would have great ramifications in European politics. In particular, the resurrection of Poland was the "wish and demand" of all Germany. According to Lamartine, emancipation of Poland ought to "lead necessarily and immediately to a war with Russia, a state so unpopular and so detested in Germany. France will be forced to take part in that war," Lamartine continued, "which will cause little bloodshed and end quickly."[12]

In response to the news of an uprising in Milan March 18–22, 1848, Lamartine turned to a trusted member of his inner cabinet, Alexandre Bixio, brother of the Genoese republican leader. Giving Bixio the title of Secretary of the Legation at Turin, Lamartine sent him to investigate the situation in northern Italy. On March 29 Bixio reported that Sardinia's military position was bleak. Although everyone had *"great illusions as to their probable chances in war,"* Bixio complained, "I am most struck here by the contrast of the audacity of enterprise and the insufficiency of means." Bixio asked for further instructions. Lamartine's annotation on the dispatch read:

> Reply that the information seems to us to conform closely to our predictions. It is necessary to insist vigorously that Sardinia complete the advance once she has begun. France will only intervene if Italy calls for it.[13]

France was committed to come to Italy's aid when the Sardinian armies inevitably collapsed.

Simultaneously the situation in northern Europe became more serious as Denmark and the German Confederation neared a confrontation over the disputed duchies of Schleswig and Holstein.[14] These two territories had been joined by a personal union when, on March 27, the king of Denmark issued a royal proclamation annexing Schleswig to Denmark. The revolutionary Provisional Government of Schleswig-Holstein gathered troops and asked for support from the German Confederation. On March 28, Marquis Auguste-Bonaventure de Tallenay, French minister in Hamburg, warned his government that "everything is ready for a war in the duchies of Schleswig-Holstein." The following day he reported that a "semi-official article" in the Berlin press referred to the disputed duchies as "territory of the German nation," which Prussia had to protect against a Danish invasion.[15]

War had become inevitable, and it commenced on April 7 with an attack by 10,000 Danes on Flensburg and a German retreat which quickly became a rout. By April 12 the Danes were masters of the entire duchy to the Eider River, and menaced Rendsburg, the last German fortress in Schleswig. Meanwhile on April 4, the German Confederation took measures to protect Holstein, one of its members. Federal troops of the Tenth German Army Corps advanced to Rendsburg, turning a local revolt into a European problem.

With wars threatening in the north and south Lamartine reviewed the situation for a joint meeting of the Council of the Provisional Government and the Commission of National Defense:

> The King of Sardinia has decided to move into Lombardy-Venetia, resolved to accept the crown of these rich countries. He awaits the recognition of France. Naples is a semi-republican state; Rome poses a republican constitution; the Pope has accepted the presidency. Florence seems calm, Genoa incandescent. With one hundred twenty thousand men under arms, Switzerland seems indisposed to contract an offensive and defensive alliance with France. Germany is exposed to profound disturbances. In Berlin, the revolution stopped at the second stage. Fear caused the King of Prussia, like the King of Sardinia, to be carried away by ambition. The English government fears our participation in the Irish troubles; but the cold response to our Republic in Spain gives her hopes of support against us. Prey to excessive irritation, the tsar searches for popularity to the point of attempting the emancipation of the serfs; he dreams of despotism in democracy; this will cause a rising of the nobles against him. He can rally four hundred thousand men. *The Polish question is on the brink of resolving itself without the need of our firing a shot.* In the face of these facts, the Provisional Government more than ever perseveres in its policies.[16]

Following these remarks, Lamartine introduced the members of the Commission of Defense, who were then given authorization to increase France's military strength and to station large armies on the Italian, German, and Spanish borders.

On April 2 the Council of the Provisional Government received from Lamartine the welcome news of Austria's full retreat and also heard that Russia was less hostile to the republic. The council then discussed the Prussian request for French support in the case of an immediate invasion by Russia.[17] In spite of its policy of peace the republic suddenly seemed threatened with the prospect of war on two fronts.

Yet the accepted wisdom is that France was unwilling and unable to fight. With rare unanimity, historians have uncritically accepted Lamartine's subsequent claim that the French army was in a precarious state soon after the February Revolution. Lamartine's colleague, the utopian socialist Louis Blanc, later recalled that:

> The total number of men available for the defense of the country did not exceed 101,000, whilst the number requisite, in the event of a monarchical coalition, to line the frontiers without unfurnishing Algeria, could not be less than 514,000!

At the same time, the country's financial condition was "actually verging on bankruptcy."[18]

Lamartine's assessment differed in detail only. On taking office, he noted, he found the French army of 370,000 troops "so reduced by garrisons, the defense of the coasts and the colonies . . . that the minister of foreign affairs and his colleagues trembled for the country's weakness."[19]

But an evaluation of the military preparedness of France from a current vantage point must take into account not only the number of troops she had at hand but also their state of training and discipline. It must consider as well the special problem of maintaining order in Paris, the comparative strength of France's allies and opponents, and, in addition, the country's non-military resources.[20]

Some historians have praised France for her "peaceful policy" and "prudence" during these days of crisis. Others have pointed out that her domestic difficulties, including an excited population of radicals and a bankrupt treasury, as well as a professional army too small for normal peacetime needs, made it impossible to consider any armed incursions on foreign soil and kept the republic peaceful.[21]

Undoubtedly, the Provisional Government feared an immediate attack by a foreign coalition, and it swiftly organized a Commission for the Organization of National Defense under General Pelet to prepare to repel an invasion of French soil. Jean Baptiste Charras, protégé of French General and later Minister of War Lamoricière, on March 2 was appointed the commission's secretary. When Eugene Cavaignac refused the post of defense minister, the commission decided to retain François Arago for the moment and to make Charras under-secretary of state. Charras took office on April 7. In his memoirs, Charras claimed that his first move was to impress on the command of troops and on the administration a "seal of energy and activity" and to demonstrate to them that their chief was a "man of will." He saw his task as being to "reestablish discipline, augment very quickly the personnel and material of the army, organize the Army of the Alps," and to prepare the organization of other armies on the Moselle and Rhine and in the north.[22]

The task was not easy. On April 7, thirty-three corps were infected with cases of "very grave insubordination." Within two weeks, Charras claimed, order was reestablished by energetic measures, as the ideologically engaged Charras refused to allow the army to be "politicized." Soon 150,000 conscripts were called to the colors, 30,000 horses bought, and arsenals and material on hand doubled and tripled. In May the portfolio of minister was offered to Charras, who had been working sixteen to twenty hours a day at the ministry, but the lieutenant colonel refused it. When Cavaignac arrived in Paris as minister on May 17, he left Charras to continue the work of reorganizing the adminstration of France's defenses. France's cavalry strength was doubled and the infantry raised to over a half-million men, "dressed, equipped, armed, and in a perfect state of maintenance and discipline."[23]

Charras's account is supported by the independent record of Charles de Rémusat, who credited him with the transformation of the army's effectiveness after the revolution. Son of a regicide, Charras had taken an active part in the Revolution of 1830 and wrote for the opposition paper, *The National*. "Charras, by his position and his qualities," Rémusat noted, "was more able than anyone else to resist an invasion of the anarchical party in the army." He held the army intact until Cavaignac could take command. By maintaining discipline and preventing the organization of radical clubs in the army, Rémusat contended, Charras was responsible for "saving France."[24]

A recent study suggested that the "morale crisis" was already ebbing before Charras's actions. "The crisis of discipline after February," wrote Witold Zaniewicki, "was immediately reabsorbed by energetic action by the cadres, above all those who were republicans."[25] Zaniewicki cited evidence that both officers and men were anxious for war. The generals Lamoricière, Bedeau, Changarnier, Saint-Arnaud, and Oudinot all wanted foreign combat. Zaniewicki noted several indications of the simple soldiers' desire to fight. Rather than immobilizing the army, the emergence of a civil war between social classes increased the popularity of foreign war. The soldier of 1848 was most often a bachelor who ardently desired battle in order to escape the *ennui* of garrison life, perhaps even more so than the officers. Until the closing of Alpine passes by winter, Zaniewicki argued that troops were ready and able to fight in Italy. Thus Zaniewicki concluded that the French were much stronger in 1848 than in 1830 or 1840. Lamartine could boast before the Constituent Assembly on May 23 that France, within a few days, would have an invincible army of 500,000 men and 80,000 horses.[26]

The fact remains that there was a short interval after the February Revolution when Lamartine seemed to depend on his eloquence and relationship to Ledru-Rollin and Louis Blanc, as they controlled storming crowds and delegations at the *Hôtel de Ville*. In March and early April, however, Lamartine's confidence in his ability to rule in this manner fluctuated.[27] Yet he completely compartmentalized his anxiety over the government's difficulties with the Paris clubs and his overwhelming confidence in France's international strategic situation. Indeed, at the very moment that he complained that he did not have a single bayonet at his disposition—nor would have until the completion of elections for officers by the National Guard units in twenty days—he expressed no apparent concern for his ability to wage war effectively. He confidently predicted a short and easy victory for France and the German states in an inevitable future battle with Russia.[28] The problem of keeping internal order not only varied from day to day, but was a powerful argument for immediate war, since the main complaint of the radicals with government was its inclination toward peace. Lamartine's first task, therefore, was to neutralize the excessive enthusiasm of the radical clubs for a war.

The Provisional Government was, indeed, less concerned with the size of the military force than with its total resources—with its potential allies, with its prospective opponents and neutrals, and with the attitude of the French population toward war. All of these were ultimately political and diplomatic matters.

Thus the question of France's ability to fight must be considered from two viewpoints. First, how strong was the French army in 1848? And second, how strong did the policymakers *think* it was? The latter consideration was the more significant and took into account the total strength of the nation, the superiority of France relative to her likely opponents. Lamartine boasted in March that the nation had never been stronger: "Foreign affairs were not more secure after Austerlitz. We shall have a French system instead of isolation."[29]

The "French system" was based on the three assumptions: France would fight with foreign allies, never alone, and Germany was the natural collaborator because of the Provisional Government's outward policy of peace. This further assumed that France had to appear disinterested. It could only be invincible in the role of protector of nations. Louis Blanc cautioned that "military protection of France, prematurely pressed upon nationalities still unprepared for the decisive struggle," might have "aroused their jealousies rather than their sympathies." The Germans in particular had a "bitter recollection of the revolutionary occupation of Mayence and Frankfort by the French."[30]

Underlying all of these premises about the role of France in Europe was a general and dominant supposition that sets off 1848 as a watershed in the history of western civilization: 1848 was an age of great faith, of overwhelming belief in the power of ideas, of the conviction that armies were powerless against the thrust of ideology. It was the last cry of "liberties to the people." This generation saw itself as witness to a great conflict of principles, with legitimacy, the holy alliance, and "reaction" (what the Duc de Broglie called the "old politics") locked in a life and death struggle with what was popularly termed "the revolution," representing the French system of liberalism, nationalism, the rights of peoples, and the espousal of freedom.

Both parties to the struggle shared this view—Nicholas I of Russia, the Comte de Chambord, and conservatives in general as much as Lamartine, Louis Blanc, or the triumphantly confident liberals of March 1848.

France's reluctance to fight might well have stemmed from her leaders' confidence that the treaties of 1815 would fall of their own accord before an inevitable rising of the peoples. This may have been what Lamartine meant when he claimed in early April that the "Polish question is on the verge of resolving itself, without our needing to fire a shot."[31]

France's great bulwark was the revolutionary ideal of liberty, equality, and fraternity for all peoples. If the republic became involved in an open war, it could only be in defense of human rights. The avowed policy of France was peace, asserted Lamartine. It would never be the aggressor; therefore, he could always rely on the total support of the French people to protect France's frontiers. The only other possible war involving France would be in defense of a neighboring nation whose revolutionary liberties were in danger of extinction by foreign armies. In the latter case, France would have as allies other freedom-loving peoples who had been emancipated. "France's only war is based on its principles," Lamartine contended. "The sole conquest that France wishes to make across the Rhine and the Alps," he asserted, "is the friendship of enfranchised populations." France could include as its friends all the free peoples of Europe, because it alone was not concerned with expansion of frontiers, only of ideas.[32]

Lamartine believed, moreover, that by her "disinterested policy" France had "paralyzed" her enemies. "The people," Lamartine later wrote, "edified by the moderation and the respect [of France], would no longer follow their governments in a crusade of a holy alliance against France, . . . and if the sovereigns tried to use their armies, the kings themselves would fall." The force of peaceful ideas had made France powerful far beyond its borders. "If democracy has a Thirty Year's War like Protestantism," Lamartine promised the French assembly, "instead of marching at the head of thirty-six million men, France marches before eighty-eight million confederates and friends, included within its system of allies Switzerland, Italy, and the emancipated peoples of Germany."[33]

In the name of the Provisional Government, Armand Marrast told a deputation of 2,000 Swiss residing in France:

> The Manifesto expressed the thoughts of the Provisional Government. We establish as a sacred principle the complete independence of nations. . . . These principles are henceforth placed under the guarantee not only of France, which is proud to march at the head of free peoples, but of all the peoples who feel the need to unite themselves as brothers to defend these principles. . . . We are certain that if absolutist

> Europe . . . ventured to infringe on the rights of that social
> sovereignty to freely organize, we shall find in all the European
> nations an immense, infinite cooperation; they feel bound by
> the invincible tie of right, and before this mass animated by
> all the ardour of liberty, provocative and foolhardy absolutism
> would draw back beyond the steppes of the desert.[34]

Likewise, Lamartine's successor as foreign minister, Jules
Bastide, who had been under-secretary of state since the February Revolution and thus evidence of the essential continuity of
Richelieu-Girondist policies throughout the revolutionary year,
shared Lamartine's beliefs. When Bastide replaced Lamartine in
the newly elected Executive Commission in May 1848, he stated
that an important element in France's strength was the sympathy
that she could expect in neighboring countries because of her
revolutionary ideals. Whereas the archenemy, Austria, could only
"invoke the right of property," the republic represented the "opposed principle of the sovereignty of peoples." If war came, it
would be precipitated only by "gravely wounding public opinion
in France." In this case, Frenchmen would carry out the threat
of Lamartine's Manifesto and the "treaties of Vienna would be
resolutely torn up," while the French waged a modern ideological
war. "We shall call for a war against the thrones." The age of
crowned heads would be over if France began such a war, because "all the peoples only await our [French] signal" to begin
the conflict. All of Italy would join France with Germany and
even "the states submitting today, however poorly, to Austrian
domination." The desire for peace never meant that the French
were unprepared for war. All the oppressed peoples awaited liberation by the French and would gladly help France against their
own reactionary governments.[35]

With Austria immobilized by internal dissension, Russia—the
only other nation able to oppose France—could bring only 200,000
troops into central Europe. Is there any doubt as to why Lamartine
believed that a war of Germany and France against Russia would
have "little bloodshed and be short"? France, joined by Prussia
and the south German states, would have presented a formidable
potential bloc against Russia or Austria.

All of Lamartine's revolutionary diplomatic strategy depended
on his continued mastery of his position in Paris. He could not
allow the excessive enthusiasm of radical clubs to push France into
war before the Provisional Government and its secret agents had

prepared the way by diplomatic means.

Contradictory language concerning France's military situation primarily reflected the leaders' concern for the timing of the outbreak rather than an opposition to war as such. France's professional army needed several weeks after the February Revolution to restore its fighting effectiveness and to raise strength to the necessary half-million troops needed for a foreign war. Equally important, France could never appear to be an aggressor. The peoples of Europe must welcome France as a liberator, otherwise the reactionary rulers would use national sentiment—the most powerful force of 1848—against France herself.

The French nation, and the clubs in particular, had to have a clear reason for fighting so that public opinion could be manipulated to gain total support for a "war of liberation." Finally, the French army had to be paid; France's allies were expected to subsidize the cost of the campaign. Premature action by the clubs might well provoke hatred of the French republic among her neighbors and, as Lamartine and Louis Blanc warned, that could be disastrous for France. By contrast, if France waited for the great war of European liberation to erupt and could intervene to protect the peoples' aspirations for national liberation, then her military strength would be invincible. The question was timing.

Thus Lamartine never "rejected" a Prussian alliance "offer," contrary to the accepted wisdom of diplomatic historians like A. J. P. Taylor and Lawrence Jennings. Their error stems from their use of Circourt's published memoirs rather than the original dispatches available in the Bibliothèque Nationale. These letters reveal a very different scenario. The original terms for an alliance initiated by Lamartine on March 25 were brought to Berlin by Czartoryski.[36] Thus Arnim's "request" for a French alliance was in reality no more than a confirmation of Lamartine's original terms. Circourt's transmittal of Arnim's query was couched in the most unfavorable terms: The French envoy indicated that an open alliance at that particular juncture might involve France in a civil war in Berlin, since Germany was in the midst of "profound disturbances" and the king of Prussia might fall at any moment. The dissolution of Arnim's cabinet, Circourt indicated, would lead to the collapse of the monarchy in Prussia, and this would result in the "political dissolution" of the state.

Since the Grand Duchy of Posen had already lapsed into anarchy, Circourt speculated that a public display of French support for Arnim might bolster his government, especially in the eyes of the Polish radicals. But such action ran counter to Lamartine's policy of avoiding overt interference in the domestic affairs of other states. Moreover, what interest had France in strengthening the Arnim cabinet against the Berlin revolution? Why should France oppose the "dissolution" of Prussia and the resulting independence for the Polish portions of that state? Why should the French prevent the creation of a republic in Berlin? After all, Circourt noted, he himself had concluded that old Prussia was dead without any hope of a resurrection.[37]

Although Arnim's request for a public and formal alliance with Prussia was apparently not discussed by the Council of the Provisional Government, on April 2 Lamartine *did* bring up the question of "French support for Prussia against an immediate invasion by Russia" and the response was positive.[38]

Dated April 4, the response in Paris to Circourt's dispatches arrived in Berlin on April 15. The message reiterated the specific terms of the alliance as Czartoryski had communicated them. Champeaux, Lamartine's personal secretary, emphasized the transitory character of the present situation and the weakness of the Provisional Government:

> Our affairs take each day a better turn . . . except for the financial situation. . . . Every day gained is in itself an improvement. We are on the eve of elections for the national guard, which will aid us in elections for the assembly. . . . You will probably not receive the new instructions that you desire and have asked for in all your letters. It would be imprudent to build on shifting sands. Also, your mission is above all to watch, to estimate, and to observe. . . . "If Russia attacks Prussia and invades her territory seizing Posen, France will support Prussia by force." You can use that phrase confidentially and in conversation but without going further; in a moment when every eventuality can be realized from one day to another, it is necessary to work with great reserve and to shun anything precise to avoid entangling the future.[39]

When informed by Circourt of Lamartine's response, Arnim was thoroughly content. Instead of regarding this answer as a "rejection" of the alliance—as Taylor and Jennings falsely conjectured—Circourt reported that "this promise gave [Arnim] a great deal of satisfaction; it made his position stronger and clearer, in effect, at least from one side"; Arnim had found the promise of help in the event of a Russian invasion reassuring.[40]

France's alliance reaffirmed a commitment to defend Prussia's eastern flank, which led Arnim, his cabinet, and the Prussian army to view the alliance as a solid reality. The monarch's adjutant, Leopold von Gerlach, recorded on April 21, "The king's entire ministry is for the war with Russia, and the king is completely alone in opposition."[41] Frederick William IV's will to resist the March ministry remained weak.[42]

The anti-Russian party included not only Arnim, but the king's most intimate friends and confidants: his ambassador in London, Baron von Bunsen; Frederick William's protegé and aide-de-camp, Friedrich Adolf Baron von Willisen; and even the minister of war and later chief of staff, Karl Friedrich Wilhelm von Reyher. Arnim's government had taken complete control of Prussian policy and openly resisted the king's will. As late as June 13 the king admitted to Gerlach that his minsters did everything for him.[43] Gerlach concluded that Frederick William was "poorly treated" by his cabinet and his mood was one of "sad resignation." On June 4, after an evening at Sanssouci with the king, Gerlach wrote, "The ministers want, or at least expect, a war with Russia in alliance with France."[44]

Lamartine and Arnim's joint plan of a Franco-Prussian war against Russia to free Poland miscarried for a number of reasons. Russia failed to act as the Prussians had anticipated—Tsar Nicholas I did not attack Prussia, and France and Prussia waited in vain to "rescue" Poland. "From the end of March," Circourt observed, "the Prussian ministry awaited a large insurrection within the Russian Empire. This expectation was frustrated. Nothing stirred." Instead of a war of the Poles and the Prussians against Russia, a rising of Poles against Prussia broke out in Posen during late April. In spite of this, Paris continued to expect the Prussian cabinet to carry out its promises to aid the Poles. Prussia remained a central focus for French policy throughout 1848 as all eyes looked toward Russia in expectation of the armed revolt which would bring freedom for the Poles and unity for Germans.[45]

French policy had involved public posturing, traditional diplomatic contacts, and dispatching of confidential agents. An apparent contradiction between France's public and private policy (promising the French public to liberate peoples while assuring the diplomatic corps that France would not resort to war), that contradiction appeared resolved by Arnim's acceptance of Lamartine's diplomatic feeler carried by Prince Adam Czartoryski to Berlin.

Although the Paris-Berlin axis could threaten Russia militarily, Lamartine failed to act. The French did not hold back because of a contemporary fear of their own military impotence; this is one of Lamartine's fabrications, later taken up by historians. The contemporary record shows Lamartine confident that French arms could carry the day in any conflict. Lamartine's deceptive claim that the republic was "inactive" because of his fear of France's military weakness has no basis in fact. It was rather a cover for his actual policy of using secret agents in Germany: Adolphe de Circourt, Adam Czartoryski, Mikhail Bakunin (as advance agent for what was hoped to be a 8,000-man army that would link up with Hecker and Struve's revolt in Baden), and Louis Blanc's associate Alexandre Rey. Undoubtedly, Lamartine's confidence fluctuated. But on March 25 he assumed that a *"bouleversement général"* was on the verge of transforming Germany into a democratic republic. In response to his expectation that the people would stand by France in a war against the universally detested tsarist horde, on March 25 Lamartine confidently ordered Czartoryski to inform Arnim that France was interested in a Paris-Berlin alliance that would free Poland in a joint campaign against the tsar. Thus Lamartine expected France to go forth at the head of an alliance of peoples when the war broke out. And Lamartine's diplomatic campaign was not limited to his use of the secret agents. He continued to pressure the old monarchs with timely pronouncements in the press.

What the Provisional Government did during the next crucial month was to avoid the dilemma of whether to engage in war or to remain at peace by initiating direct diplomatic negotiations with Russia and Austria. Lamartine wished for the eastern powers to follow Prussia's example of capitulating to French objectives and thereby freeing subject peoples in return for some territorial compensation for their losses in prerogatives.

NOTES

1. James Chastain, "Michael Bakunin," in *Crucible of Socialism*, Louis Patsouras, ed. (Atlantic Highlands, 1987), pp. 3–19.

2. Apponyi to Metternich, Paris, March 17, 1848, HHSA, K. 377, III, fo. 280–81.

3. Apponyi to Chancellor, Paris, March 23, 1848, HHSA, K. 337, III, fo. 286–87.

4. Garnier-Pagès, *Histoire*, VII, 267–75; The account is complicated by the fact that one of the leaders, Adalbert Bornstedt was in the pay of the Prussian government to spy on German radicals; Karl Marx, Frederick Engels, and Stephan Born resolutely opposed the armed putsch and distanced themselves publicly from the certain failure of the expedition; Jenny Marx to Joseph Weydemeyer, Paris, March 16, 1848, in Marx-Engels, *Werke*, XXVII, 604; For the background of the Legion use with caution the memoirs of the President of the *Société des Démocrates Allemandes*, Heinrich Börnstein, *Fünfundsiebzig Jahre*, I, 405ff.

5. Ligne to Hoffschmidt, Paris, March 23, 1848, Ridder, I, 242. Lamartine "assured me that he had at his disposal only a corporal and four men and that he had, at this moment, only moral influence." A few days later he no longer feared the clubs, perhaps because a number of the most radical leaders had left Paris in the recent dispersion toward the frontiers: Hatzfeldt to Foreign Minister, Paris, March 26, 1848, GSA, fz. 855, fo. 133; Yet in April, Lamartine told the chargés of various German states that the government was again in a difficult and dangerous position: "In Paris the most menacing argument of the violent men against the government is that it had little sympathy for foreign enterprises for liberty and gave them little aid"; he and several of his colleagues lived under constant menaces of assassination. Bose to Foreign Minister, Paris, April 13, 1848, Kretzschmar and Schlechte, *Gesandtschaftsberichte*, p. 81.

6. Circourt to Lamartine, Berlin, March 29, 1848, Circourt Papers, Bibliothèque Nationale, Mss. n.a. fr. 21, 684, fo. 348.

7. James Chastain, "Bakunin as a French Secret Agent in 1848," *History Today* XXXI (August 1981), 5–9.

8. Lamartine to Alexandre Rey, instructions, Paris, March 27, 1848, AEF, MD, Allemagne 171, fo. 175.

9. Lamartine to Salignac-Fénélon, Paris, March 31, 1848, DDF, I, 532–33.

10. Lamartine to Lefebvre (Minister in Karlsruhe), instructions, March 13, 1848, DDF, I, 173–74; cf. instructions for De la Cour (chargé

in Vienna), March 12, 1848, DDF, I, 164–65; Garnier-Pagès, *Histoire*, VI, 253–54.

11. The claim that France opposed the creation of German unity originated in the periodical press and Frankfurt assembly of 1848: Heinrich von Treitschke, in his lecture delivered before 1870, charged that France in 1848 had inevitably opposed German desires for national union because of its reason of state, "Frankreichs Staatsleben und der Bonapartismus," in *Historische-Politische Aufsätze* (5th ed.; Leipzig, 1886), Vol. III; after World War I German archives were opened to the public, and the first works on Franco-German relations based on a full range of the unpublished sources were Otto Pfisterer, "Preussen und Frankreich im Jahre 1848" (diss. Tübingen, 1921), and Friedrich Ley, "Frankreich und die deutsche Revolution 1848–49," which emphasized the traditional French opposition dating from Richelieu to German aspirations for unity in 1848; these formed the foundation for published works by Erich Marcks, "Die europäischen Mächte und die 48er Revolution," *Historische Zeitschrift*, CXLII (1930), 73–87, and Alexander Scharff, *Die Europäischen Grossmächte*; French as well as other European archives were used by the Vicomte de Guichen, *Les grandes questions européennes et la diplomatie des puissances sous la Seconde République française* (2 vols.; Paris, 1925–29), who printed documents from the archives with little explanation and analysis of their meaning; Paul Henry did not deny German charges, as Frenchmen had generally defended their government against Italian complaints, but praised the foresight of statesmen in 1848 for recognizing the German menace more clearly than their successors at the quai d'Orsay, "La France et les nationalités en 1848, d'après les correspondances diplomatiques," *Revue Historique*, vol. 186 (1939), 48–77, vol. 188 (1940), 234–58; and *La France devant le monde de 1789 à 1939* (Paris, 1945); Scharff after World War II was able to consult the French archives and emphasized the French opposition to the Frankfurt assembly's policy in Schleswig-Holstein, e.g., "Schleswig-Holsteins Erhebung im Spiegel französischer Akten," in *Aus Schleswig-Holsteins Geschichte und Gegenwart: Festschrift für Volquart Pauls* (Neumünster, 1950), pp. 173–94; cf. S. A. Kähler, "Die deutsche Revolution von 1848 und die europäischen Mächte," in *Vorurteilen und Tatsachen* (Hamelin, 1949); Gerhard Ritter, *Europa und die deutsche Frage: geschichtliche Eigenart des deutschen Staatdenkens* (Munich, 1948); Wilhelm Mommsen, *Grösse und Versagen des deutschen Bürgertums: Ein Beitrag zur politischen Bewegung des 19. Jahrhunderts, insbesondere zur Revolution 1848/49* (2d. ed.; Munich, 1964); Paul Bernstein, "The Rhine Problem during the Second Republic and the Second Empire," (Ph.D. diss., University of Pennsylvania, 1955). Another group of historians has seriously questioned that the French would ever have used force to prevent German unity: Valentin, *Geschichte der deutschen Revolution*; Stadelmann, *Social and Political History*; Alois Mertes, "Frankreichs Stellungnahme zur deutschen Revolution im Jahre 1848," (diss., Bonn, 1951), Robert Hahn, "The Attitude of the French Revolutionary Government"; James Chastain, "French

Kleindeutsch Policy in 1848" (Ph.D. diss., University of Oklahoma, 1967). Werner E. Mosse shifted the historical controversy by questioning whether too much had not been made of the Schleswig-Holstein question, whether French opposition to Germany's actions in the Baltic duchies had not been confused with opposition to German unity as such, in *The European Powers and the German Question, 1848–1871: with special reference to England and Russia* (Cambridge, 1958), cf. review by W. N. Medlicott, *Slavonic and East European Review*, XXXVII (1959), 542; most recently, Frederick A. de Luna, in *The French Republic under Cavaignac, 1848* (Princeton, 1969) discovered that the French were sympathetic to German unity until the election of Louis Napoleon in December 1848 and William J. Orr, "La France et la révolution allemande de 1848–49," *Revue d'histoire diplomatique* XCIII (1979), 300–30, accurately summarized the central thesis of my doctoral dissertation: that the French in 1848 suspended the old antagonism toward Germany's unity.

12. Apponyi to Chancellor, Paris, March 25, 1848, HHSA, K. 337, III, fo. 292–96.

13. Lamartine to Bixio, Paris, March 15, 1848, instructions, DDF, I, 224–25; Bixio to Lamartine, Turin, March 29, 1848, DDF, I, 490–92; the controversy concerning French policy toward Italy dates back to the events themselves, as the French foreign ministers were heavily criticized in France and Italy for their failure to give aid; Lamartine's defense was his *Histoire de la Révolution de 1848*, and Jules Bastide answered Cavour's taunts with *La République Française et l'Italie en 1848: récits, notes et documents diplomatiques* (Brussels, 1858). The standard Italian answers are found in the works of Nicomede Bianchi, especially the *Storia documentata della diplomazia in Italia dalla' anno 1814 all'anno 1861* (8 vols.; Turin, 1856–72). Luigi Chiala charged that the French were playing a double role in Italy, claiming sympathy while egotistically looking for an occasion to seize Savoy, *La vita ed i tempi del Generale Guiseppe Dabormida* (Turin, 1896). More recently, Ruggero Moscati, *La diplomazie europea e il problema italiano nel 1848* (Florence, 1947) accused the French of duplicity in promising help, then abandoning Italy in its moment of need. The standard analysis is A. J. P. Taylor, *The Italian Problem in European Diplomacy*, who generally agrees with the critics of French policy that it was disingenuous, interested more in not being involved in war than in protecting the accomplishments of the northern Italian revolutions. French honor has been defended in a series of articles written by Ferdinand Boyer, which have been incorporated into *La Seconde République, Charles-Albert et l'Italie du nord en 1848* (Paris, 1967). Boyer correctly places a considerable portion of the blame on the devious and mistrustful government of Charles Albert in Sardinia, who feared French motives and refused to ask for, or even allow any, French aid until it was too late.

14. The common problem among works on French policy toward the Schleswig-Holstein question is the tendency to vastly overestimate

the importance that this matter had for Paris, as well as to exaggerate the understanding that the French had of the basic facts of an extremely complicated matter that Palmerston said only three men ever understood; cf., Alexander Scharff's "Europäische und gesamtdeutsche Zusammenhänge der schleswig-holsteinischen Erhebung," in *Stufen und Wandlungen der deutschen Einheit: Festschrift für K. A. von Müller* (Stuttgart, 1943), pp. 196–223; "Revolution und Reichsgründungsversuche: 1848–51," in *Deutsche Geschichte im Überblick: Ein Handbuch,* ed. Peter Rassow, pp. 430–53; and "Das Erste Londoner Protokoll: Ein Beitrag zur europäischen Problematik der schleswig-holsteinischen Frage," in *Festschrift für Otto Schell: Beiträge zur deutschen und nordischen Geschichte* (Schleswig, 1952), pp. 314–34; Lawrence C. Jennings, "French Diplomacy and the Schleswig-Holstein Crisis," *French Historical Studies,* VII (1971), 204–25. Scharff's conjecture that French opposition to the policy of the German states in the Schleswig question caused a rejection of German unity is questionable; Jennings shares his mistake of considerably overstating the importance of Schleswig-Holstein for France. In spite of the evidence Scharff and Jennings amass, the conclusion seems inescapable that the distant duchies *per se* were an extremely remote interest for France. This is indicated by the fact that the French never even discussed the matter with the Prussian chargé until August 1, at which time Hatzfeldt had to request instructions outlining his government's policy, GSA, Frankreich 861, fo. 100, and reply of August 4, 1848, Frankreich 856, fo. 234.

15. Tallenay to Lamartine, Hamburg, March 28 and 29, 1848, DDF, I, 464–65, 481; the dispatches from Hamburg gave a full picture of the developing crisis.

16. Garnier-Pagès, VII, 310–11.

17. *Ibid.,* VII, 311–12.

18. *Ibid.,* VII, 312; Louis Blanc, *1848: Historical Revelations inscribed to Lord Normanby* (London, 1858), pp. 223–24.

19. Lamartine, *Histoire,* II, 51; Tersen, *Le gouvernement,* p. 64; Lamartine's monthly figures are incorrect; for accurate numbers see note 23 below; Garnier-Pagès, *Histoire,* VI, 268–71, VII, 311ff.

20. The principal sources of information for the following are the "statistical bureau" files of the French army and foreign ministry. Under the command of General Pelet, the army office gathered information from the normal sources: diplomatic, consular, and military attaché reports, newspapers, spies, travelers, and other informants. The bureau assembled background data helpful for estimating the military effectiveness of foreign units as well as maintaining detailed charts of current strengths for the foreign armies, which it often compared with the French army. Lengthy reports, studies, and memoranda with information on the armies of Europe fill hundreds of boxes at the Service Historique de l'Armée (SHA) (Château de Vincennes) Mémoires et Reconnaissances (MR) section that are supplemented by the Cavaignac Papers. General Pelet was a member of the

Commission for the Organization of National Defense, which planned the great expansion of the French army soon after the February Revolution. His unit gathered information to assist the under-secretary of war, Lt. Colonel Charras, in writing such detailed reports on the strength of the forces of European powers as that read by the minister of war on April 5, 1848 before the Council of the Provisional Government, Garnier-Pagès, *Histoire*, VI, 268–69, VII, 311–312; Cavaignac Papers, 1 Mi 2 R 20.

21. Wilhelm Mommsen, *Grösse und Versagen des deutschen Bürgertums*, p. 109; Otto Pfisterer, "Preussen und Frankreich," p. 29; Alois Mertes, "Frankreichs Stellungnahme," p. 26, are typical.

22. Ms. of Charras's autobiography, BN, Mss, Fonds Hetzel, fz. 9, fo. 420–22.

23. *Ibid.*, fo. 422–38; *Moniteur*, December 21, 1849. One of the first actions of the Provisional Government was to expand greatly France's active army. The forces rose from around 375,000 men in January 1848 to over 462,000 men on July 1, 1848. The method of expansion was also very important; the veterans of the class of 1841 were not allowed to leave early, as was the custom when the new recruits arrived in July, but served their full service period until December 30. The French army carried its strength as follows:

February 1, 1848	370,681
March 11	368,546
April 1	369,945
May 1	377,623
June 1	432,498
July 1	462,731
August 1	496,731
September 1	501,753
October 1	502,753
November 1	502,075
December 1	502,365

Situation générale de l'armée, January 1, 1848 to January 1, 1849, SHA: *Moniteur*, May 24, 1848, No. 145, p. 1142; Garnier-Pagès, *Histoire*, II, 157; Witold Zaniewicki, "L'Armée française en 1848: introduction à une étude militaire de la Deuxième République (22 février–20 décembre 1848)" (3ᵉ cycle thèse, University of Paris, 1966); this exemplary dissertation is the first attempt at a full study of the French army in 1848 and supercedes all previous works; Jonathan M. House, "Public Force in Paris, February 22 to June 26, 1848" (Ph. D. diss., University of Michigan, 1975) unravels the complicated problems of public order.

24. Charles de Rémusat, *Mémoires de ma vie* (Paris, 1962), IV, 260–65; Garnier-Pagès, *Histoire*, VII, 315–319.

25. Zaniewicki, "L'Armée française," I, 127, 161–71; *Moniteur*, May 24, 1848.

26. *Ibid.*; P. Chalmin, "La crise morale de l'armée française," in

Bulletin de la Société d'Histoire de la Révolution de 1848: Etudes, XVIII (1955), 28–76 (hereafter *Bulletin*) and "Les Crises dans l'armée française, 1830–1848," *Revue d'histoire de l'armée,* XVIII (1962), no. 4, 45–62; Giradet suggested that perhaps Chalmin had exaggerated the elements of dissension and minimized cohesion. "Above all," Giradet cautioned, "one ought to strive to learn the duration of the crisis described" by Chalmin, suggesting that the solidarity of the officer corps was very quickly restored before the menace of social subversion and the symptoms of revolutionary penetration among the troops. "Autour de quelques problèmes," *Bulletin,* XVIII (1955), 7; Giradet's reservations were reinforced by Zaniewicki, "L'Armée française."

27. Lamartine's speeches of May 6 and 8, *Moniteur,* May 7 and 9, 1848.

28. Apponyi to Chancellor, Paris, March 25, 1848, HHSA, K. 337, III, fo. 292–96; cf. Jennings, *France and Europe,* pp. 63–70.

29. Lamartine to Monsieur Rocher, Paris, March 5, 1848, *Correspondance de Lamartine* publiée par Madame Valentine de Lamartine (2d. ed.; Paris, 1882) IV, 274; I have not intended to minimize Lamartine's sincere wishes for peace; I have only suggested that his rejection of an offensive war was not caused by his supposed belief of French military weakness; for Lamartine's peaceful wishes see *Histoire,* II, 12–13, but note also that Lamartine had little confidence that peace could be maintained, as he almost doubled the size of France's standing army.

30. Louis Blanc, *1848,* p. 222; General Pelet, April 7, 1848, "Sur une guerre de Pologne: Note demandée par le Ministre des Affaires Etrangères," SHA, MR 2111, No. 16, pp. 161–70, which inherently assumes that Prussia and other German states would be active allies.

31. Garnier-Pagès, *Histoire,* VII, 311.

32. *Moniteur,* May 7, 1848, May 9, 1848; Lamartine had claimed in the Manifesto that France would "happily" accept war if this were declared against it, "in spite of its moderation," Lamartine, *Histoire,* II, 39.

33. *Moniteur,* May 9, 1848; Lamartine, *Le passé,* p. 63.

34. *Moniteur,* March 13, 1848; cf. Lamartine's similar remarks to an Irish delegation, "The fallen monarchy had treaties and diplomats; we have people for diplomats and their sympathies for treaties!" *Moniteur,* April 4, 1848.

35. Bastide to De la Cour, Paris, September 26, 1848, AEF, Autriche 436, fo. 229 bis; cf. Bastide to Arago, Paris, September 8, 1848, AEF, Prusse 302, fo. 264; Bastide to Le Flô, Paris, October 5, 1848, AEF, Russe 202, fo. 107; Arago to Bastide, Berlin, November 25, 1848, AEF, Prusse 303, fo. 123.

36. Circourt to Lamartine, Berlin, March 29, 1848, BN, Circourt Papers, fo. 348.

37. *Ibid.,* March 27, 1848, fo. 339–41; *Souvenirs,* I, 326–27.

38. Garnier-Pagès, *Histoire,* VII, 312.

39. Champeaux to Circourt, April 4, 1848, *Souvenirs*, I, 329–40; and BN, Mss. n.a. fr. 21, 684, fo. 401; Circourt's allegation, "The Provisional Government of France dare not engage any affair abroad," does not reflect the evidence. France was quite willing to act; it merely declined to put this in writing. Cf. *Souvenirs*, I, 328.

40. Circourt to Lamartine, Berlin, April 17, 1848, BN, Mss. n.a. fr. 21, 684, fo. 401; Circourt's erroneous charge that Lamartine "rejected" Arnim's alliance "offer" has been accepted uncritically by historians who failed to consult the documents, see Scharff, "Revolution und Reichsgründungsversuche," p. 433; Lewis Namier, *1848: The Revolution of the Intellectuals*, (New York, 1964), p. 75; Valentin, *Geschichte der deutschen Revolution*, I, 542. The "betrayal" was cited as proof that France was interested in preserving peace, but never sympathetic toward Polish or German aspirations, absorbed only by its desire for political survival. France, they charge, was unfaithful to its promises, realistic but never frank; see Scharff, "Revolution und Reichsgründungsversuche," Marcks, "Die europäischen Mächte," pp. 76–77, and *Die Aufsteig des Reiches*, I, 259–61; France's chargé told the British ambassador that "France had always been on terms of alliance and friendship" with Prussia, Westmorland to Palmerston, Berlin, September 4, 1848, PRO, FO 64/289.

41. Gerlach, *Denkwürdigkeiten*, I, 154.

42. *Ibid.*, I, 153.

43. *Ibid.*, I, 164; not even the ultra-reactionary Gerlach could withstand the overwhelming sentiment pressing Prussia toward war, *ibid.*, I, 149; cf. account, in the liberal German press welcoming the war against Russia, *National Zeitung*, April 30 and May 1, 1848.

44. Gerlach, *Denkwürdigkeiten*, I, 163; cf. Jennings, *France and Europe*, pp. 92–93n.

45. Circourt, *Souvenirs*, II, 57; Sur une Guerre de Pologne: note demandée par le Ministre des Affaires Etrangères, No. 16, April 7, 1848, SHA, MR 2111, fo. 161–70; Arnim's request for naval assistance to Prussia in the Baltic presented special difficulties. The Danish had clear superiority over the German Confederation on the sea. Denmark also had the full cooperation of the Swedish and Russian fleets. The geographical situation of the entrance of the Baltic demanded the cooperation of Sweden and Denmark to maintain and supply a French naval presence in the north. England had to be consulted also, yet Lamartine thought that the English were as belligerent toward France as Austria. Sending French ships to the Baltic would have depended heavily on circumstances at the outbreak of hostilities, most of all, England's attitude. France's sea power had been concentrated by Guizot at Toulon for use against the Italian revolution.

Chapter Three
French Policy Moves East
APRIL-MAY 1848

*E*LECTION OF A FRENCH Constituent Assembly in late April placed increased stress on Lamartine. Since an overwhelming majority of the new parliamentarians were provincial notables hostile to Lamartine's placating of the Parisian mob, tensions rose and ultimately boiled over in the June Days revolt the following month. Partisans of the February ideal of conciliation shrank in number, to be replaced by militants. Lamartine's popularity was jeopardized when he refused to join the newly formed Executive Commission, which replaced the Provisional Government, unless it included as well the socialist Ledru-Rollin. Although this incident marked the beginning of Lamartine's personal decline, it failed to materially alter the momentum of the Richelieu-Girondist policy of replacing the house of Habsburg as European arbiter. However, initiatives by Lamartine and Bastide in the east underlined an increasing preoccupation with the lower Danube as a determinant region that would assist Poland and Italy in escaping from foreign domination. Thus another major French agent, Carl Ludwig Bernays, would join Bakunin in agitating in Germany, then later travel on to Budapest. But most of the work was done by Czartoryski's army of agents, who covered every part of the Balkans. Undoubtedly, Czartoryski played an important role in convincing Lamartine and Bastide to attempt to outflank Austria in the east and thereby to force the Habsburgs to compromise in the west. For decades Czartoryski had tried to persuade French and British leaders that southeastern Europe should be an area of concern; he finally had an audience.

Even those remote corners of Europe hitherto untouched by the spread of revolutionary violence found themselves threatened in April 1848. In London on April 10, the Chartists presented their "great petition" to Parliament, and it looked as if Great Britain might become the next victim of unrest.

An uprising led by Frederick Hecker and Gustav Struve in Baden on April 12 led to the proclamation of a republic and placed increasing pressure on the governments of all the German states. Coincidentally, on April 15 Bakunin was traveling through the entire Rhineland as an advance agent for Georg Herwegh's German Legion, which had left Paris for the German states. Bakunin tried unsuccessfully to convince Marx and Engels, then in Cologne, to join in the general uprising for a German republic.

The internal situation of the French Provisional Government had been strengthened by favorable demonstrations by the organized trades in Paris on April 16. (We can now, in retrospect, recognize this as a defeat of the social revolution and a victory for "moderation.") The confidence of the Provisional Government, in its efforts to combat spontaneous violence, was further reinforced with the return of troops to the city on April 20.

France's close relations with Prussia became clouded when, on April 23, the local Prussian commander in Posen took steps to suppress Polish rebellion against Prussian authorities in the province. Here, as in Paris, there was a fine line between order and chaos. The essential question for France was not whether Prussia would allow a handful of Poles to destabilize a Prussian border area and so excite Russian counter-measures, but whether Prussia was firmly committed, with France, to resist the anticipated armed incursions of Russian troops into central Europe.

France's patient policy of waiting for the eventual collapse of Austria appeared to be bearing fruit the final week of April. In Vienna on April 25, the proclamation of an imperial Austrian constitution promised responsible government throughout the Danubian monarchy. The same day, the Papacy joined the Kingdom of Piedmont-Sardinia, sending troops for the common war against Austria. Also on April 25 in Cracow, the Austrians suppressed a Polish revolt, increasing the alienation of the national Polish movement from Vienna. And before the week was over, on April 30, at the battle of Pastrengo, Italian forces under the command of the Sardinians defeated Austria's army. Austria's final disintegration seemed only a matter of time.

The strongest threat to the integrity of the Austrian Empire came from the German national movement, since Germans were scattered through all parts of the empire. This threat became the greater when, in early May, Germans from the confederation and other territories elected delegates to a liberal parliament charged to meet in Frankfurt am Main to write a constitution for a united Germany.

Yet a note of caution should have been sounded. The united German assembly had not even met when, on May 2, an army of the confederated German states invaded Jutland. The liberal Frankfurt assembly would be forced to begin its deliberations while the states were at war with Denmark over Schleswig-Holstein.

In an action that was equally unsettling for the French, the Prussian army completed the pacification of the rebellious Poles in Posen on May 2 and divided the province along alleged national lines.

At the end of April, the French had finally elected their Constituent Assembly, which was scheduled to begin its deliberations in the first week of May. As the representative assemblies opened proceedings in Paris and Frankfurt, the new French Executive Commission, which replaced the Provisional Government, looked for an early announcement of a "democratic alliance" between the two assemblies dedicated to securing freedom for Poland and Italy.

The situation in Austria remained unstable. On May 15, popular riots in Vienna forced the emperor to flee the capital and seek refuge in the mountains of Tyrol. The end of May brought news of yet another military setback when on May 30, at the second battle of Gioto, the Sardinians once again defeated the Austrian troops.

And the Prussians took an important step toward defusing French dissatisfaction over their conflict with Denmark by accepting English mediation for armistice discussions on May 19. France could at least hope that the war in the north might end quickly with a negotiated peace.

THE LEGATION COUNCILLOR OF BADEN in Paris, Baron F. A. von Schweizer, reported to his government on May 3 that "new agents left daily to make contact with foreign democrats, to stimulate the revolutionary spirit which one says here has begun to lie dormant in Germany."[1] Even though we have direct evidence of only a handful of these agents, their method of operations corresponded closely to Schweizer's description, in particular, the movements of two old associates of Karl Marx, the Russian anarchist Mikhail Bakunin and Carl Ludwig Bernays. Their method of operations was very similar to that of Circourt and Czartoryski, whose missions had forged a military link between the French and German peoples. Bakunin's sights were turned first of all toward a military insurrection of the Germans, while Bernay's most important sphere of activity would be among the Magyars in Budapest. In all cases, objectives clearly extended beyond mere agitation to the inciting of violence. Thus latter day critics of the French government cannot fault France for failing to try to stimulate the revolutionary spirit beyond its borders any more than its leadership cannot be praised for an alleged prudence.

Just as Schweizer described the secret agents, Bakunin entered Germany "to stimulate the revolutionary spirit." Bakunin, as the advance scout of the German Legion as well as an agent of the French Provisional Government,[2] brought instructions and letters of introduction from the leader of the insurrectionary German army, the communist poet and old friend of Karl Marx, Georg Herwegh, addressed to German democrats.

Herwegh described Bakunin to the radical democrat from Königsberg, Dr. Johann Jacoby, as "one of my dearest friends," deserving his trust, since Bakunin would "explain everything to you that Germans as well as French wish to know. You can regard him as the only authentic source about me." Herwegh urged Jacoby to include Bakunin in his "circle of acquaintances," since Bakunin brought a "sack full of revolutionary inclination *(Lust)* to clean out your constitutional atmosphere."[3]

Bakunin was received enthusiastically by the German democrats. He impressed them as well-educated and capable, "determined to act." And Bakunin spread the good word that: "The party of the *red* flag is very strong in Paris."[4] Over the next couple of weeks, Bakunin met at least fifty "energetic and influential" German democrats to explain to them Herwegh's plans and obviously to urge them to join Herwegh in a general uprising, instead of wasting time on writing a German constitution. Bakunin crisscrossed the middle Rhine to Mannheim, Mainz, and Heidelberg, arriving in Cologne on April 12—the same day that Hecker and Struve raised the flag of rebellion in Constance. Bakunin lingered in Cologne from April 12 to 20 to gain his bearings. Shortly before Bakunin's arrival, Marx and Engels had converged on Cologne as the most likely center of insurrection in the Rhineland. During the eight days in Cologne Bakunin justified to Marx and Engels the Paris-hatched plan for taking a gamble on an immediate coup.

But the fathers of scientific socialism had the better of the argument in Cologne. Bakunin wrote back to Paris on April 17 in an "inexpressible depression," recalling that he had left France "crazy," and during his first weeks in Germany was a person with a "fever." But he now had to admit that there was no chance of an immediate revolution in the Rhineland. The Philistines were in complete control of Cologne. The German bourgeoisie were doing three things, Bakunin wrote: preparing for the elections to the German parliament; using all possible means, including the exercise of terror, against the people to prevent them from arming themselves; and sending the poor young men of Cologne to Denmark to "save the German brothers in Schleswig and Holstein." That Schleswig-Holstein movement was "completely reactionary," Bakunin charged, intended to glorify the Prussian king as savior of the German nation, even though half of the people in the provinces spoke Danish. The German states were on the brink of a horrible uprising of peasants and proletarians; the symptoms indicated that a country-wide democratic revolt was no more than two or three months away. The radical leaders "gradually organize[d] their power," and Bakunin found plenty of "intelligent" and "capable" individuals preparing for the inevitable blow-up.[5] Bakunin concluded that Marx and Engels were correct. Herwegh's course was hopeless. The princes had been toppled, but a more dangerous foe had taken their place: the middle class. The bourgeoisie used the Schleswig-Holstein cry to confuse the masses, to direct mass energies toward a foreign war, and the forces of order reestablished a militarist regime throughout Germany. The time was not ripe for a workers' revolt, and Herwegh had to be notified at once. Bakunin later admitted in his "Confession," composed in captivity for the tsar, that he had written to Flocon from Cologne.[6]

The Parisian reaction in mid-April to Bakunin's warning of failing revolutions across the Rhine was panic. Flocon called in the president of the German Democratic Society in Paris, Heinrich Börnstein, to sound the alarm that Herwegh's operation must immediately be cancelled.[7] When Herwegh's wife responded that the members of the legion refused to listen to reason,[8] Carl Ludwig Bernays was ordered by the French foreign minister on April 26 to intercept Herwegh's forces before they crossed the French border to certain disaster.[9]

After the fiasco of the German Legion's incursion onto the soil of Baden, Bernays continued to the capital, where he directly

BASTIDE.

Cet honorable membre de l'Assemblée nationale est représenté tel que, naguère, il apparaissait
aux regards des mortels, lorsqu'en sa qualité de ministre des affaires étrangères il montait à la
tribune pour ne pas répondre à toutes les interpellations qu'on voulait bien lui adresser.

Jules Bastide, French Minister of Foreign Affairs, by Honoré Daumier, Bibliothèque Nationale (Paris).

intervened with the government of Baden by pleading for clemency for the members of the German Legion.[10] And we shall soon see Bernays at the end of May in Budapest attempting to persuade the Hungarian cabinet to break with Austria and form a military alliance with the French government.[11]

But we should note two results of Bakunin's analysis of conditions in Germany: His characterization of the German war in Schleswig-Holstein as "reactionary" would stick in the mind of the French foreign minister and would reappear repeatedly during the year and affected thinking in Paris.

The French government continued along three distinct and parallel courses, with the use of public statements, traditional diplomacy, and secret agents. French revolutionary councils once more reassured vocal domestic critics of the sincerity of France's promises to defend the right of sovereignty of oppressed peoples. During early May, grandiose pronouncements that the government would act to free Italians and Poles from tyranny echoed through the newly elected French Constituent Assembly. Meanwhile, confidential agents traveled across central Europe, in particular to the Hungarian capital of Budapest. At the same time, Lamartine in Paris attempted to open negotiations for "alliances" with the ambassadors of Austria and Russia. The common thread in all three lines of action (public, secret, and diplomatic) was an effort to arrange matters peaceably and thereby to avoid the necessity of French military intervention against Austria and Russia. Thus the French republic's policy of negotiated peace (with menace of war) continued, as the French Constituent Assembly replaced the Provisional Government with an elected Executive Commission.

The Executive Commission's Minister of Foreign Affairs, Jules Bastide, who shared in navigating the course of foreign affairs as under-secretary since the February Revolution, maintained the same course. For the remainder of the year he would continue the Richelieu-Girondist policy of antagonism to the house of Habsburg. The essential continuity was underlined by the promotion of Bastide's *chef de cabinet*, Jules Hetzel, to Bastide's old post of under-secretary of state. Hetzel remained the confidential intermediary between the foreign ministry and secret agents, and his papers in the Parisian Bibliothèque Nationale are a key to identifying the Second Republic's network of confidential emissaries. Bastide emphasized now-familiar themes of France's hopes for peace in his first circular to French diplomats dated May 12. Bastide hinted at some of the advantages of war in France's current situation. The same troublesome radicals who were "accustomed to combat in the streets" and "dangerous" for the French government would become "most useful auxiliary" troops for France on the battlefield. The foreign members of the radical clubs who had been such a constant element of disorder would form the nucleus of the "friends that the republic counts abroad."[12]

Bastide went on to point out that war would do away with unemployment and the unsatisfactory attempts to relieve it through the system of National Workshops. Indeed, the military establishment, "whose maintenance costs an enormous amount," would be "nourished" by war.[13]

Bastide's circular suggested that although France desired peace, there were definite limits to her forbearance:

> If, by the fault of Europe, peace became . . . impossible, what an imposing force the government of the republic would have at its disposal; with the energy of populations accustomed to combat in the streets, dangerous today for [the republic], fully prepared tomorrow to become a most useful auxiliary if it is necessary to fall on the frontiers; with a million soldiers animated with the same patriotism whose maintenance costs an enormous sum and which the war would nourish; and last, with the great number of friends that the republic counts abroad. Who can hold back the *élan* of these, who would rise at the first signal to serve her cause?[14]

Principal among those friends was Prussia, whose armed powers the intelligence departments of the French army and foreign ministry estimated at close to a half-million men. In executing the decision of April 2 to defend Prussia against "an immediate invasion" by Russia, Lamartine ordered General Pelet to draw up a detailed memorandum for the operations of a French expeditionary force in Germany. Pelet assumed that Prussia would be France's "ally." The south German states would "probably not oppose the interests of Poland," but principal support would come from the north German states, which were "more enlightened." These, having already begun their revolutions, "will freely aid a Polish crusade." Pelet was confident that Austria would be unable to take an active part because of her war in Italy. This left England, "our eternal enemy." France under no circumstances should risk an affront to England by questioning its control of the seas. While Pelet reminded Lamartine that the French army was weak—at this

time not the equal of the German Confederation—by the end of
the summer, France would be "able to support any combination
in foreign policy."[15]

Lamartine used the detailed information from Pelet to explain
his Polish policy to the Constituent Assembly. Geographical and
political necessity demanded that France work with the Germans
for Polish freedom. If France sent any army across Germany against
German wishes, Lamartine pointed out, "it would find 500,000
Germans on its flanks before it arrived in Poland," and a Russian
army of 250,000 would have already annihilated the Poles. "To
send 100,000 or 120,000 of our boys would be a slaughter." France's
only possible course was to work with Germans "interested like
us in the resurrection and reconstruction" of Poland.[16]

The Prussian chargé saw Lamartine on the evening of May
14 and discussed his speech before the chamber for the following
day. Lamartine asked Hatzfeldt if he could assure the French assembly that "the government of Your Majesty was resolved to carry
out its work of the reorganization of the Polish nationality in the
Grand Duchy of Posen in spite of the events in that land."

Hatzfeldt replied, "Nothing has changed in the intentions of
my government." Lamartine agreed that French recriminations
against Prussia's actions would do no more than "excite the easily
offended susceptibilities of Germany." Hatzfeldt recalled "the sympathy that had welcomed the Polish emigrés a few weeks earlier
in Germany, and what interest had been manifested for their nationality." He blamed the disturbances in Posen on the activities of
the party of disorder, which had exasperated the German population
by its "hatred, spirit of exclusion, and persecution."[17]

Arnim approved of Hatzfeldt's language and authorized him
to show Lamartine his dispatch promising, "Nothing has changed
in the benevolent dispositions of the king in regard to the Polish
nationality in the Grand Duchy of Posen; you will find confirmation
in the address of the crown that his majesty read yesterday on the
occasion of the opening of the national assembly, and you will see
there that the king's government has decided to continue in its
work of reorganization and holds to its promises in spite of the
lack of gratitude that its good intentions have received."[18]

Lamartine and Bastide were "most satisfied" by Arnim's communication. Bastide agreed that the Poles' own conduct had caused
a reversal of opinion in Germany, which originally had been favorable. "He told me," Hatzfeldt reported, "that it was the misfortune

of the Poles to tie their cause to an unruly and evil faction in all
countries and thus to weaken sympathies" in their behalf.[19] Bastide
was particularly aware of the Prussian government's Polish problem,
since he had one of his own. In its ardent zeal to do something
for Poland, a strong faction in Paris threatened to involve France
in a premature war with Russia and the German states as well.

In an attempt to dampen the enthusiasm of the Foreign Affairs
Committee of the Constituent Assembly, Bastide told it that he
"feared if one were too energetic at the moment, the Polish cause
would be destroyed." Pleading that France lacked the resources
for an immediate war, he advised a more careful policy. The committee rejected an address to the Frankfurt parliament because
there was "no regular means to deliver" such a message, and instead
adopted a proposition drawn up by Bastide to invite the Executive
Power "to pursue the reconstitution of Poland." This was presented
to the assembly as a "unanimous resolution" calling for a "fraternal
pact" with Germany. As an afterthought, the committee also added
the "enfranchisement of Italy" without a dissenting vote.[20]

In Bastide's view, Polish freedom depended on the progress
of revolution in the German states. As reactionary cabinets were
transformed into liberal states, public opinion would press, as it
had in France, for the reconstitution of a Polish state. Bastide's
immediate problem was to wait for events in Germany to move
the revolution into a more radical phase. Poland could only be
rescued by peace. He told a German ambassador that France:

> depends on the good will of Germany, which we sway by
> example and by moral influence. The reported victory of the
> people of Vienna of the 15th will aid the Poles. The more the
> Austrian Empire and Germany break with the old system,
> the more Poland will find support in these very nations, and
> I think that it will soon be possible to organize a diplomatic
> intervention of the entire continent on Poland's behalf.[21]

Meanwhile, Franco-Prussian relations were threatened from a
new quarter. By late April the Danes had been defeated, and on
May 4 the commander of the German forces, Wrangel, crossed the
border into Jutland. Germany's involvement in Schleswig, an area
at best only half German, was a major error, and helped seal the
doom of the Frankfurt assembly. In *The European Powers and the
German Question*, W. E. Mosse accurately noted the gravity of the
mistake. "It was above all German intransigence in the question
of the duchies," Mosse concluded, "which provoked the hostility

of the powers toward the national assembly and its government."
Alexander Scharff likewise found that the "Schleswig-Holstein
question is the key to understanding the opposition that the German
revolution encountered."[22]

Scharff's statement is accurate in the sense that Schleswig
symbolized the momentous problem caused by competing claims
over the same territory by the German states and their neighbors.
The inherent difficulty of readjusting the borders of central Europe
to fit the new doctrine of nationality was complicated by the
political inexperience of both the French and German revolutionaries. The international committee of the Heidelberg preparliament,
for example, in its report of April 12, naively laid claim to portions
of Holland, Switzerland, Alsace, and Lorraine—where German
was the chief language—as compensation for the loss of provinces
in Italy and Poland. No matter how consonant this was with the
theory of nationality, politically it was disastrous, for it set Germans
unnecessarily against their neighbors by defining the nation on its
most doubtful borders instead of quickly consolidating power at
its nucleus. Schleswig was the least important of a series of German
demands on the territory of surrounding states that ultimately
brought a clash with the French government.

The French were no less naive. Bastide followed Bakunin's
appraisal of the situation in Schleswig and shared the bias of his
secret agent and thereby oversimplified the complexities of the
national situation in the Duchy in Schleswig and falsely assumed
that the province was overwhelmingly Danish.[23] He was equally
misinformed about the political complexion of the revolutionary
movement in Schleswig-Holstein, describing it inaccurately as a
"factitious aristocracy" while the Danish king was "the most liberal
sovereign in Europe," with an assembly emanating from universal
suffrage and "soon to receive the most democratic institutions."[24]

In fact, the national movements in both countries were popular
in nature, and in Germany the enthusiasm for Schleswig-Holstein
infected all political groups *except* the "aristocratic" extreme right.[25]

Bastide always viewed the Germans as the outsiders in the
Schleswig situation. While Holstein was both part of Germany
and under the crown of the Danish king, Schleswig had never
been part of the German Empire nor of the German Confederation.
Legally and historically it seemed to belong to Denmark. Bastide
thought that Schleswig was essentially "Danish," and its incorpo-
ration into Germany would be an "oppression" of the Danish

nation, which ran contrary to French policy. The true nationality question in the Schleswig affair, Bastide assumed, was "rather Danish and even Scandinavian." Denmark defended her territory in an unjust war.[26]

Bastide was interested in the victory of "liberty" as much as in national self-determination. He therefore feared the domestic ramifications of an extended struggle over the liberal revolution in Germany and Denmark. Denmark could be held back in its evolution to freedom because of a necessity to seek aid from reactionary Russia. "Russian protection," Bastide warned, "could only be exercised at the expense of the triumph and progress of liberty in the north." If the tsar used the Schleswig question as an excuse to act, not only would Russian meddling extinguish freedoms in Denmark, but in Germany as well. Bastide was visibly exasperated that "Germany does not understand that the intervention of Russia in favor of Denmark must give to that enemy of liberal and democratic Germany another means to bear down and make war on it." France wanted a quickly negotiated end to the Schleswig war because the conflict was "as disastrous for Prussia as for her adversary."[27]

France's friendship with Denmark was platonic. Although Lamartine objected to the German policy toward Denmark in the Schleswig issue, he assured Hatzfeldt that the matter was not of "major and pressing importance for France." He was vaguely aware that "a certain treaty existed whereby France had made engagements *vis-à-vis* Denmark relative to Schleswig."[28] A few days later, Lamartine told the Danish government that France would not intervene in the Schleswig problem because her "position" did not allow it.[29] France's interest in the question was to bring peace as rapidly as possible.

By the end of May, it appeared that a truce on the Schleswig-Holstein issue was imminent, when Prussia accepted mediation by Britain's foreign secretary Palmerston under conditions set out in a British note of May 19. The Prussians abandoned Flensburg on May 25, allowing northern Schleswig to revert to the Danes. Berlin had bowed to foreign pressure to end hostilities, but suffered a political embarrassment at home, for the cause of Schleswig-Holstein was close to the hearts of German liberals. Schleswig had been for years a touchstone of commitment to the cause of German unity, and the setback for Prussia was a grave moral defeat in the eyes of the political Left.

Meanwhile, France's most pressing concern had been northern

Italy's revolt against Austria. German liberals shared the French aspiration to create a new era of European freedom, to bring liberty not only to Poland but also to Italy, and to defeat the mutual foe, the holy alliance.[30] Lamartine stressed that, as far as France was concerned, Austria was an ideological adversary, a class enemy, rather than a traditional territorial opponent. Should liberals remain in control of German governments or establish a united German regime, then Austria's long-range chances of retaining her Italian provinces seemed remote.

Until late summer there was little probability of French military involvement in northern Italy. Remembering clearly the annexations made by the first French republic, many Italian nationalists were, at best, equivocal as far as France was concerned. They "feared seeing France impose her protection," wondering if this would be compatible with Italian independence. Apprehensive of French help, they preferred, if possible, to do things alone, reported the French consul in Ancona in a dispatch to Lamartine.[31] From Turin, Bixio assured Lamartine, "No one wants to substitute France for Austria." If the French sent an army across the Alps counter to Italy's wishes, "it would mean the end of French influence and French ideas in Italy for an extended period." Only a striking defeat of the Sardinian king's forces would cause Italians to request aid from Paris.[32]

Not only did Italian patriots have little confidence in France's Provisional Government, but it, in turn, did not trust the motives of Charles Albert, king of Sardinia, suspecting him both of exploiting the Italian national movement merely to avoid being swept from his throne, and of being involved in secret negotiations with Austria. Moreover, his frequent hesitations in the field caused many Frenchmen and some Italian nationalists to question his abilities as a military leader. The French chargé thought "the inaction of Charles Albert could make one suppose that he is in secret partnership with the Austrians." He was no friend of democracy, so his government "is hardly disposed to arm the Piedmontese people in fear that one day these arms will be turned against it."[33]

France had little choice but to wait. Bastide was forced to reject a forward policy in Italy, and put his hopes on the power of ideas to transform Europe. The French minister in Bern, General Count de Bissy de Thiard was informed, "We would prefer, without a doubt, for the triumph across the Alps [in Italy] of a democracy like ours; we desire that the republican party, the most numerous, the most able, and the most sympathetic to the masses would make its principles prevail."[34] The victory of democracy was, for Bastide, a question of ideology, of making "principles prevail." French arms could as easily hinder as aid the spread of such principles. Bastide therefore told the Saxon ambassador on May 20 that there would be no need for French intervention in the Italian dispute because "the pen is mightier than the sword."[35]

At no point did France seriously contemplate armed action *against* Sardinia. Bastide wrote Thiard that France was fully aware of the serious political consequences of an aggrandizement of Sardinia:

> The French republic has proclaimed her respect of nations which seek to reconstitute themselves, has recognized the law of peoples to organize themselves as they judge right within the capacity of their civilization, their interests, and their needs; could she openly oppose that which northern Italy asks for today: an independent nation, welfare, and security? We are aware of disadvantages before it matures, and in Italy, as in Germany, a monarchy founded on democratic institutions seems destined to serve as the transition to the pure republic.[36]

Sardinia would have to be allowed to free Italy of the Austrians unaided. Any French attempt to assist the Italian provinces in a revolt against Austria without the concurrence of Sardinia would encounter violent opposition.[37] Also important in any French attempt to foster the nationalist aspirations of the Italian provinces under Austrian rule was her relationship with the Hungarians. A major portion of Austria's army in Italy was in fact drawn from the Hungarian portions of the empire. And these eastern provinces were themselves in revolt against Habsburg authority.[38] This tendency in Budapest to distance itself from Vienna had immediate meaning for France. Any weakening of Austria's hegemony over northern Italy increased the possibility of a widening of the French sphere of interest. An autonomous policy in Budapest interested France because of the likelihood that this independence could separate the conduct of military and foreign affairs. Such an eventuality of an independent Hungary would in turn significantly aid Charles Albert in his war against the Habsburgs.

Under the circumstances, France urged the Magyars to take a bold line in foreign affairs, one that was independent of the imperial Habsburg government. More immediately, the French asked the Hungarians to withdraw their contingents from the

Habsburg army in northern Italy in the hope that this would force the Habsburgs to negotiate an end to the conflict with King Charles Albert of Piedmont-Sardinia.

Echoes of France's concerns reverberated in two places in Hungary. The first place was the Hungarian cabinet. On April 12, 1848, the Ministerial Council decided to seek allies among the liberal peoples of western Europe: the British, the Germans, and the French. The minutes of April 16, 1848, reflected an awareness of the *quid pro quo* that the French demanded from the Hungarians in return for a military alliance, namely, freedom for Italy. On April 16, 1848, the Ministerial Council also ordered its Foreign Minister, Prince Pál Ésterházy, to press Vienna for the return of Hungarian soldiers serving in Italy.[39] But the Hungarian cabinet itself was under pressure from a group of young Hungarian radicals who identified themselves with the revolutionary idealism of France. This group protested the delay of the Hungarian cabinet and army in "clarifying" the relations between Hungary and Austria.

Yet even the radicals were ambivalent. Like the Ministerial Council, they seemed unsure whether Hungary should go it alone or whether the Magyars might impose their will over Vienna and thereby control the common policy of the entire Danubian monarchy. On the one hand, the radicals urged that it was time for Budapest to exert direction over a *common* policy of foreign affairs, war, and finance. On the other hand, they warned in their paper *March Fifteenth* that "the war with Austria is as certain as two and two are four."[40] The radicals doubted that the Habsburgs would give up power peacefully. In their cafe, Hall of Liberty, they organized a "March Club" to "spread the principle of liberty" and called for arms to be distributed to the people. When the octogenarian General Baron Ignaz Lederer refused their demand for arms, two thousand radicals took to the streets on May 10, 1848, to march on his home. Troops concealed near the house struck down an unarmed crowd, wounding many and killing at least one student. The Hungarian cabinet found itself facing a serious crisis.[41]

While the radical youth attempted to force the Hungarian government to break with Vienna, the French government was confronted with a crisis of its own. In early May it seemed only a matter of time before King Charles Albert of Piedmont-Sardinia was defeated in the field and the French government was publicly committed to come to his aid were this to happen. The Austrians' most dependable forces were from Hungary and Croatia. From a military as much as a political standpoint, therefore, it was essential to Paris that Hungary set itself apart from the Viennese cabinet. Thus the French government sent a confidential agent, Carl Ludwig Bernays, to Budapest,[42] to urge the Hungarian cabinet to declare Hungary separate from the Habsburg dominion.[43] Bernays promised Louis Kossuth, the leader of the European revolution and darling of Hungarian radicals, that Hungary would not suffer if she dared to break openly with Austria. France would provide not only moral support but military help as well. Kossuth told Bernays that he was prepared to sever all ties with Vienna.[44]

The French and their Hungarian sympathizers seemed to have won a major victory. The Magyar historian Aladár Urbán believes that the May incident was the crucial turning point in 1848 and has suggested that the Hungarian government at this point gave in completely to a radical demand to take definite command of the army, requiring the entire military to swear a new oath to defend the Hungarian constitution.[45] István Hajnal, the modern Hungarian historian, also considered May the fateful period when the Hungarian cabinet stepped forth and initiated its own foreign policy as an independent country.[46] Under pressure from the Budapest radicals and fearing imminent tsarist interference, the Hungarian government adopted the principal demands of the Hungarian radicals—and of the French envoy Bernays.

On May 14, 1848, Lajos Batthyány, premier in the Hungarian government, sent two liberals, László Szalay and Dénes Pázmándy to Frankfurt as deputies of the "Hungarian government" to the German Assembly to arrange diplomatic relations based on "common independence, freedom, and material prosperity."[47] The Hungarian Minister of Interior Bertalan Szemere wrote Szalay on May 25 urging an alliance between Hungary, Germany, France, and England against the Slav danger. "I believe and Kossuth does too that you should go to England. . . . On your return, either you or Pázmándy can go to Paris." Szalay was further instructed to explain the liberal principles motivating Hungary's policy toward "the eastern countries." Szalay should indicate that Hungary's policy did not differ from those of France and England and to assure them that the Hungarian cabinet desired an "intimate alliance" with the English and French.[48]

The Magyar defection from the Habsburg cause raised the possibility of a victory for the forces of nationality and liberty throughout the Austrian Empire. The French chargé in Vienna,

De la Cour, believed that the Austrians were aware of the untenability of their situation in Italy. "They will resign themselves to concede . . . much easier than one could have hoped in other circumstances," he reported. The Austrian foreign minister, Count Karl Ficquelmont, "frankly agrees that Austria cannot reasonably hope to retain the Italian provinces."[49] De la Cour advised his government, therefore, not to embarrass Austria by intervening in northern Italy and "humiliating" it. This would only compromise the liberal Viennese revolution.[50] A powerful new Austrian liberal faction wanted an entente with France and "would not decline revolutionary solidarity" to cooperate in bringing freedom to Europe.[51]

Bastide agreed that there was no reason for France to complicate matters by becoming involved in Austria's conflict with northern Italy. Austria was far too weak to retain her Italian provinces. The flight of the Austrian emperor to Innsbruck on May 15 "left the capital to the chance of events. The Austrian monarchy is dismantled and weakened, breached by the increasingly dissolving action of the diverse nationalities." The Bohemians, Hungarians, and Germans, Bastide believed, had made the emperor a "more nominal than real leader. . . . Disunion, defiance, and anarchy are universal; a serious and respected authority, a government worthy of the name no longer exists."[52]

After the Bolshevik Revolution of 1917 opened tsarist archives, the Soviet historian Pokrovsky published an essay revealing the startling fact that Lamartine had speculated about a possible Franco-Russian alliance during 1848. German historians like Alexander Scharff charged that such talk by the French leader was proof of the existence of an alliance of the flanking powers who were hostile to German unity in 1848. Likewise, Polish historians like Josef Feldman felt betrayed by the discovery of Lamartine's apparently hypocritical behavior, seemingly sacrificing Polish freedom to Lamartine's "realistic" interest in French survival.[53] On first examination the evidence seems to undermine our thesis that Lamartine was doing more than biding his time as director of foreign policy for the French republic, but before accepting the overhasty generalizations, let us examine the evidence.

The Russian chargé in Paris saw Lamartine in April when Nicholas's fears of daily invasion by a Polish-Prussian revolutionary army were greatest. Kiselev read only parts of Nicholas's letter assuring the French government of the impossibility of Russian intervention in the internal affairs of France. The tsar hoped to prevent a war over a misunderstanding of Russian intentions.

Lamartine was pleased by the communication and added a declaration of his own peaceful intentions to those of the tsar. He acknowledged that French public opinion was sympathetic to the Poles. He attempted to pose as the "man of order" in the midst of chaos, the one who by his own genius stood in the way of a hasty march on Warsaw. Lamartine assured the Russian chargé that, though no one had hindered the Polish revolutionaries from leaving France, he had to get rid of those disorderly people somehow. Lamartine then went on to speculate about a "natural alliance" between France and Russia. He explained:

> During my diplomatic career . . . I have often thought about the mutual hostility of France and Russia and have come to the conclusion that the most natural alliance for France is an alliance with Russia. If the Polish question had not produced a certain sympathy in France, . . . this alliance would have long ago existed to aid both peoples, whose spirits are much more closely related than are those of any other two peoples. All of this is only a question of time and good circumstances.[54]

This was not Lamartine's only attempt to secure detente. Count Karl Robert Nesselrode, the Russian chancellor, confided to Baron Peter von Meyendorf, Russian ambassador in Berlin, on May 20, "Lamartine is making us enthusiastic advances, which one here by all means does not take negatively."[55]

On closer examination there seems less here than accepted historical wisdom has imagined. Above all, matters remained on the level of no more than "diplomatic conjecture" (Rudolf Stadelmann), and no alliance ever materialized between France and Russia. Lamartine had actually done little more than to speculate on what might happen if Russia would liberate the Poles. Under such circumstances of a free and independent Poland, an alliance between France and Russia might be negotiated. Thus Feldman and A. J. P. Taylor erroneously concluded that France had abandoned the Poles. On the contrary, Lamartine made Polish freedom the price for normal relations between Paris and St. Petersburg. In other words, Lamartine only reiterated the language of his earlier public circular to the three northern courts and the "Manifesto to Europe." If Poland were reconstituted, then a "natural alliance for France" would be with Russia. There is even less proof for Scharff's charge that Lamartine used the threat of a Franco-Russian alliance to thwart German unity. Lamartine neither mentioned a united Germany nor seemed threatened by the apparition. Most telling, the discussion never advanced to the point where the terms of this "alliance" were an issue. However, we may wish to speculate on the shape of possible terms of such an understanding by turning to Lamartine's somewhat more detailed discussions with the Austrian ambassador for a similar "alliance."

Lamartine offered Austria the Danubian principalities as a compensation for the loss of Austria's Italian provinces. The offer to Austria of territory in the east was renewed twice by Bastide, and places the entire question of France's policy toward Austria in 1848 in a new context. Rather than waging an "undeclared philosophical war" against Austria—as Lamartine later claimed to be doing—he was attempting to appease Vienna.[56]

Lamartine's effort to interest Austria in the Danubian principalities signified a major new component in the French republic's design to reconstruct European politics. In the border area where Romanov and Habsburg ambitions contended, French revolutionary diplomacy found a new eastern orientation. Commencing with Lamartine's conversation in early May, the east of Europe increasingly became a preoccupation of the French. But as their stratagems in this area developed, Lamartine and Bastide never swayed from the ultimate objective of Richelieu-Girondist policy, which was to free Poland and Italy from foreign rule. A significant change in that strategy, beginning in May, would be greater concern for the Magyar revolt. But when Lamartine spoke with Apponyi early in the month, his immediate purpose was to steer Austrian expansion toward the Balkans.

The proposal of a new "mission" for Austria was first made when Apponyi visited Lamartine before taking leave of Paris. Lamartine took the opportunity to explain the French position at length. He reiterated that Italian affairs were the most threatening to European tranquility. "He hoped that the court of Vienna would succeed in resolving peaceably the questions pending today in the [Italian] peninsula." Lamartine and Bastide often suggested their sympathy for Austria to her representative by voicing distrust of King Charles Albert of Sardinia. Lamartine told Apponyi that Charles Albert's conduct was marked by "weakness and extreme versatility." He indicated that he would not be surprised if the sovereign were secretly negotiating with Austria and only making a "comedy of resistance." Lamartine volunteered to Apponyi a possible recompense for Austria's losses in Italy:

The court of Vienna *could find in the Danubian principalities a compensation for the loss of her states in Italy:* The French government desires *that Austria should be strong in the east* and, if it is necessary, it would be prepared to arrive at an understanding for that end.[57]

Lamartine repeated that France's primary interest was Italy, ignoring entirely the conflict of the German Confederation in Schleswig. He did not mention Poland nor the Austrian possession of Galicia. Instead of talking of old frictions between Paris and Vienna, he shifted the discussion to the east, a favorite subject for the romantic poet, Lamartine.[58]

Lamartine's delusive proposal to place the Danubian principalities under Austrian suzerainty places his offhand reference to an alliance between France and Russia within a new context. It seems apparent that in both instances (his fantastic proposals to Austria and to Russia) Lamartine hoped to divide Austria from Russia. If France could sow seeds of dissension between the Habsburgs and the Romanovs, then the survival of the French republic was assured. As we shall see, Lamartine's successor in foreign affairs, Jules Bastide, mistakenly believed that Russia might assist France in moderating Austria. The patent absurdity of such an illusion only underscores the misdirected and amateurish enthusiasm of France's revolutionary command. And Bastide's self-deception is reflected in newly discovered instructions for a special envoy to St. Petersburg. We shall examine later this mission, which shared with Lamartine's first overtures to Russia a misevaluation of the basic abhorrence for revolutionary France that was felt by the tsar.

There was never any point of departure for Lamartine's alliances with either Austria or Russia. These were trial balloons that never left the ground. An alliance of the flanking powers never materialized to threaten German unity, although the French, Schweitzer perceptively realized, thought that "success was only a matter of time and patience."[59]

In spite of superficial difficulties caused by the Polish and Schleswig situations, the French assumed that they had created an invincible armed front with Prussia and the minor German states. Metternich's holy alliance was in shambles. Reassured of Prussia's support, France looked for new members for the liberating coalition. Lamartine made advances to the Russian and Austrian governments, seeking potential allies for a peaceful regeneration of Europe.

The policy of this French republic was much like that of Louis Philippe's adviser François Guizot, Schweitzer alleged, with the difference that Guizot desired "peace by the action of governments," while now Lamartine "wants it by that of the people." Republican peace, however, was combined with "revolutionary propaganda abroad," which was a "plague as destructive as war itself."[60] Paris would intervene in its own fashion and at its chosen time to free Italy and establish Poland out of the decomposition of Austria, but only with Germany's cooperation.[61] The new "policy of Tartuffe" was based on a belief that France had "the right of monopoly to peacefully revolutionize Europe."[62] France never had a fixed policy; it was "always in a state of expectation on nearly all points." Underhandedly, it republicanized Europe by continuing revolutionary discussions in the wings while offering the velvet glove to the governments. It only awaited the right moment to fish in the troubled waters of Italy and Germany.[63]

Strong circumstantial evidence confirms Schweitzer's testimony that French secret agents were, in fact, already doing this in Germany. The favorable reception of France's emissary in Germany, Mikhail Bakunin, strongly suggests collaboration with official circles in Prussia.

Obviously disappointed by the peaceful condition of Cologne, Bakunin left the Rhine to travel east. In Berlin, he was advised to agitate in Cracow (Austrian Poland) rather than go to Posen where a civil war was raging between Poles and Prussians. Instead, Bakunin overslept the next morning, missed his train, and soon appeared before the Berlin police president.

Bakunin's relations with the Berlin police president were determined by the fact that emissaries in foreign countries—like Bakunin—carried "in reserve" formal credentials as traveling envoys of France's foreign ministry for presentation in just such an eventuality,[64] and that from March to June 1848, France and Prussia were bound together in an alliance to fight Russia in order to secure German and Polish unification as nation states. The police president of Berlin had formerly served in Posen and was strongly sympathetic to both the Polish and German national movements.

Bakunin handed over two passports. One was in his own name, identifying him as a Russian emigré who had been tried in absentia and who was wanted by the Russian government. The other had been made out under a pseudonym by the Paris prefect of police. Instead of informing the Russian ambassador in Berlin of Bakunin's presence there, the police president confiscated the passport in Bakunin's name and returned the false French passport with a handwritten annotation "to Leipzig, not good for Posen." He then presented Bakunin with a second passport identifying him as a Prussian citizen "travelling to Leipzig and Breslau."[65] He did this even though Bakunin explained to the Berlin police president that his actual mission along the Russian border was "to excite the countries of Slavic language into an insurrection, to republicanise them, and to provoke a war between Prussia and Russia."[66] But this was consistent with the Prussian policy at that moment. Thus the Prussian police saw nothing out of the ordinary in Bakunin's activities. Indeed the police president of Berlin continued to assist Bakunin as a co-conspirator for the next few weeks.

The conclusion seems inescapable that Bakunin's insurrectionary machinations were approved as part of a joint Franco-Prussian liberal policy of creating war against the tsar. This also explains the initiative of the French envoy to Prussia. As soon as the official French diplomatic agent learned that Bakunin was in Berlin, he asked the Prussian foreign minister to promise that under no circumstances would Bakunin be extradited to Russia. This sort of sympathetic treatment at the highest level was obviously reserved for special cases; the French diplomat immediately reported his intervention on Bakunin's behalf to Paris, where he apparently knew that his own foreign minister would be interested.[67]

So Bakunin's explanation that he was up to no more than causing havoc among the Poles and thereby inciting a major European war appeared completely respectable to the Berlin police president. Bakunin was on his way within an hour.[68]

But Bakunin did not head toward Posen, which would have been possible with his newly acquired Prussian passport, nor to Cracow. In fact, he never arrived in Poland. Instead he remained in the German states. Bakunin's hitherto unexplained behavior is disentangled by the discovery that he was a French agent ordered to Germany—not to Poland, which he subsequently claimed was his destination. The Franco-Prussian strategy was based on an assumption of a joint undertaking of the French and German peoples to free Poland. An integral part of this policy was, therefore, agitating for the election of delegates to the coming German parliament who were sympathetic to this Polish policy. Bakunin thus traveled to Leipzig to see his old friend from pre-1848 Paris, Arnold Ruge. Ruge was a candidate for this German constituent assembly and one of the most outspoken champions of a "war to end all wars" to be fought by the Germans and Poles united with the French to force back Russian influence to the steppes of central Asia. When Ruge failed to gain support from the city fathers of Leipzig, Bakunin promised to get him elected in Breslau. Therefore Bakunin never continued his journey on to Cracow to stir up the Poles. He remained in Breslau to agitate for Ruge so that he might argue in Frankfurt for a great war against the tsar. To elect Ruge, Bakunin was able to put together a solid bloc of democrats and constitutionalists with the outstanding exception of Marx's faction.[69]

Official protection for Bakunin extended to Breslau. When the Breslau police president inquired about Bakunin's presence in Prussia, the Berlin police president lied twice. Indeed he even misinformed the Prussian minister of the interior. Important higher officers seem to have approved of Bakunin's activities in Breslau. Bakunin tried to influence opinion toward a general program that he had developed in his manifesto of March 13—a European-wide revolution to overthrow the tsar. Since this was also the aim of the Prussian and French governments, Bakunin never needed to sacrifice idealism for cooperation with the Prussians. Even when the Russian ambassador in Berlin learned that Bakunin was in Breslau, where he reportedly offered a great deal of money to two Poles to assassinate the tsar, Bakunin was only warned of the danger.[70]

Bakunin's activities in Prussia showed that Schweizer's information was not wide of the mark. French emissaries like Bakunin were sent "to excite the countries of Slavic language into an insurrection, to republicanize them, and to provoke a war between Prussia and Russia." Moreover Bakunin's behavior reflects an extremely close collaboration with the Prussian administration at the highest levels in the help he received in inciting the Poles to rebel in neighboring Russian territory. Finally, Bakunin's decision in May to divert his main efforts from direct agitation among Poles to the elections for the Frankfurt parliament in the Silesian capital of Breslau once more emphasizes the extremely close tie between the Polish and German issues. France could never hope to bring her policies of revolutionizing all Europe to fruition without intimate cooperation between French and German popular forces. European-wide action against Russia was the objective of Bakunin's agitation in Breslau for Ruge's election to the Frankfurt assembly, and Ruge never wavered in that course of pressing for a German war against tsarism. The road to Warsaw and Moscow seemed to lie from Paris and Berlin through the old German city of Frankfurt am Main, and for the next several months French hopes would center on a positive response to the French national assembly's call of May 24 for a unanimous resolution between the parliaments of Paris and Frankfurt to enfranchise Italy and Poland.

Even as Bakunin was diverted from traveling to agitate among the Poles, he remained faithful to the ultimate French goal of liberating all Europe from tyranny. France's agents concentrated on eastern Europe because behind the Habsburg's despotism stood the tsar's armed forces. Thus, since the immediate objective was the overthrow of the house of Habsburg, the ultimate enemy of the people and upholder of oppression was the Russian tsar. If Habsburgs were to be brought down, the tsar as well could not be ignored. Bakunin joined Bernays and Czartoryski's Balkan agents in their efforts to mobilize all men of good will.

Historical wisdom erroneously insists that Jules Bastide's replacement of Lamartine as foreign minister on May 12 initiated a change in policies. That false impression originated in the confusion of axioms of diplomacy with mere modalities in their outward behavior. The supposedly more cautious Bastide merely preferred a more restrained public style in contrast to Lamartine's flamboyant declarations. But Bastide did not modify the essential nature of Lamartine's policies. Certainly it was neither more cautious nor conservative, but remained committed to the Richelieu-Girondist formula. In fact, Bastide was the author of the French assembly's unanimous resolution of May 24, which was an unequivocal reassertion of France's commitment to join with Germans to free Italy and reconstitute a free Poland.

The actual major reconstruction of the second republic would come after the June Days revolt under Cavaignac, but this was purely a domestic matter and did not affect foreign policy. A primary historical misconception is the confusion of domestic and external affairs. While in the realm of foreign policy, French radicals since the February Revolution had been the most vocal proponents of liberating sovereign peoples from oppression, that rhetorical extravagance ought not be confused with a difference in goals with Lamartine and Bastide. Let us now turn to a closer examination of actual changes that were taken in France's posture during June.

NOTES

1. Baron F. A. von Schweitzer to Dusch, Paris, May 3, 1848, BGLA, fz. 48/2037, fo. 445.

2. Henri Boernstein, Bulletin des nouvelles de l'Allemagne, July 17, 1848, AEF, MD, Allemagne 129, fo. 42; Börnstein was president of the German democratic club responsible for the Herwegh expedition; the following first appeared in my article, "Bakunin as a French Secret Agent in 1848," reproduced with the permission of the editors of *History Today*.

3. Otto von Corvin-Wiersbitzski, *Ein Leben voller Abenteuer*, ed. Hermann Wendel (Frankfurt, 1924), II, 431; Herwegh to Jacoby, Paris, March 30, 1848, in Gustav Mayer, "Briefe von Alexander Herzen und Michael Bakunin an Johann Jacoby," *Archiv für die Geschichte des Sozialismus und der Arbeiterbewegung*, I (1911), 482.

4. *Ibid.*

5. Bakunin to Annekov, Cologne, April 17, 1848, quoted in Tannewitz, "M. A. Bakunins publizistische Persönlichkeit," pp. 183–84.

6. *The "Confession" of Mikhail Bakunin with marginal comments of Tsar Nicholas I*, trans. Robert C. Howes, introduction and notes by Lawrence D. Orton (Ithaca and London, 1977), p. 59.

7. Börnstein, *Fünfundsiebzig Jahre*, I, 412.

8. *Ibid.*, I, 412–13.

9. Ch. L. Bernays to Foreign Minister, Strasbourg, April 29, and Karlsruhe, April 29, 1848, AEF, MD, Allemagne 170, fo. 21–24; Lefebvre to Foreign Minister, Karlsruhe, April 29, 1848, DDF, I, 1088–89; Bernays arrived too late to prevent Herwegh's men from crossing guided by two messengers, reportedly from Struve, who was also fighting the government in Baden; annex to Bernays' report written by a participant, fo. 22–23.

10. *Ibid.*

11. See above, p. 94.

12. Bastide to French diplomatic agents, Paris, May 12, 1848, DDF, II, 184–86.

13. *Ibid.*

14. *Ibid.*

15. Sur une guerre de Pologne: note demandée par le Ministre des Affaires Etrangères, No. 16, April 7, 1848, Pelet Papers, SHA, MR 2111, fo. 161–170.

16. Lamartine speech of May 23, *Moniteur*, May 24, 1848; Louis Bertrand, *Lamartine*, pp. 223–24.

17. Hatzfeldt to Frederick William IV, Paris, May 15, 1848, GSA, fz. 856, fo. 55–56; also quoted in Feldman, *Sprawa Polska*, pp. 220–21n.

18. Arnim to Hatzfeldt, Berlin, May 23, 1848, GSA, fz. 856, fo. 86; Garnier-Pagès, *Histoire*, III, 230–31.

19. Hatzfeldt to Frederick William IV, Paris, June 3 and 4, 1848, GSA, fz. 856, fo. 122–26; cf. the puzzling misconception of Jennings that "French relations with both Prussia and the government in Frankfurt were adversely affected by the events in Poland," bringing a progressive estrangement between the French Republic and Frankfurt, as well as between France and Prussia, *France and Europe*, pp. 92–95.

20. Procès-verbaux de l'Assemblée constituente: Comité des affaires étrangères, May 24, 1848, Archives Nationales, C 926 [C277] 561, fo. 1–6; *Moniteur*, May 25, 1848.

21. Bastide thought in terms of pacific diplomatic and revolutionary action. He expected to deliver Poland with "all" of Europe as allies, not in battle, but peacefully. Könneritz to Foreign Minister, Paris, May 22, 1848, Kretzschmar and Schlechte, *Gesandtschaftsberichte*, pp. 101–02.

22. W. E. Mosse, *The European Powers and the German Question*, p. 25; Alexander Scharff, "Revolution and Reichsgründungsversuche," p. 434; cf. Scharff, "Schleswig-Holsteins Erhebung im Spiegel französischer Akten"; Garnier-Pagès, *Histoire*, II, 341–47.

23. Bastide believed that "only 125,000 of 350,000 speak German" in Schleswig; in reality, a modern researcher concluded that, "It is impossible to estimate with any accuracy the number of those speaking German and Danish in Schleswig in the first half of the nineteenth century." In the complex situation of dialects, including an estimated 23,000 to 27,000 speaking Frisian and 47,000 to 75,000 speaking equally both German and Danish, probably approximately an equal number spoke some sort of Danish or German idiom. Bastide's misconception of the overwhelming Danish character of the area had great ramifications, of course, in his attitude toward German demands that all of Schleswig belonged in the German "nation"; Bastide to Arago, Paris, June 29, 1848, DDF, II, 1158; W. Carr, *Schleswig-Holstein 1815–48: A Study in National Conflict* (Manchester, 1963), pp. 70–71, 318.

24. Bastide was probably referring to the dynastic claims of the Duke of Augustenburg which Frederick William IV of Prussia, with Arnim's advice, had favored in a letter of March 24, 1848, Huber, *Deutsche Verfassungsgeschichte*, II, 668; Bastide to Arago, Paris, June 29, 1848, DDF, II, 1158.

25. *Protokolle der Deutschen Bundesversammlungen*, §215, March 31; §228, April 4; §267, April 12; §596, June 5, 1848; Huber, *Deutsche Verfassungsgeschichte*, II, 672–73. For a rapid survey of the background of the Danish-German conflict see the excellent articles by Troels Fink and Alexander Scharff in *Bibliografi og Ikonografi 1864* (Neumünster, 1970) pp. 11ff. E. R. Huber, *Deutsche Verfassungsgeschichte seit 1789*, II, 660ff.,

and the documents in Huber, *Dokumente zur Deutsche Verfassungsgeschichte* (Stuttgart, 1961), I, 451ff.; the basic problem was constitutional, with the Danish liberals of the Eiderdanish party wishing to remake Denmark to bring Schleswig into an integral national state, while the Germans of Holstein and southern Schleswig asked to be included in unified Germany; Holstein was a member of the German Confederation and at the same time was part of the Danish state, and the real conflict was over Schleswig and the German contention that an "indissoluble union" existed between Danish Schleswig and German Holstein.

26. Bastide to Arago, Paris, June 29, 1848, DDF, II, 1158.

27. Bastide to Arago, Paris, June 29 and September 7, 1848, DDF, II, 1158 and AEF, Allemagne 302, fo. 251; Jennings apparently never considered that France's fear of Russian intervention might have influenced its Schleswig policy. "French diplomacy and the first Schleswig-Holstein crisis," *French Historical Studies*, VII (1971), 204–25.

28. Hatzfeldt to Berlin, Paris, April 24, 1848, GSA, fz. 855, fo. 192–93; Lamartine was being coy? More likely he knew nothing more about the treaty.

29. Hatzfeldt to Arnim, Paris, April 27, 1848, GSA, fz. 855, fo. 198; Lamartine to Adolphe Dotézac, Paris, May 2, 1848, DDF, II, 24. Jennings, "French Diplomacy," p. 208, is correct that Lamartine's excuse was a "specious argument" since the French policy was active elsewhere at the same time, but his conclusion that he sacrificed Denmark for a Prussian alliance is strained; France was quite willing to give strongly worded protests to Prussia over the Posen question, but neither French foreign minister even discussed Schleswig at length with the Prussian chargé until August, cf. James Chastain, "French *Kleindeutsch* Policy in 1848," p. 99.

30. Circourt to Lamartine, Berlin, April 2, 8, and 17 and May 8, 1848, BN, Circourt Papers, fo. 366, 380, 403, and 464–67; Rossi to Pareto, Berlin, April 7, 11, and 29, 1848, AST, 31/607, 608, and confidential letter.

31. Armand-Charles Duault (French Consul) to Lamartine, Ancona, April 9, 1848, DDF, I, 741–42; When Lamartine told the Sardinian minister that the French army would only intervene "for the defense of oppressed nations and to impede the European equilibrium being upset to the advantage of oppressing states," Brignole replied that the Sardinian army was in Lombardy "not only in the hope, but in the conviction that we will never find ourselves in a situation to invoke the armed help of the French government." Marchese Antonio Brignole de Sales to Pareto, Paris, April 12, 1848, AST, 277/1805; Boislecomte draft for cipher telegram, Paris, April 19, 1848, BN, Hetzel Papers, 6/31.

32. Bixio to Lamartine, Turin, April 20, 1848, DDF, I, 931.

33. Count Gustave de Reiset (chargé) to Bastide, Turin, June 5, 17, and 20, 1848, DDF, II, 684, 970–71, and 1041; Adrien Benoît-Champy

(a lawyer typical of the new diplomatic corps) to Foreign Minister, Florence, April 29 and May 19, 1848, DDF, I, 1104–05 and II, 347–48, Henri Vicomte de Poilly (Secretary) to Bastide, Florence, June 29, 1848, DDF, II, 1170; Thiard to Foreign Minister, Bern, April 20 and May 14, 1848, DDF, I, 939–41 and II, 231; Bixio to Lamartine, Turin, April 27, 1848, DDF, I, 1060; For the French fear of England's hostility to its Italian policy see: Auguste Marquis de Tallenay (Minister) to Foreign Minister, London, May 4, June 5 and 8, 1848, DDF, II, 52, 679, 741; Bastide to Tallenay, Paris, May 31, 1848, AEF, Angleterre, 670, fo. 80; Tallenay to Bastide, London, July 26, 1848, AEF, Angleterre 670, fo. 273.

34. Bastide to Thiard, Paris, May 23, 1848, DDF, II, 427.

35. Könneritz to Foreign Minister, Paris, May 22, 1848, Kretzschmar and Schlechte, *Gesandtschaftsberichte*, p. 101; Reiset to Bastide, Turin, June 8, 1848, DDF, II, 746; Benoît-Champy to Bastide, Florence, June 6, 1848, DDF, II, 699–700, expressed similar confidence in the eventual victory of Italian republicans. Bixio to Foreign Minister, Turin, May 10, 1848, DDF, II, 160 and Benoît-Champy to Foreign Minister, May 19, 1848, DDF, II, 347, are typical of the requests for a more active French policy in Italy, and repudiated by Foreign Minister to Bixio, Paris, May 10, 1848, DDF, II, 159.

36. Bastide to Thiard, Paris, May 23, 1848, DDF, II, 427.

37. Jules Bastide, *La République française et l'Italie*, p. 26.

38. Istvan Deak, *The Lawful Revolution: Louis Kossuth and the Hungarians, 1848–1849* (New York, 1979); Edsel Walter Stroup, *Hungary in Early 1848: The Constitutional Struggle Against Absolutism in Contemporary Eyes* (Buffalo, N.Y.–Atlanta, GA, 1977); the claim of legality was Lajos Batthyány's defense at his trial, Árpád Károlyi, *Németújavári gróf Batthyány Lajos elsö magyar miniszterelnök föbenjáró pöre* (Budapest, 1932) 2 vols.

39. Deak, pp. 110–11; Aladár Urbán, "Zehn kritische Tage aus der Geschichte der Batthyány-Regierung (10–20 Mai 1848)," *Annales Universitatis Scientiarium Budapestitenis . . . Sectio Historica* (1960), II, 93–94; Hajnal, pp. 30 and 85.

40. Laszlo Deme, "Nationalism and Cosmopolitanism among the Hungarian Radicals," *Austrian History Yearbook*, XII-XIII (1976–77), 36–44.

41. Deak, pp. 135–47; Urban, pp. 91–124; Laszlo Deme, *The Radical Left in the Hungarian Revolution of 1848* (New York and Boulder, Colorado, 1976).

42. Helmut Hirsch, "Karl Ludwig Bernays: Heines Kampfgefährte aus den vierziger Jahren," *Heine Jahrbuch*, XIII (1974), 85–102; Börnstein, *Fünfundsiebzig Jahre*; vol. I; Helmut Hirsch, "Karl Ludwig Bernays: Ein Emigrierter Schriftsteller als US-Konsul in der Schweiz," *Jahrbuch des Instituts für Deutsche Geschichte* (Tel-Aviv), IV (1975), 147–65.

43. Charles Louis Bernays to Foreign Minister, St. Louis, Missouri, February 23, 1849, dossier personnel, AEF.

44. James Chastain, "Iratok Franciaország Magyarországi Politikájának Történetéchez 1848-ban," *Levéltari Közlemények* (Budapest) XLVII
(1976) No. 2, p. 277, cited as footnote 28* added by the Hungarian editor
Dr. Karolyi Vörös; I wish to thank Dr. Vörös for this key reference and
my colleague Joseph Ipacs for his help in translations from Hungarian.

45. Urban, p. 113.

46. István Hajnal, *Á Batthyány-kormány külpolitikája* (Budapest,
1957), pp. 48–66; Edsel Walter Stroup graciously allowed me the use of
his English translation of this book.

47. Karolyi, I, 1; Lászlo Szalay, *Diplomatische Aktenstücke zur Beleuchtung der ungarischen Gesandtschaft in Deutschland* (Zurich, 1849), pp.
5–6; Deak, p. 147; Hajnal, pp. 50–53; on the Hungarian revolution, in
addition to the works cited above see Wilhelm Alter, *Die auswärtige Politik
der ungarischen Revolution 1848/1849 unter Benutzung neuer Quellen* (Berlin,
1913); Dragoslav Stranjakovic, "La collaboration des Croates et des Serbes
en 1848–1849," *Le Monde Slave*, n. s. XII (1935), 394–404; Milan Mar-
kovich, "La révolution serbe de 1848 et les français," in *Actes du congrès
historique du centenaire de la Révolution de 1848* (Paris, 1948), pp. 193–201;
Jaroslav Sidak, "Revolucija Godine 1848–49," *Historijski Zbornik*, I (1948),
25–42; J. Marriot, "Great Britain and Hungary in 1848," *Hungarian
Quarterly* (1938), 58–67; Gerald Govorchin, "Croatian nationalism and
the Revolution of 1848," *Red River Valley Historical Journal of World History*,
I (1976), 6–16; Marcel Handelsmann, "La question d'Orient et la politique
jugoslave du Prince Czartoryski après 1840," *Académie des sciences morales
et politiques (Paris). Revue des travaux et comptes-rendus*, (1929), 394–433
and "La politique jugoslave du Prince Czartoryski après 1840," *Polska
Akademia Umiejetnusei, Cracow. Bulletin International. Roeznik* (1929), 107–
12; Zoltan I. Toth, "The Nationality Problem in Hungary in 1848–1849,"
Acta Historica, IV (1955), 235–77; Rudolf Maixner, "A. T. Brlić, émissaire
du Ban Jelačić en France," *Annales de l'Institut français de Zagreb* (jan-mars
1939), 1–49.

48. Hajnal, pp. 56-57.

49. De la Cour to Lamartine, Vienna, April 28 and May 2, 1848,
DDF, I, 1070 and II, 20; The Prussian Ambassador in Vienna noted a
pessimistic lack of will to resist events a week *before* Metternich's fall. He
described him as "depressed, disgusted, and very changed. He abandoned
the greatest part of work to Count de Münch and Baron Werner. . . . Dis-
couragement publicly abounds. One sees matters in the darkest terms."
Arnim to Foreign Minister, Vienna, March 3 and 7, 1848, GSA, fz. 691
Oesterreich, fo. 58 and 70.

50. De la Cour to Foreign Minister, Vienna, May 12, 1848, DDF,
II, 191–92.

51. *Ibid.*, May 16 and 31, 1848, DDF, II, 265, 581–82.

52. Bastide to De la cour, Paris, June 6, 1848, DDF, II, 690; On
his return from Innsbruck to Vienna, De la Cour thought that the Austrian

cabinet had resigned itself to the "inevitable sacrifice" of its Italian affairs, letter to Bastide, Vienna, June 20, 1848, DDF, II, 1037; De la Cour to Bastide, Vienna, May 25, 1848, DDF, II, 445; Bastide apparently ignored the warning that matters were not so simple; even some liberal Germans who desired "democratic principles" at the same time applauded Austria's victories in Italy; these liberals' "German spirit" was stronger than their "democratic ideal." Klein to Foreign Minister, Strasbourg, May 10, 1848, DDF, II, 152.

53. There is no real work on Franco-Russian relations, merely fragments; all discussion is based on a short article by Mikhail Pokrovsky, "Lamartine, Cavaignac und Nikolaus I.," in *Historische Aufsätze* (Vienna, 1929), pp. 95–122.

54. Pokrovsky, pp. 106–09.

55. *Ibid.*, p. 98.

56. Paul Henry's statement, "there is not a word in the diplomatic correspondence regarding the future organization of Austria," is misinformed, "La France," *Revue historique*, vol. 188 (1940), 256.

57. Thom to Ficquelmont, Paris, May 1, 1848, HHSA, IV, 86–87, italics in Vienna.

58. In a year of French statesmen so self-consciously trying to imitate the Great Revolution it is possible that the foreign ministry could have been inspired by an old memorandum submitted to Napoleon after Austerlitz, recommending similar compensations for Austria along the Danube. See the documents in Pierre Bertrand, "M. de Talleyrand, l'Autriche et la question d'Orient en 1805," *Revue historique*, XXXIX (1889), 63–75.

59. Baron F. A. von Schweitzer to Dusch, Paris, May 3, 1848, BGLA, fz. 48/2037, fo. 444–45.

60. *Ibid.*, May 24, 1848, fo. 519.

61. *Ibid.*

62. *Ibid.*, July 18, 1848, fo. 731–35.

63. *Ibid.*

64. cf. Lamartine to Rey, Paris, March 27, 1848, AEF, MD, Allemagne 171, fo. 175.

65. Josef Pfitzner, "Michael Bakunin und Preussen im Jahre 1848," *Jahrbücher für Kultur und Geschichte der Slaven*, n. s. VIII (1931), 240–41.

66. Bakunin, *Confession*, p. 63.

67. Circourt to Lamartine, Berlin, April 28, 1848, *Souvenirs d'une mission*, II, 77.

68. Pfitzner, p. 242.

69. *Ibid.*, pp. 249–52.

70. *Ibid.*, pp. 257–58.

Part Two

THE DEMOCRATIC ALLIANCE

JUNE-AUGUST 1848

Chapter Four

The Unanimous Resolution of May 24

JUNE 1848

*J*UNE WAS THE DECISIVE MONTH for the revolution in France. Symbolic of this new phase were Circourt's replacement in Berlin by Emmanuel Arago and the June Days revolt in Paris. The contrast between the two illustrate the distinction between external affairs and politics at home. It was a supreme irony that at the moment the French suppressed Parisian radicals in a bloodbath, the foreign policy most closely associated with this faction predominated during the summer months of 1848. That is, Bastide emphasized the Girondist over the Richelieuist aspect of that strategy; he preferred as an ally the new German constituent parliament to the Prussian government of King Frederick William IV because he perceived the former as more attuned to his "democratic" sentiments.

In Paris there had been warnings during May that the French assembly was impatient to purge the old Provisional Government of its self-styled socialists (Ledru-Rollin, Flocon, Albert, and Louis Blanc) when it elected an Executive Commission. By June Lamartine's influence had waned because of his insistence that the Executive Commission include Ledru-Rollin. The critical domestic event of the revolution, however, was the spontaneous workers' revolt of the June Days. A period of dictatorship by Cavaignac merged into the organization of a new cabinet, which included few traces of the original leaders from the optimistic February days. Accepted wisdom has divided 1848 into an earlier period dominated by Lamartine and his stirring public proclamations to revolutionize Europe, and the later, more conservative, prudent, and realistic government of "honest republicans" who worked with General Eugene Cavaignac and sought to restore public order after the destructive divisions of the bloody June Days. The rest of Europe

The Uprising by Honoré Daumier, The Phillips Collection (Washington, D.C.).

felt shock waves after the revolt in France was suppressed. The extreme Parisian radicals had been the most vocal proponents of a European-wide revolt to bring down the old monarchies and thereby to free Poland and Italy along with the other oppressed peoples.

The eminent historian of the 1848 revolution, Veit Valentin, shared the belief that the tide of revolution broke by June, allowing the impetus of revolt to recede so that reactionary forces could commence their recovery. In succeeding years, the partisans of the various national revolts, searching for the cause of their failure, have regretted that the popular rising was not assisted by French troops in a manner similar to French aid in the Great Revolution of 1789.

Yet the chorus of radical voices which has heavily criticized France for "inaction" was misinformed. All of the changes of personnel at the top of the French government had little influence on external policies. Lamartine's under-secretary, Jules Bastide, continued to direct foreign affairs without interruption until the election of Louis Napoleon in December, when Bastide's offer to stay on was turned down. It was business as usual for French secret agents; both Bakunin and Carl Ludwig Bernays attended the Pan-Slav Congress in Prague in mid-June, where they agitated among Slavic speakers. A primary thrust of the French plan of universal insurrection centered on the German assembly in Frankfurt because German legions were vital to any program of liberation of the oppressed Poles and Italians. And the French did not cease to dispatch envoys to urge Germans to join in the good fight for freedom.

The third front that Carl Ludwig Bernays opened up in Budapest became ever more active; the Hungarian public overwhelmingly called for the return of all Hungarian troops from Radetzky's army that was fighting Charles Albert of Sardinia in northern Italy. Even as the revolt raged in Paris, an envoy from the Hungarian cabinet arrived in the French capital to sound out the French on the possibility of a formal diplomatic recognition of Hungarian independence. The road to Warsaw might lie along a detour from Frankfurt to Budapest. In the following months, talks would revolve around a possible French military alliance with the peoples struggling against the Viennese government within the Austrian Empire itself.

The most misinformed generalization is the tendency to characterize Bastide as a more "prudent" or "realistic" promoter of French

interests than was Lamartine. Bastide had a similar taste for grandiose statements of solidarity with the oppressed of the earth. Bastide's key public announcement, recalling Lamartine's "Manifesto
to Europe" of March 4, was a "unanimous resolution" of the new
French assembly on May 24 requesting that the German national
assembly meeting in Frankfurt am Main join the French parliament
to free Poland and Italy. The statement contained the essential
thrust of France's diplomacy: free and sovereign states in united
Germany, Italy, and Poland brought about by the action of the
peoples themselves united in democratically elected assemblies.
That public statement was reinforced on the diplomatic level. On
June 9 France's newly appointed envoy in Berlin, Emmanuel Arago,
delivered a protest to the Prussian government against its handling
of the question of Poland. Thus, on the diplomatic plane, France
was bringing pressure on Arnim's cabinet by registering a complaint
over Prussia's delay in implementing Frederick William's promise
of autonomy to the Poles of Posen. Still, the French had not given
up on the Germans—Bastide merely exhibited impatience. Finally,
France's confidential operatives like Carl Ludwig Bernays turned
the screws on the European cabinets as they maintained direct
communications with the leaders of the rebels in other countries.
All three of the strata of public, diplomatic, and secret contacts,
each in its own distinct manner, were part of the French government's campaign of liberation.

This threefold effort to enfranchise the nations miscarried,
not in the least, because of an ideological fallacy. That liberal dream
of a Europe of free peoples rested on the assumption that popular
governments could succeed where the old monarchs had failed
because past international turmoil originated in the unfulfilled aspiration of the nations for independence. This was a crucial misconception. The opportunity of the reactionary princes to recover their
position materialized because of historical antagonisms among the
peoples themselves. That French image of universal brotherhood
broke on the rock of conflicts among the "oppressed peoples."
Instead of rallying to the French tricolor in a united front of popular
forces in a war against the thrones, the people began to fight among
themselves.

On June 6, the Serbs in southern Hungary reacted against
attempts at "Magyarization" by the dominant ethnic group. Here
were two "fraternal" peoples at each other's throats, and, as with
the earlier conflict over Schleswig-Holstein, the French confronted

a situation totally at variance with their ideology of the "peoples" versus the "tyrants." Equally ominously, on June 10, the liberal Hungarian cabinet of Lajos Batthyány took the opposite course from the one urged by France and promised troops to Austria for her war against the Italians.

But the greatest disappointment of all was the "liberal" German parliament. Rather than responding in kind to the generous French offer of a "fraternal alliance" to free Poland and Italy, the Germans, too, seemed about to join the Magyars in aiding the despotic Habsburgs. On June 17, the Frankfurt assembly protested the Italian "threat" to Trieste. By June 20, a "war-like giddiness" had seized the assembly, which seemed determined to fight a war, even if as yet unsure against whom. Then on June 29 a majority in the supposedly liberal body chose as the "imperial vicar," the chief executive of new Germany, a Habsburg archduke. It looked as if the German states might begin their history as a united nation in a war against France and in support of Habsburg oppression of Italy.

As fighting broke out in Paris during June, marked by three days of fierce street battles between the popularly elected assembly's army and the city's lower classes, some serious rethinking of assumptions seemed called for. Matters might be more complicated than they had seemed in the optimistic days of February and March. But as yet no one was questioning the "inevitability" of the progress of the revolution. Only in retrospect have historians seen June as the crucial point when history failed to turn.

At this very moment, the French government was undoubtedly encouraged by the arrival of a special diplomatic mission from Budapest which pledged secretly the solidarity of the Magyars with the French cause. At the same time, the fall of the Camphausen-Arnim cabinet in Berlin meant a further erosion of Prussia's commitment to the liberal alliance with France.

A sense of frustration at the inability to shape these events may have prompted France in late May and early June briefly to consider a major shift of her political energies from Berlin to Frankfurt. The popularly elected national assembly, which had begun deliberations on May 18 in Frankfurt for a constitution for a united Germany, seemed a more likely ally than Frederick William's cabinet in Berlin. The replacement of Circourt by Emmanuel Arago as French envoy at Berlin and the unaminous resolution of the French Constituent Assembly to the Frankfurt parliament of May 24 proposing a common policy anticipated a change of course.

Paris expected that the close alliance between the German and French representative bodies would lead to a redress of the wrongs suffered by the Poles and Italians. The German democrats and liberals, the French thought, would cooperate to transform Europe.[1]

Bastide's replacement of Lamartine's friend Circourt with Arago in Berlin was an important juncture. The aristocratic Circourt naturally had a close relationship with Arnim's cabinet of Junkers, and Bastide's longtime comrade-in-arms (and son of a member of the Provisional Government), the militantly republican Arago, was more intimate with parliamentarians and socialists in Berlin. After leaving Breslau and taking up residence in the Prussian capital, Bakunin was a frequent visitor to the French legation. Bastide underlined Arago's elevated status as his spokesman by replacing not only Circourt but the legation head, Brunet-Denon, as well, appointing Arago as the only French diplomatic agent in Berlin. And as Arago expressed Bastide's official displeasure with Prussia's prolonged delay in giving the Poles their national organization, Bastide clearly expressed a preference to collaborate with the new Frankfurt assembly. Thus Arago's appointment signaled a significant shift of emphasis in Franco-German relations.

Bastide on June 3 noted the progress of the Frankfurt assembly in according unity and equality as the priority over all the German sovereigns.[2] On June 8 Bastide indicated the new direction for France in a dispatch to his chargé in Frankfurt, Henri-Charles Joseph Savoye.[3] The French national assembly, Bastide reminded him, had proclaimed the necessity of a fraternal pact with Germany for the reconstruction of Poland. A "close alliance" between Paris and Frankfurt would undo the great iniquity of Poland's division. He commended Savoye's close relations with the parliamentarians and stressed the importance of good and frequent communication with members of the German assembly.[4]

The following day, Bastide underlined the altered relationship with Arnim's government in a strongly worded protest to his new chargé in Berlin against the division of Posen into German and Polish zones. Emphasizing that Posen had never formed part of Germany, he complained, "This is in fact a fourth division of Poland," and an "infraction of the principal treaty of Vienna (articles 1 and 2)." He instructed Arago to read the dispatch and leave a copy with Arnim if he so desired.[5]

Thus A. J. P. Taylor was mistaken in assuming that by early June the French had lost interest in the cause of Poland. Taylor alleged that Arago's arrival signaled the end of French involvement on behalf of the Poles; Bastide "instructed him to drop the Polish question and to keep quiet; 'do not publish anything in the papers and do not excite peoples.' " Taylor asserted that "in Bastide's view, the principle of nationalism had sunk to fourth place."[6] France was uninterested in the Poles and was leaving them to their fate because of a change of spirit which came over French foreign policy when Bastide replaced Lamartine.[7]

On June 16 Bastide expressed strongly his exasperation with Prussia's failure to help the Poles, objecting to her usurpation of Polish territory. Although France sincerely desired the "most intimate union" between France and Germany, he noted, "Our policy cannot be exclusively German." It was a crime to divide Posen, he asserted, and informed Savoye of his protest in Berlin on June 9.[8] Strains in the relationship with the Prussian cabinet, however, did not extend to Germany as a whole. Bastide emphasized on June 12 the "proven loyalty of our conduct toward Germany" and the "friendly relations between the two lands."[9]

Savoye confirmed the favorable sentiment of the majority in the Frankfurt assembly on June 11 and the next day responded to Bastide's dispatch of June 8. Savoye assured him:

> I hope to announce in a few days that the parliament deliberated on an address in reply to the solemn declaration of the national assembly in Paris [of May 24]. Whatever the result of that deliberation, it will at least have the advantages of allowing us to distinguish our friends from our enemies.[10]

Savoye was encouraged by assurances of the Frankfurt assembly speaker, Hans von Gagern, to a Polish visitor to Frankfurt, Ladislas Platter, of his good intentions and those of the majority of the assembly "relative to the reconstruction of the Polish nationality," and a motion proposed in Frankfurt for Franco-German cooperation to free Poland and Lombardy.[11]

The project to replace Berlin with Frankfurt as France's partner in an intimate alliance that would free Poland and Italy ended suddenly in mid-June when the German assembly abruptly became a major cause of concern by threatening France's most vital interest—Italy.

Bastide had been cautioned a month earlier that German nationalists elected from Austria to the Frankfurt assembly hoped to enlist that body's support for Austria's war in northern Italy.[12]

Governments of the smaller states seemed unlikely to respond to France's offer of the fraternal pact to enfranchise Italy. The head of the liberal cabinet in Baden, Ferdinand von Dusch, impressed on the French chargé in Karlsruhe that the fate of Venice concerned not only Austria, "it interests also all Germany. Trieste is the outlet for German commerce in the Adriatic, but Trieste alone is not enough for us; we need a military port."[13]

The French consul in Trieste, Gabriel de Lesparda, likewise advised that "the city, by its customs foreign to the peninsula, is attached by its commercial interests not only to Austria, but to all of Germany."[14] And, indeed, the Italians clashed not only with Austrian reactionaries, but also with Germans who thought Austria's position in Italy was important to Germany's interest, safety, and independence.[15] For all of these reasons, most Germans at the Frankfurt assembly were especially concerned about the port of Trieste, part of the Holy Roman Empire and its successor, the German Confederation, since 1382.

The Sardinian agent in Berlin, Rossi, found the hostile tone of a portion of the German press concerning Italy an "enigma"; he concluded that financial ties of southern Germany to Austria and Trieste were the principal cause; material interests predominated over all other considerations.[16]

The Belgian chargé compared the intensity of German feeling for Trieste to the extreme fanaticism of the French over the Polish problem.[17] Paris learned in May from special agent Carl Ludwig Bernays that the sole concern of the Frankfurt assembly in the south was to keep Trieste as part of Germany, so that southern Germany would have a port on the Adriatic. Germans assured Bernays that France could have a free hand in Italy as long as she left Trieste to Germany.[18]

German apprehension over Trieste was so intense that Sardinia's diplomatic agents in Munich and Berlin warned their countrymen not to interfere with the port. When news reached the Frankfurt assembly that Trieste was under blockade from the fleets of Sardinia, Naples, and Venice, the reaction was one of extreme alarm. Sardinia's agents noted that if reports of an actual bombardment were verified, the Frankfurt assembly might well declare war on Sardinia. The political consequences of such an attack on the only port of the German Confederation with access to the Mediterranean markets could be fatal for Italy.[19]

The Belgian chargé also warned his foreign minister, C.

d'Hoffschmidt de Resteigne, of a political reaction in Germany:

> This measure could well change the dispositions of Germany
> relative to the war in Piedmont, which has been in this country,
> at least until now, unpopular. One generally desired here that
> Italy should constitute herself in repose. But touching Trieste,
> on whose behalf the council of fifty had sent commissions to
> Vienna recommending that they not give up the important
> maritime point, could change that goodwill to hostility.[20]

On June 17, a protest was sent to Sardinia in the name of the
German Confederation against "all acts of hostility on the part of
the combined naval forces of Sardinia, Naples, and Venice on the
port of Trieste and against all violations of the territory of the
German Confederation in general."[21] The protest by the old Diet
of the German Confederation was followed a few days later with
a remonstrance from the Frankfurt national assembly. It declared,
"An attack on Trieste would be considered a declaration of war
against Germany."[22] Moreover, according to the Belgian chargé,
the vote at Frankfurt was unanimous.[23]

The complaints of the Diet and national assembly in Frankfurt
naturally greatly disturbed the French. A lengthy "Note on Germany and Austria" was drawn up by the French foreign ministry
following an investigation of the legal basis for the German declaration of June 20.[24] Bastide told Hatzfeldt that he had advised the
cabinet in Turin to be careful not to violate the rights of the German
Confederation. France was visibly troubled by the possibility of
Germany's coming to Austria's aid in Italy.[25] In late July, the minister in the central power, Ritter Anton von Schmerling, informed
the Frankfurt assembly that the maintenance of the Trieste blockade
had impelled the Austrian Empire to send the Sardinian envoy a
new note, which was much "more energetic" than the first communication.[26]

Bastide was concerned with the protests of some vocal members
of the Frankfurt parliament who implied that Austria's war in Italy
should concern Germans. And, like the conflict in Italy, the French
watched the German-Danish war for signs that it might impede
the peaceful and liberal evolution of both peoples toward an international solidarity of free peoples under French tutelage.

During June, France's relations with Germany were disturbed
by the Schleswig-Holstein question, though not enough to cause
Bastide to do anything. He briefly considered a protest in Berlin

but quickly dropped the idea. In early June he wrote his ministers in Copenhagen and London noting that Prussia had evacuated Jutland and Denmark had taken the offensive while Russia threatened to invade Prussia. In these circumstances, Bastide concluded:

> It seems neither proper nor opportune to me to place France in any manner with these manifestations and these oppositions, against Prussia, above all at a time . . . when the quarrel appears on the verge of pacification.[27]

Jennings has cited the former dispatch as proof that, "Bastide ordered French ministers in the various capitals concerned with the crisis to second *any* diplomatic move favorable to Denmark." Jennings stated correctly that Bastide promised "energetic declarations" in Berlin and Frankfurt showing "serious disapprobation of Germany's proceedings toward Denmark," but he gave no evidence for his conclusion that "Bastide immediately complied with this Danish request." Rather, Bastide wrote, "I considered action in Berlin favoring Denmark," but went on to say that he had given up that idea; Bastide did not join "Russia and Sweden in steadfastly opposing by diplomatic means Germany's designs on Schleswig," but, on the contrary, instructed his diplomats not to interfere in this matter beyond seconding England's efforts to mediate for a peaceful solution.[28]

Danes got only meaningless assurances of friendship from Paris, in contrast to the firm protest which Bastide sent the following day to Berlin on behalf of the Poles. Obviously, Schleswig had a low priority in Paris. France was far more interested in the resolution of the French assembly of May 24, which called the alliance with the Frankfurt assembly to redress injustice in Poland and Italy, than in distant and insignificant Schleswig-Holstein. As the mediation between Germany and Denmark bogged down in June, Bastide vented his anger in intemperate letters to his chargés in Berlin and Frankfurt—but not with the Prussian chargé, Hatzfeldt. For the time being, France took no active part.[29]

Indeed, in this same dispatch Bastide complained of the injustice of Germany's conduct in usurping other's lands, yet still looked forward to "a close alliance" between France and Germany to free Poland. This is evidence that France's objection to Germany's Schleswig policy does not in itself explain the break between Paris and the Frankfurt parliament.[30]

Bastide feared the Russians would use the Schleswig question as an excuse to halt Germany's progress toward freedom, and at the expense of liberty in northern Europe.[31] This was in accord with what he heard from his minister in London, who cautioned that Russia's actual objective in its involvement with Schleswig was to destroy republican ideas in Germany and to gain an English alliance against France.[32]

Normanby informed Palmerston on June 29 that Bastide had "more than once lately" expressed uneasiness over the "external danger to Prussia in the East."[33] Bastide shared the universal conviction that Prussia and Russia were headed toward an inevitable clash. The Sardinian envoy in Prussia, for instance, noted that, "The attention of Germany turns with worry towards the north, and numerous newspapers contain more or less exact accounts of Russia's military preparations." Nicholas I, he believed, intended to invade Germany "to compromise the élan of the peoples toward liberty" and "to establish despotism." The Prussian prime minister's assurances that Russia was only taking defensive measures and not concentrating forces on the Prussian border, the Sardinian envoy reported, "were greeted coldly by the [Prussian] chamber, which hardly seemed convinced of the absence of a danger of intervention." Prussians judged that a war was "inevitable without knowing against whom it will be directed." He went on to say that Prussian reserves had been called up to constitute a force of 300,000 men and that all fortresses had been readied for a state of siege.[34]

Members of the Frankfurt parliament[35] and the Prussian cabinet[36] agreed that a Russo-Prussian conflict was certain. Tsar Nicholas I had thought in April that war was inevitable.[37] The Belgian foreign minister viewed Prussia's solicitation of an alliance with France and Berlin's "friendly attitude" toward Arago as results of the Russian threat to Germany.[38]

On the morning of June 17, Bastide was "very alarmed by Russia's attitude and by the march of Russian troops."[39] The Saxon ambassador reported on June 19 that Bastide was "very despondent and anxious." He was convinced that an "immediate war between Russia and Germany was inevitable."[40]

Arago urged Bastide to use the greatest circumspection in dealing with German matters. Allow time for conditions to ripen, he admonished, and French ideas would triumph. Arago was confident that a great majority of Germans were sympathetic to the French and manifested a profound aversion to Russia:

The Polish cause is odious for Russia. In this question [of

Poland] Germany is divided. We should support Poland without becoming embroiled with Germany, which is menaced by Russia. Wait patiently a while, which will not be long. Germany, whose progressive ideas approach those of France, will throw herself completely into France's arms when Russia attacks her. United with Germany for the inevitable triumph of the great principle that will regenerate Europe, we shall reinstate Poland with the cooperation of the entire German Confederation. I do not know a single German patriot who does not absolutely agree that Germany's unity necessarily means a free and independent Poland.[41]

Arago suggested that the new cabinet did not represent accurately the actual trend of Prussian opinion, which increasingly favored France and Polish freedom. In his view, this government, imbued with "racial hatred," would do nothing for Poland. The "resurrection" of Poland was intimately tied to the triumph of democratic unity in Germany. The union of the German states daily made "great progress," but was "only realizable by democracy." Until a new revolution swept across Germany, "promises will be made, but we shall obtain nothing serious." However, the young democratic party was "destined" to become "master of the situation" very soon.[42]

News from Frankfurt was likewise mostly discouraging. Savoye warned on June 20 that a "war-like giddiness" had seized the assembly. Involved in a war with Denmark over Schleswig, the assembly threatened to send troops into northern Italy because of the blockade of Trieste, and to Prague to disperse the Czech insurrection. Relations between the Germans and Poles had suffered as well because of the April rising in Posen. Savoye advised avoiding all appearance of interference in German domestic politics. Most politicians, he assured Bastide, tended toward France's position on Posen. France, under these circumstances, should unobtrusively promote Polish interests while waiting for Polish and German tempers to cool.[43]

A speech by Raveaux, who represented Cologne in the Frankfurt parliament, honored France and her assembly. Savoye observed on June 24 that the address brought the Frankfurt national assembly to its feet, with the exception of a handful of reactionaries. Savoye at first thought that the election of a Habsburg prince, Archduke John, to fill the post of imperial vicar *(Reichsverweser)* was a favorable development, considering the alternatives. He read Bastide's objections to the division of Posen to the speaker of the assembly,

Heinrich von Gagern, and Archduke John's advisor, Ritter Anton von Schmerling.[44] At that point Bastide could hope that his firm protest against the division of Posen was heard sympathetically in Frankfurt.

Bastide, however, had begun a retreat from the exposed position of the unanimous resolution of May 24, slowly realizing that he must adapt to a situation unanticipated by his ideological preconceptions. It was now less than obvious that all freely elected popular assemblies could be counted on to reflect faithfully the peaceful disposition of the masses. There was increasing evidence of a divergence of views between Frankfurt and Paris on Polish and Italian independence. Bastide reconsidered his relations with the German states, scrapping Lamartine's plans to centralize all French diplomacy in Frankfurt, because "one cannot make diplomacy with an entire national assembly." France's policy toward German unity was a determination to have no policy. "We shall avoid any interference as much as possible; we shall also not concern ourselves with what happens in Germany." France in return asked only for "peace and quiet" from Germany. The whole French nation wanted just to be left alone. The French cabinet was willing to allow the Germans to fulfill their national destiny, choosing to ignore "the German problem."[45]

Bastide appreciated Arago's observations on maintaining good relations with both the Poles and the Germans, agreeing that it was now best to go no further with complaints to the Prussian government against the division of Posen along national lines. "That protest [of June 9] subsists; that is enough for the present."[46] The Poles would have to wait for changes within Germany before France could offer any material assistance.

Bastide's caution was undoubtedly increased by the contradictory and confusing picture of German conditions filtering back to Paris. He was repeatedly assured that Germany was far closer to a civil war than to unity of any sort.[47] A number of observers reassuringly reported that a republican movement was sweeping across Germany, bringing a more radical phase to the German revolution.[48] The minor courts were powerless and resigned to their fate. The court of Baden was prepared to accept a "very strong and very vigorous power invested with the confidence of all Germany that can guarantee them against the double danger that menaces all—the subversive republican party and the proletariat."[49] The situation was little different in the larger states.

Gerlach and the other unofficial advisors around Frederick William IV in Potsdam, the infamous camarilla, "build castles in the air, concentrate troops, augment the Berlin garrison gradually to 25,000 men, but there is no courage for a *coup d'état*."[50] In Vienna "governmental anarchy overflows."[51] Even the armies of Prussia and the other German states were infected with insubordination and disaffection.[52] These reports suggested that Germany was on the verge of a greater and far more violent revolution.

Nevertheless, developments in Frankfurt were anything but reassuring. Rather than a definite answer to the call of the French national assembly for an offensive and defensive alliance of France and Germany, the decision on such an association with France, Savoye reported, had been adjourned until the *Zentralgewalt* (the new central authority) was installed.[53]

Savoye was quite discouraged by the composition of the parliament. He regretted the "absence of representatives from the heart of the people," and the "prodigious agglomeration out of all proportion" of salaried functionaries, of titled men, and of professors. All of these showed a "certain disdain" for the people, he thought.

It was not surprising that the French were displeased by the membership of the parliament and of the newly formed central authority.[54] Its chief, or "vicar," the *Reichsverweser*, was Prince John of the Austrian house of Habsburg, and his cabinet was conservative. The Austrian diplomat, Ritter Anton von Schmerling, was appointed minister of interior and Dr. Johann Heckscher was named foreign minister. The latter, Savoye warned, loved to argue more to show his own brilliance than to clarify the situation. Heckscher too was not thought to be friendly to France. General Edward von Peucker, the minister of war, was a competent Prussian general, evidently reflecting the views of the Prussian cabinet. Savoye cautioned against expecting any sympathy for France from him.[55]

A republican refugee from the Palatinate, Savoye presumed that the assembly was unrepresentative of the true views of the German masses. According to Savoye, Germans wanted a revolutionary alliance with France, but this objective was thwarted because of the presence of a great number of counter-revolutionaries in the parliament. Thus Germans were alienated from a body which was hostile to the wishes of the people as well as inhospitable towards France. Savoye warned that instead of being likely confederates of Bastide's Girondist policy, a great number of parliamentarians were partisans of the Habsburgs and enemies of the French republic. Savoye had little hope for the Frankfurt parliament and he doubted that a new, more liberal cabinet would be formed soon. "The sentiments of the people with regard to France will never be represented by that majority of functionaries, servants, and partisans of the old monarchical system, who doubt and hate France."[56]

Instead of announcing an intimate alliance between the Frankfurt and Paris assemblies, the Germans showed enmity toward France in the debate on augmenting the numbers of the federal army. The bill passed by a vote of 303 to 149. "It is clear," observed Savoye, "that the reason for the increase is less a fear of Russia than a mistrust of France." The main speakers for the bill had been old Prussian militarists: General Hans von Auerswald, "a man without capacity, imbued with the old Prussian ideas against France"; Prince von Lichnowski, who "glories to be the sworn adversary of the French republic"; and, most importantly, General Joseph Maria von Radowitz, who "detests the system of the government of France."[57]

Although Arago, too, was alarmed by the election of the Austrian prince to head the government in Frankfurt, he did not reject the assembly as summarily as Savoye did. He held to his *idée fixe* that the "unitary tendency" in Germany would be beneficial to France. "It is necessary to consider the cause of unity as having taken a retrograde step" in choosing Archduke John as imperial vicar. John was not anti-democratic, nevertheless, and depended on the majority of the parliament, which Arago assumed was "democratic." He thus concluded that France, without departing from a "prudent caution," ought to establish "intimate relations with the ministers who surround the archduke." France should convince them of the utility of an alliance. The two principles that divided Europe between east and west were absolutism and democracy, France and Russia. France's task was to reconstitute independent Poland as the first rampart of the west.[58]

Bastide was undoubtedly held back from precipitate action by indications that the Magyars might pressure the Austrians from the east to give in to France's peaceful policy of encouraging national liberation.

On May 28, 1848, a Hungarian envoy was sent to Belgrade with instructions that mentioned that the Hungarian government "has sent commissioners to London and Paris."[59] And on June 6 the Ministerial Council decided to establish Hungarian consulates in Constantinople and in the Danubian principalities.[60] But the bold step of appointing an ambassador with formal credentials to France involved diplomatic recognition of the French government by Hungary. On May 24, Hungary's interior minister, Bertalan Szemere, had written to Frankfurt that he was inclined to approach first Palmerston, then Lamartine. However, on May 27—most likely after talking with France's envoy, Bernays—he decided that Szalay ought to travel first to Paris and only incidentally to London. By June 20, the Hungarian government was considering appointing László Szalay as "ambassador in Paris"—a legal move that would have had grave international repercussions, including the possible division of the Danubian monarchy.[61]

Szalay's mission to Paris between June 23 and 25, 1848, presaged a formal diplomatic exchange between Budapest and Paris.[62] By June 30, the Budapest newspapers published the name of the soon-to-be appointed French diplomatic agent, Pascal Duprat. Apparently the French were about to open direct diplomatic links to the first of the break-away governments from the former Danubian monarchy.

Events in southern Hungary assumed increasing importance; the people of this region of the Croatian military frontier (Grenzer) were organized into disciplined armed units, which included Radetzky's finest soldiers in Italy. However, with the civil disturbances in southern Hungary, an aide to the Slavic national leader, the Patriarch Rajačić, drafted a plan toward the end of June that proposed extensive military and diplomatic action against Austria and Hungary. The scheme called for "sending Hikalovič to Paris along with Medakovič to explain our position there and to win the sympathy of the French government. Once he has succeeded in this mission he should go to Charles Albert's headquarters in Piedmont with a letter of recommendation and from there call upon the Grenzer to revolt."[63] Through the extensive Polish diplomatic network of Prince Adam Czartoryski, word of this scheme drifted back to Paris, and the "plan did not remain a dead letter," according to Alan Sked.[64] The subterranean world of secret contacts through European subversives provided Bastide with knowledge of the complexities of a national awakening in the Danubian basin. And the French themselves were formulating their own far-reaching plans to completely reconstruct the entire lower Danubian region as a series of satellite states looking to Paris as an arbiter of their various national destinies.

In June, mixed signals came back to Paris, but it appears that French leadership ignored the danger on the horizon. Agents warned that international relationships could defy simple categories of peoples defying wicked oppressors. The ideological French government seemed predisposed to divide the world into two simple categories: on the one hand, malicious and aristocratic rulers, and on the other, beneficent and peaceful peoples. The March revolutions in central Europe were expected to replace the evil old regimes with the direct rule of peoples and thereby to inaugurate the universal brotherhood of mankind. Thus, Bastide supposed that the popular election of a German national assembly would necessarily mean a democratic alliance linking Paris and Frankfurt. Instead, that democratically elected Frankfurt assembly seemed disposed to support historical and tyrannical claims of the German princes to oppress neighboring peoples. France's chargé in Frankfurt cautioned that some Frankfurt parliamentarians might favor retaining Trieste and Schleswig-Holstein, which should have alerted the French of the dangerous potential. Likewise, the outbreak of conflict between the Magyars and their non-Magyar subject peoples had ominous implications.

Still, the French had no reason to lose hope. Their new chargé in Berlin, Emmanuel Arago, delivered a sharply worded protest against the Prussian delay in implementing the promised national reorganization of Poland. Despite the fall of the Camphausen-Arnim cabinet, Bastide believed that the Prussian government wished to cooperate with the French. Even more encouraging were indications of the break-up of the Habsburg empire. The mission of a Hungarian agent to Paris could prepare the way for the establishment of Czartoryski's proposed "Danubian confederation" of autonomous states in east central Europe that would replace the old Danubian monarchy. Above all, progress in unifying Germany in Frankfurt encouraged Bastide, who assumed that such a unity was a prelude to greater French and liberal influence. The author of the French assembly's unanimous resolution of May 24 believed that a "democratic alliance" between the political assemblies of France and united Germany was a prerequisite for any political change.

Meanwhile, the chief sphere of operations of France's secret agents continued to move to the east during June. The suppression of the June Days revolt had removed the danger that Parisian radicals might precipitate an international blow-up before France's underground emissaries could construct an effective coalition of armed nations that would provide popular auxiliaries for a great revolutionary army.

Whereas we must not minimize the symbolic importance of the June Days revolt, it was the culmination of a process that dated back several weeks. Above all, the historical wisdom that Cavaignac and Bastide transformed both domestic and foreign policies by the victory of their party of order bears reexamination. Cavaignac was the son of a regicide and brother of one of the most distinguished republican leaders. Bastide was a high-minded republican fanatic. What they shared with their colleagues in power since the February Revolution was an abhorrence for disorder and anarchy. The importance of their June victory then was not a conservative alteration of foreign policies; there was no such fundamental change. Its real significance was that it ended Bastide's anxiety that the Parisian radicals would precipitate a premature declaration of war. As a matter of fact, Bastide's major departure in policy bore no direct connection to the June Days, but preceded it by a month.

The chief divergence from Lamartine's policy was Bastide's attempt at a democratic alliance with the delegates to the Frankfurt parliament. But this was not the result of a more conservative bent or a decreased interest in freeing Poland, but sprang from Bastide's impatience with the slow progress of Arnim's liberal cabinet in effecting the promised reorganization of Prussia's Polish provinces. The substitution of Arago for Circourt indicated a movement away from a purely Richelieuist tactic, the drawing together of all groups hostile to Habsburg supremacy in Germany. Bastide opted for a more Girondist emphasis, an augmenting of the peoples' zeal by rallying ideological militants for a war of principle against the thrones. But hardly had Arago arrived in Berlin than the French envoy in Frankfurt sent the first warnings that a great number of the parliamentarians were hardly democrats at all, but partisans of the Habsburgs and enemies of France. During July French attention would focus on these same arenas: in his hopes for the reconstitution of a Polish state and the enfranchisement of the Italian people, Bastide expected succor from a broad coalition of peoples headed by the Magyars and Germans.

NOTES

1. Bastide later attributed this interlude of a "democratic alliance" between the French and German parliaments to Lamartine, and described it as favoring "democratic and unitary tendencies in Germany." Hatzfeldt to Foreign Minister, Paris, August 12, September 1, and 4, 1848, GSA, fz. 863, fo. 15, fz. 861, fo. 135 and 181; Könneritz to Foreign Minister, Paris, June 19, 1848, Kretzschmar and Schlechte, *Gesandtschaftsberichte*, pp. 118–19.

2. Bastide to Humann, Paris, June 3, 1848, DDF, II, 643.

3. Joseph Savoye, a lawyer from Zweibrucken, came to France as a political refugee from the Bavarian Palatinate in 1832. BGStA, Gesandtschaft Paris, fz. 4692, 4694, and 4659.

4. Bastide to Savoye, Paris, June 8, 1848, DDF, II, 731.

5. Bastide to Arago, Paris, June 9, 1848, DDF, II, 762–63.

6. A. J. P. Taylor, *The Struggle for Mastery in Europe*, pp. 15–16.

7. de Luna, *The French Republic*, p. 346.

8. Bastide to Savoye, Paris, June 16, 1848, DDF, II, 929.

9. *Ibid.*, June 12, 1848, II, 803.

10. Savoye to Bastide, Frankfurt, June 12, 1848, DDF, II, 805.

11. *Ibid.*, June 5 and 11, 1848, DDF, II, 675–79, 793.

12. De la Cour to Foreign Minister, Vienna, May 12, 1848, DDF, II, 193–94.

13. Lefebvre to Foreign Minister, Karlsruhe, May 15 and June 21, 1848, DDF, II, 239 and 1049; Günter Wollstein, *Das "Grossdeutschland" der Paulskirche: Nationale Ziele in der Bürgerliche Revolution 1848-49* (Düsseldorf, 1977) analyzes the attitude of the delegates to the Frankfurt Assembly toward Germany's neighbors.

14. Lesparada to Bastide, Trieste, June 3, 1848, DDF, II, 650.

15. Theodor Schieder, "Das Italienbild der deutschen Einheitsbewegung," *Studi Italiana*, III (1959), 146–47.

16. Rossi to Pareto, Berlin, June 14, 1848, AST, 31/627.

17. Briey to Hoffschmidt, Frankfurt, May 29, 1848, AEB, Allemagne, IV, 88.

18. Bernays to Boislecomte, Frankfurt, May 19, 1848, AEF, MD, Allemagne 170, fo. 27.

19. Federico Curato, "*Il Parlamento di Francoforte e la prima guerra d'indipendenza italiana,*" *Archivo storico italiana*, CX, 280; Rossi to Pareto, Berlin, June 21, 1848, AST, 31/629.

20. Briey to Hoffschmidt, Frankfurt, May 29, 1848, AEB, Allemagne, IV, 88.

21. Savoye to Bastide, Frankfurt, June 17, 1848, DDF, II, 958; Briey to Hoffschmidt, Frankfurt, June 18, 1848, AEB, Allemagne, IV, 102.

22. *Stenographischer Bericht über die Verhandlungen der deutschen constituirenden Nationalversammlung zu Frankfurt am Main*, (Frankfurt/M., 1848), I, 391; Savoye to Bastide, Frankfurt, June 20, 1848, DDF, II, 1033.

23. Briey to Hoffschmidt, Frankfurt, June 20, 1848, AEB, Allemagne, IV, 104.

24. AEF, MD, Allemagne 162, fo. 352–60.

25. Hatzfeldt to Foreign Ministry, Paris, July 6, 1848, GSA, fz. 861, fo. 54.

26. Briey to Hoffschmidt, Frankfurt, July 24, 1848, AEB, Allemagne, IV, 131.

27. Bastide to Dotézac, Paris, June 7, 1848, DDF, II, 724; to Tallenay, June 6, 1848, AEF, Angleterre 670, fo. 106.

28. *Ibid.* and Jennings, "French Diplomacy," pp. 211, 214.

29. Bastide to Savoye, Paris, June 8, 1848, DDF, II, 731.

30. Bastide to Tallenay, Paris, June 12, 1848, DDF, II, 805–06; Bastide to Savoye, Paris, June 16, 1848, DDF, II, 929; and Bastide to Arago, Paris, June 29, 1848, II, 1157–59.

31. Bastide to Arago, Paris, June 29, 1848, DDF, II, 1158.

32. Tallenay to Bastide, London, June 22, 1848, DDF, II, 1070.

33. Normanby to Palmerston, Paris, June 29, 1848, PRO, FO 27/810.

34. Rossi to Pareto, Berlin, June 30, 1848, AST, 31/632.

35. Comte de Briey to Hoffschmidt, Frankfurt, June 3, 1848, Ridder, II, 93.

36. Gerlach, *Denkwürdigkeiten*, I, 154, 163.

37. Bloomfield to Palmerston, St. Petersburg, April 8, 1848, quoted in Feldman, *Sprawa Polska*, p. 339.

38. Hoffschmidt to Nothomb, Brussels, June 17, 1848, Ridder, II, 112.

39. Könneritz to Lamaistre, Paris, June 17, 1848, Kretzschmar and Schlechte, *Gesandtschaftsberichte*, p. 117.

40. *Ibid.*, June 19, 1848; Meneval to Bastide, Dresden, June 19, 1848, *Ibid.*, p. 120; Arago to Bastide, Berlin, June 20, 1848, DDF, II, 1036; Kraetzer-Rasserts to Bastide, Mannheim, June 19, 1848, AEF, MD, Allemagne 129, fo. 19–20, warned that the Russian fleet in the Baltic was making preparations for a great blow; Ligne to Hoffschmidt, Paris, June 19, 1848, AEB, IV, France, fo. 219.

41. Arago to Bastide, Berlin, June 20, 1848, DDF, II, 1036.

42. *Ibid.*, and June 17, 1848, II, 959–64; Essard to Bastide, Hamburg, June 27, 1848, DDF, II, 1133.

43. Savoye to Bastide, Frankfurt, June 20, 1848, DDF, II, 1032–33.

44. *Ibid.*, June 24, 1848, II, 1096–97; Archduke John earlier favored an entente with France, De la Cour to Bastide, Vienna, May 25, 1848, DDF, II, 446.

45. Könneritz to Foreign Minister, Paris, June 19, 1848, Kretzschmar and Schlechte, *Gesandtschaftsberichte*, p. 118; cf. A. J. P. Taylor, *Struggle*, pp. 3–4, France traditionally "had no clear-cut Germany policy . . . they ignored 'the German problem' until it was thrust under their noses by events."

46. Bastide to Arago, Paris, June 29, 1848, DDF, II, 1157.

47. e.g., Engelhardt to Bastide, Mainz, June 13, 1848, DDF, II, 819; Tallenay to Bastide, London, June 13, 1848, DDF, II, 820–21; Lefebvre to Bastide, Baden, June 14, 1848, DDF, II, 850–52; Savoye to Bastide, Frankfurt, June 12 and 14, 1848, DDF, II, 804–05 and 849; Fontenay to Bastide, Stuttgart, June 15 and 24, August 6, and September 9, 1848, AEF, Wurtemberg 72, fo. 14, 15, 44–45, and 57–58; Rothan to Bastide, Kassel, June 18, 1848, DDF, II, 981; Arago to Bastide, Berlin, June 15, 1848, DDF, II, 908; Humann to Bastide, Munich, June 7, 1848, DDF, II, 718; this leitmotif was especially strong in Heinrich Börnstein's reports from beginning to end, e.g., No. 2, 84–96, 98, 104, 112, and 123. The dispatches of the secret agent, Dr. Kraetzer-Rasserts were equally apocalyptical, MD, Allemagne 129, fo. 21–22, 147–51, 187, 197, 211, 230.

48. cf. reference 42 above; Börnstein reassured that "political reaction is impossible in Germany." Bulletin No. 20, No. 28, and No. 84, AEF, MD, Allemagne 129; Kraetzer-Rasserts to Bastide, Strasbourg, June 10, 1848, AEF, MD, Allemagne 129, fo. 5; "that traditional love of the German people for its princes spoken of by Heinrich Heine has almost completely disappeared," Rothan to Bastide, Kassel, June 11 and 18, 1848, DFF, II, 796 and 981–82; Engelhardt to Bastide, Mainz, June 13, 1848, DDF, II, 819.

49. Lefebvre to Bastide, Karlsruhe, June 14, 1848, DDF, II, 850–51.

50. Börnstein, Bulletin, July 15, 1848, No. 15, AEF, MD, Allemagne 129.

51. No. 16; "If the reactionary party perseveres in that way the republic will be proclaimed in Vienna within a month." No. 25; everyone in Vienna had forgotten the existence of an Emperor of Austria, No. 27, No. 28; anarchy in Vienna, No. 30, No. 39.

52. Börnstein, Bulletin No. 6 (Nearly all the armies of the German Confederation demoralized and insubordinate); *ibid.*, Fontenay to Bastide, Stuttgart, June 24, 1848, AEF, Wurtemberg 72, fo. 15; Gerlach, *Denkwürdigkeiten*, April 21, 1848, I, 154; July 6, 1848, I, 173; July 18, 1848, I, 176–77; and September 12, 1848, I, 195, expressed doubts as to the political reliability of the Prussian army.

53. Savoye to Bastide, Frankfurt, July 2, 1848, AEF, Allemagne 805, fo. 210.

54. *Ibid.*, July 7, 1848, fo. 211.

55. *Ibid.*, July 15, 1848, fo. 217–18.

56. *Ibid.*

57. *Ibid.*, Wiessner (extreme left) spoke on behalf of a Franco-German alliance, and the gallery applauded "vivement." July 7, 1848, *ibid.*, fo. 211–12.

58. Arago to Bastide, July 1, 1848, AEF, Prusse, 302, fo. 140–41; On July 7, Arago too was worried that John was more Austrian than German and might drag Germany into Austria's struggle with Italy, *ibid.*, July 7, 1848, fo. 148.

59. Hajnal, *A Batthyány-kormány külpolitikája*, p. 58.

60. *Ibid.*, p. 59.

61. *Ibid.*, p. 107.

62. *Ibid.*, pp. 107–08.

63. Sked, *Survival of the Habsburg*, pp. 68–69.

64. *Ibid.*

Chapter Five
The Frankfurt Assembly and Austria
JULY 1848

*D*URING JULY BASTIDE WAS DISTURBED by the failure of the German constituent assembly to respond to the French assembly's unanimous resolution of May 24. But priorities in Paris and Frankfurt were clearly divergent. The Germans' primary concern was to define the borders of their new nation. While the French sought their assistance in the liberation of oppressed nations from Austrian control, a significant number of Germans sympathized with the house of Habsburg's imperialist mission. These Germans naturally never shared the French enthusiasm for a democratic alliance to free the Poles and Italians, but first had to face the question of which European provinces were German. And in the process of discussing what constituted German soil, claims were made on areas that Germany's neighbors felt were historically theirs. What seemed for Germans a rightful defense of legitimate ownership appeared to their neighbors as encroachment and expansionism. Thereby the high-minded call for universal emancipation degenerated into petty bickering over real estate. The debate in Frankfurt over the seating of delegates from Prussia's Polish-speaking provinces shocked Bastide and prompted a major reassessment of France's attitude toward the German parliament.

Meanwhile, changes in Paris made Bastide's position more secure. The June Days anarchy prompted the French assembly to dissolve the Executive Commission to give General Cavaignac full powers to suppress the workers. But this was not a new juncture in foreign affairs. A reflection of essential continuities was Cavaignac's use during the fight of the June Days as his *chef de cabinet* of Jules Hetzel, a close friend of Bastide and clandestine agent in Belgium. When Cavaignac named his government, Bastide remained foreign minister with Hetzel becoming under-secretary of

General Eugene Cavaignac (1802–57), painting by Ary Scheffer, Musée de Versailles.

state. An old close friend of Cavaignac's brother Geoffrey, Bastide had the confidence of the new chief of state.

Policy-making was centralized at the top; Cavaignac got daily summaries of all incoming diplomatic couriers, and his marginal comments show that he read them with some care. Broad direction of diplomatic strategy—which ultimately meant decisions regarding war and peace—was a matter for the full cabinet, although day-to-day operations were left to Bastide. Beginning in late July, Bastide seems more confident (earlier in the month there was a question of his replacement), and the records of his very frank conversations with the Prussian and Austrian chargés in Paris multiply dramatically. As Pouthas recognized, business was routinely carried on directly between Bastide and the foreign envoys. Since Bastide and Lamartine, despite personal oaths of loyalty exacted at the threat of dismissal, still mistrusted the professional staff at the ministry, they had removed all confidential matters to a secret inner cabinet in the ministry, served faithfully by Jules Hetzel. The French career diplomats in the field suffered from the same suspicion of primary fidelity to the former monarch; therefore, France's regular diplomatic corps was supplemented by special agents, whose devotion to the republican cause was unquestioned. Usually relieved of the tedium of daily contacts with heads of state, the envoys could move freely at all social levels. Once abroad, they took advantage of the opportunities presented by circumstances: consulting sources unavailable to a normal diplomat; carrying back to Paris the most sensitive requests; and personally conveying in return the sort of information that could not be put in writing. Although the record is necessarily incomplete, the examples of Bakunin, Bernays, and Czartoryski give us a good idea of their manner and scope of operations. Confidential correspondence was carried on through intermediaries, particularly Bastide's under-secretary Jules Hetzel.

Two individuals in particular did not have to conform to this system. One of them was Bastide's old ideological comrade-in-arms, Arago, who was appointed chargé in Berlin. The other was Heinrich Börnstein, former publisher of the German language newspaper, *Vorwärts!*, whose editors included Bernays, Bakunin, Marx, Engels, and Arnold Ruge. Beginning in July, he wrote a daily summary of conditions in Germany drawn from the German press and letters that he received from friends in Germany (particularly his son-in-law Carl Ludwig Bernays). During the month of July we shall see Bastide's perception of conditions in Germany molded by these trusted ideological comrades, who contributed to Bastide's mistrust of the Frankfurt assembly as a potentially "democratic" ally.

Cavaignac in turn entrusted French foreign affairs to Bastide, who could continue to conduct these on the now familiar three levels of public promises to liberate peoples, confidential dealings with the foreign diplomatic corps, and clandestine operations. For a major thrust against the Habsburg citadel it was business as usual: France used her secret agents. Bastide appointed Carl Ludwig Bernays as secretary to the French legation in Vienna with verbal instructions to fish in the troubled waters of the lower Danube. Bernays's essential charge was to threaten the Habsburgs by keeping the peoples of the Austrian Empire in a state of agitation. Later we shall see that this was part of a far-reaching scheme to transform the entire region into a series of French satellite states as a "Danubian Confederation." Bernays was not an isolated case, but one of an army of French secret agents that Baden's legation councillor had observed leaving France "daily" since the beginning of May.

Bernays's charge reflects a continuity of policies despite a change of cabinets in Paris. French interests remained the emancipation of Poland and Italy, as had been determined by the unanimous resolution of May 24. The unrest in the Danubian valley was used as a means to strike at the house of Habsburg while holding off Austria's eastern ally, tsarist Russia. At the same time, Bastide hoped once more to cement friendly relations with Prussia's cabinet in order to deny reinforcements to France's primary enemy. The isolation of Vienna from its associates seemed all the more important after the collapse of the Italian armies at Custozza toward the end of July.

Hungary's growing importance for France was underlined by a unanimous vote of the Hungarian assembly on July 11 to establish a Hungarian army of 200,000, independent of Viennese control. Since a great portion of the Habsburg army fighting in Italy came from Hungary, this decision could have important consequences.

Even more positively, in Bratislava (Pressburg) between July 20 and 23, the Hungarian radicals denounced any military aid to Austria in her war against Italy. Consequently, Carl Ludwig Bernays, accompanied by Charles Didier, who had very close links to the Polish revolutionary underground, traveled to Budapest to investigate the situation more closely. A formal declaration of Hungarian independence from Vienna became highly desirable in view of alarming news from Italy.

In late July the Habsburg army of General Radetzky routed the forces of King Charles Albert of Sardinia at the Battle of Custozza. At any moment now, France might be forced to live up to her formal pledge to "enfranchise" Italy in a war against Austria.

At this critical juncture, July 24 to 27, the Frankfurt assembly threatened the entire structure of the free alliance of peoples devised by France with an acrimonious debate on the seating of delegates from Posen. The upshot was the permanent estrangement of the German and Polish national movements. With the news of the unfortunate rhetoric in Frankfurt, the French changed their policy from pursuing a formal alliance with the Frankfurt parliamentarians to one of seeking a closer tie with Prussia, as the more likely center of anti-Habsburg sentiment.

The month ended with the ominous news of the entry of Russian troops into the Danubian principalities, bringing them to the Hungarian border. This forced the Magyars to face the issue of their attitude toward France and Italy.

The new direction of French diplomacy was clearly aimed at Berlin and Budapest, the two locales where France might hope to find a sympathetic ear for a military effort to counterbalance the Austrian Habsburg and Russian tsarist ambition to crush the forces of freedom in Italy and Rumania.

French policy drifted throughout July, more than ever "always in the expectative."[1] The goal remained the same: the transformation of Europe into national states, necessarily led by Paris. The means was to be an alliance of peoples rather than governments. The May 24 resolution committed the French to a pact with the German assembly. Bastide expressed frustration and anger as the Frankfurt parliament hesitated to respond to the French proposal. The attitude of the Frankfurt congress toward Italy, Poland, and Schleswig, moreover, was anything but reassuring. After several indecisive weeks, Bastide came to see the German assembly as possibly France's most formidable foe. It alone offered France's reactionary opponents a vital weapon: the ability to initiate a popular crusade of German nationalism against France.

Bastide, however, was still not hostile to the Frankfurt assembly when he replied to Cavaignac's request for information on the election of an imperial vicar. In his note of July 15, Bastide indicated that the nomination of Archduke John of Austria "concentrated all the rights and all the attributions of the central executive power of Germany. His position *vis-à-vis* the German sovereigns is that of a supreme chief." The choice of an imperial vicar had "mediatized and divested" the princes of their political importance. Now at Frankfurt, under the direction of the *Reichsverweser* and by the intermediary of his ministry, the questions of international law, war and peace, military organization, internal administration, public order, commerce, industry, and constitutional law would be addressed for the German Confederation. The German princes alone suffered with regret the "omnipotence that destroys them." The people welcomed the advent of the imperial vicar as "the preliminary to the formation of German unity."

Bastide concluded that France should return to Lamartine's policy which the French had rejected on June 20; namely, to concentrate all of its diplomatic efforts in Frankfurt. "The relations and the negotiations of foreign powers with Germany ought to converge on this center."[2] It seems that Bastide assumed that the realization of German unity in Frankfurt was inevitable. Whatever the cause, France once more looked to Frankfurt as the focus of its diplomatic activity in Germany, again turning its back on the German princes.

From his post in Berlin, Arago pleaded that France's true friend and ally was not in Frankfurt, but in Berlin. Over the next several weeks, he argued that it was in France's interest to support Prussia because her leadership of Germany would benefit France's client nations, particularly Poland. Arago detected a favorable shift in German attitudes toward the Poles, an indication that the clashes between the two nations were diminishing. The Berlin assembly appointed on July 4 a commission of inquest into General Pfuel's line of demarcation across Posen separating it along national lines. Arago believed "that decision . . . destroys all the proposed divisions of Posen."[3]

Arago claimed on July 6 that the investigation indicated a "happy alteration in the influence of France."[4] If Poland were not reconstituted, at least the partition of Posen was being questioned. The Prussian inquest could only do good. Bastide was very pleased about the inquiry. He believed that France had done all that she could, for the present, in making Germany appreciate right and equity in the Posen question.[5]

A few days later, General Louis Mieroslawski, the leader of the April and May uprisings against the Prussian army in Posen, was released by Prussia. Arago claimed this was proof that the

Prussians "wished to have a good solution to the affairs of the grand duchy."[6]

In a July 21 letter to Savoye at Frankfurt, Bastide implied that Arago had influenced opinion in Berlin to conform more closely to French ideals with regard to Poland. "The inquest ordered by the Berlin assembly in the events in the Duchy of Posen is the first favorable symptom" of a change.[7] Bastide went on to urge Savoye to plead for Poland with "all who are accessible to considerations of justice, of right, and of true liberalism." Germany, that "wished and ought to desire the reconstruction of Poland in its own interest, cannot offer to Europe the spectacle . . . of carving up a Polish province for her own advantage."[8] The debate on the annexation of a portion of Posen was another opportunity for the French to identify their friends and foes at Frankfurt. Bastide hoped that the Frankfurt parliament would reject Pfuel's division of Posen into German and Polish zones.

The Frankfurt assembly had to pass on the credentials of twelve delegates elected from the "German" portion of Posen. Were the Germans in Posen to be given the right of representation in the Frankfurt assembly, or were they to be excluded from their own nation? This was the difficult decision before the German parliament. The preparliament, which had annexed Schleswig, East Prussia, and West Prussia, left the problem of Posen open for the national assembly to decide. The preparliament termed the divisions of Poland a "disgraceful injustice," and pledged that the resurrection of Poland was the duty of the German people.

The Polish debate of July 24 to 26 led to a division along ideological lines. Most democrats advocated liberating Poland, because this would weaken the old conservative triad dominated by St. Petersburg. It would mean a war with Russia which the far left would welcome. "The last war," Arnold Ruge proclaimed, "the war against war, the war against the barbarism that war is."[9] Most liberals vacillated; they recognized the justice of reconstituting Poland, but they also did not want to perpetrate an injustice against the Germans in Posen.

A majority of the left stood firmly with the Poles and opposed the division of Posen, although a small group, led by Wilhelm Jordan of East Prussia, was willing to divide regions overwhelmingly populated by Germans. Other delegates were worried about strategic considerations in light of the threat of a Russian war. Robert Blum offered a motion to appoint a commission to study division of Posen instead of making a decision at that time, a response similar to that of the Prussian assembly on July 4. This motion failed by a vote of 333 against, 139 for, and 85 absent. Most of the left then withdrew before the final vote approving the division of Posen. Thus these delegates from Posen were allowed to take their seats by a vote of 342 to 31, with 31 abstaining and 157 registered as absent. Since Bastide had instructed Savoye to test France's influence in Frankfurt by working in Poland's behalf, this outcome could not have been more crushing.[10]

Also troublesome in July was the situation in Italy, with France's attitude appearing as contradictory as ever. At times Bastide warmly assured the Austrian chargé that France had no objection to Austria's retaining at least part of her possessions in northern Italy, as long as she granted them a measure of autonomy. It is just as clear that Bastide at other times, especially after Sardinia faltered, was willing to declare war on Austria to force her out of Italy.

Bastide contributed to the confusion by publishing his own defense ten years after the event, in 1858, claiming that the Italians refused French support when it would have been efficacious, and that later France, in concert with Britain, tried to arrange a negotiated settlement favorable to Italy. He insisted that a federated Italy might have been an acceptable compromise between a completely liberated and united Italy and Austrian domination of Lombardy and Venetia.

On July 12, 1848, Bastide told the Austrian chargé in Paris, Thom, "Confidentially, we have no interest in seeing Sardinia expanded, and we desire sincerely that you conserve a great portion of your possessions in Italy."[11] A week later, Bastide was preoccupied with the possibility that Sardinia might lose the war. A great Austrian triumph would cause serious difficulties for the French government. If Austria gained a crushing victory, France might have to declare war in spite of herself. Thom concluded on July 25 that France was embarrassed by her internal and external situation. One could not be certain, then, of continued French neutrality.[12]

The French continued to hope that somehow they could achieve their goals without fighting. "We do not say, like the former government," Bastide confided to Hatzfeldt, "peace at any price," but he indicated that they valued it highly.[13] France would do everything possible to evade military involvement in Italian affairs, and would investigate all alternatives of diplomatic negotiation before resorting to force. Cavaignac wanted to avoid armed action, Hatzfeldt believed, but the course of events might change his position.[14]

A. J. P. Taylor has suggested that Bastide's policy was "equivocal and contradictory" because he was a novice in diplomacy:

> Bastide was the only leading figure in 1848 completely without experience in public life and he displayed as a result all the faults of the amateur diplomat: he could never look ahead and see clearly the more remote results of any particular step he might take.

Taylor added, "It would be impossible to discover exactly what Bastide did intend in Italy and it is probable that he did not know himself."[15]

An additional element of uncertainty for Paris was its relationship with its potential military ally, Sardinia. The Turin government remained mistrustful and distant, anything but cordial. Bastide complained with some justice that:

> The French revolution found applause and echoes everywhere, confidence and allies nowhere; in Italy only a few republicans dared to offer us a hand in asking for ours. The overwhelming majority . . . rejected our help and invited us to draw the sword against Germany, against Russia, against Austria, everywhere except in Italy.[16]

While France wanted only peace "based on French interests and on true democratic principles," Bastide remonstrated, France was "the object of injurious defiance on the part of governments and peoples."[17] The French continued to blame Italian distrust of France on Charles Albert. Under his leadership, Italy would be a "source of hostilities against France." Bastide wished Italy to be free and for it to "adopt the glorious form of the republic."[18]

The diplomatic agent of Baden in Paris, Schweitzer, reported to his government on July 20 that Bastide was worried about Venice. The Frankfurt parliament had claimed it as part of Germany, which meant that France might be involved in a war with Austria and perhaps with Germany. Bastide denied that he would ever lead France into a general war, because it was not in France's interests. Moreover, the Sardinian king would be ungrateful. Between 1820 and 1822, Bastide maintained, Charles Albert had "conspired with the secret societies in Italy and in France, but

nevertheless had betrayed the party to which he belonged." Bastide
accused members of the Bonapartist family in the French assembly
of pushing for an intervention in Italy so as to "be able to fish in
troubled waters." Bastide denied that the province of Savoy would
be more than a "modest indemnity for the dangerous chances of
a European war." It was clear, Schweitzer concluded, that France
did not want a united monarchy in Italy.[19]

On July 23 Bastide acknowledged that "the idea of seeing a
French army cross the Alps becomes daily less popular in Italy."[20]
The same day, Bastide informed the Prussian chargé that the foreign
affairs committee of the French assembly "wished to force an
alliance on the government with the king of Sardinia," who did
not care for it. France, Bastide complained, "could not impose her
assistance at gunpoint."[21] Not only did the Italians not seek French
support, but by July 23 a new situation in Germany held France
back from military intervention in Italy.

Warning signals flowed into Paris that the Frankfurt assembly
was hardly receptive to the French chamber's resolution of May
24 calling for an alliance to free Italy from foreign domination.
France's minister in Baden, Armand-Edouard Lefebvre, predicted
that Archduke John's role as a mediator and diplomat in reconciling
the German princes would prove dangerous for France. Placed at
the head of Germany, with immense forces at his disposal:

> He will not forget that he is Austrian and an Austrian prince.
> He will endeavor to draw the entire confederation to the Italian
> war. He will make the maintenance of Venetia under the
> imperial scepter an entirely national question. And remember
> that if we have the German people for us, or at least neutral,
> it is not the same with the princes; a war would bolster their
> power and deliver them of a proletarian mass very menacing
> to the upper classes.[22]

Bastide's attention was now focused on Frankfurt and the
"gravity of the consequences which could result in our relations
with Germany" if France's army crossed the Alps.[23] He considered
Archduke John's speech before the opening session of the Austrian
Diet as evidence of Austria's resolution to push the war to a victory
with all possible vigor.[24] The French ministry's special adviser on
German affairs, Heinrich Börnstein, cautioned on July 24 that the
war in Italy was "very popular" in Vienna, and even the radical
party, which until then had advocated evacuation of Lombardy
and Venetia, was now forced into silence.[25] The public mood in

Germany was impossible to misunderstand, the French attaché Gustave Rothan wrote from Kassel. It was increasingly outspoken against a French intervention in Italy, which was regarded as a "German question."[26]

As with Posen, the extremist and imperialist demands came from the Frankfurt assembly. On July 17 Börnstein warned of a proposition introduced in Frankfurt urging Austria to retain Lombardy and Venetia because their loss would harm German prosperity. Börnstein was informed by sources in Frankfurt that the resolution had wide support in the assembly and "Archduke John would be delighted with its passage as a diplomatic boulevard for Austria against Italian pretentions. . . . It is a declaration of war by Germany in its entirety against Italy."[27]

On August 2, Arago warned Bastide that the Frankfurt assembly seemed disposed to embrace now the quarrel of Austria and Italy.[28] The British minister Charles Wellesley Lord Cowley reported from Frankfurt that Archduke John seemed anxious for a settlement in Schleswig and northern Italy. "I would give up Lombardy," the archduke indicated, "I would abandon the Minico. I would not insist upon keeping either Mantua or Peschiera, but the line of the Adige with Verona is necessary to us, that is, to Germany in general." John believed that "Venetia should be separated entirely from the other Austrian states except in respect to military services and revenues."[29]

Alarmed by this development, Bastide questioned Hatzfeldt on July 28 about the rumor that the Frankfurt parliament might declare Venetia part of the German Confederation. At this critical juncture, Bastide received the "sad news from Italy" of Charles Albert's defeat at Custozza. His army had been pushed back to Alexandria, and the Sardinian government at any moment would formally request French military intervention. France was on the brink of war in Italy while the Frankfurt assembly threatened its western flank. Germany was now a primary enemy instead of a natural ally.

The direct confrontation between Frankfurt and Paris, however, came not over Italy, but over the Schleswig question. On August 2 Bastide drew up for Cavaignac a note on the question of Schleswig and Holstein. He inaccurately assumed that the insurgent provisional government in Rendsburg was under the control of the Duke of Augustenberg, the revolt of a reactionary feudal prince against a reforming, liberal Danish monarch. Prussian intervention was "illicit" and an "unjust war against Denmark." Bastide denied the historic and legalistic allegation of an undissolvable tie between the two duchies. The French foreign minister alleged that the administrative and legislative union of the two duchies had "lost much of its force" with the peace treaty of June 14, 1720. He ironically asserted:

> The Germans base their claim on the pretext that of 330,000 inhabitants composing the population of Schleswig, 124,000 speak German. But, in the absence of right, Germany follows the impulse of that spirit of conquest and encroachment which, under the name of unity and German nationality, it pushes beyond its limits.[30]

Bastide's policy was thus still founded on the false assumption that two-thirds of the people in Schleswig were "Danish" and that the Germans were utterly in the wrong.

The potential danger was again signaled by Börnstein's "Bulletins." On July 14 he warned Bastide that the Frankfurt assembly was raising objections to negotiations between Denmark and Prussia and hotly criticized the evacuation of Schleswig. On July 20 the relations between Frankfurt and Berlin were strained to the breaking point. "The refusal of the Frankfurt national assembly to ratify the armistice concluded by Prussia with Denmark produced a great sensation in Berlin." German unity at its birth was exposed to serious dangers by this action. On July 26 matters had reached a crisis. The armistice between Germany and Denmark had been prolonged for three days, but no one believed that peace would be concluded. "The conditions proposed by Prussia have no chance of acceptance in Frankfurt. On the contrary, they will call for the resumption of hostilities, and Prussia will be given the alternative of invading Jutland or of dissociation from Germany." If Prussia "broke with Germany, it is forced to throw itself into the arms of Russia," Börnstein concluded.[31]

Learning of the entry of Prussian troops into Jutland, Bastide assured the British Normanby that the French government desired strong measures, "perhaps an armed intervention." Cavaignac alleged that the attack by the Diet was "perfectly unjustifiable." But Bastide backed away immediately from his initial intemperate reaction; he asked for a "combined diplomatic remonstrance," and promised to do nothing until he heard from London.[32] French relations with Prussia, though, were tense.

But the expansion of Germany's borders at the expense of the

Italians, Poles, and the Danes was not enough. The Frankfurt assembly menaced Limburg, which was part of the German Confederation and at the same time belonged to the Kingdom of Holland. Bastide charged that the threat to Limburg was another clear violation of the principle of nationalities. "The inhabitants of Limburg do not speak the German language," and one of its delegates elected to the Frankfurt assembly did not know a word of German.[33]

The modern historian Frank Eyck argued that the Frankfurt assembly was not so much deceptive as naive. It "was gullible about alleged pro-German tendencies" and thus "taken for a ride" by Limburg's elected representative, Scherpenzeel, who did not even speak German. The difficulty was that the Duchy of Limburg had a dual status as a territory under the constitution and administration of the king of Holland while at the same time under the jurisdiction of the constitution of the German Confederation. This arrangement had to end with the rise of the German national state.[34] Eyck concluded that the Limburgers probably preferred to be reunited with the rest of Limburg, which was ruled by the king of Belgium.

The assembly's "abrupt and thoughtless" decision with regard to Limburg was sharply censured in Prussia. It was realized in Berlin that this could only force the Dutch monarch to seek Russian support, just as the king of Denmark had already done.[35] Instead of placating its neighbors, the Frankfurt parliament appeared determined to antagonize and alarm them. Its public relations were a disaster.

Matters were hardly helped by the assembly's foreign minister, Johann Gustav Heckscher, a Hamburg lawyer. Instead of calming the "specious fears" of the small states on Germany's borders, he startled them with territorial aspirations. The French chargé in Vienna, De la Cour, reporting to Bastide on July 26, 1848, described how Heckscher explained the Limburg question to the Viennese diplomatic community. He traced the policy that Germany would henceforth follow, the vigor and perseverance that Germany would bring. He developed his favorite theme of unity and centralization with self-satisfaction, describing the map of the new empire without showing the slightest doubt of "the legitimacy of the pretentions of German patriotism."

In the course of the conversation, Heckscher was asked whether the "German Rhine" would extend to the Texel and the Zuider Zee, and whether France and England "in spite of their sympathy for regenerated Germany" wished Maestricht and Venloo incorporated into Germany. Heckscher lacked the common sense to consider carefully the objection, and answered naively, "Germany found in her patriotism, in the sense of right *(droit)*, the necessities of her political existence, and in the power of expansion of her nationals the means and will to overcome the obstacles that she will meet in her march."[36] The Belgian representative objected heatedly to the "new spirit of usurpation." Heckscher seemed almost happy to increase the number of enemies of the Frankfurt government.

The fate of France's May 24 resolution exemplified the growing gulf between Frankfurt and Paris. Although the Frankfurt parliament's committee on international affairs welcomed the French offer of a fraternal tie, it refused to recommend an exclusive intimate alliance.[37] The plenum discussed the question of alliances on July 22, but rather than responding to the enthusiasm of the French representatives, its members passed to the order of the day. When the offer came before the full assembly, it exhibited little sympathy for a military pact with the French to free Italy and Poland, asserting that an alliance exclusively with France was "presently inopportune."[38]

By the end of July, there was scarcely an issue of importance to France on which the Frankfurt assembly had not lined up against Paris. As far as France was concerned, German policies toward the Poles, Italians, Danes, and Dutch were in utter contradiction to their own principle of nationality and threatened France herself in Alsace and Lorraine.

Bastide discussed German affairs in general with Hatzfeldt on July 23, repeating several times that "they were almost incomprehensible to him." He asked Hatzfeldt a month after the election of Archduke John as imperial vicar "to give him some explanations, particularly with regard to the establishment of the new central power."[39] A month later, the Prussian king's aide-de-camp, during a special mission to France, testified that matters had not improved. While in Paris, General Friedrich Adolf Baron von Willisen informed several German diplomats that "the French government cannot understand the present situation of Germany."[40] On July 24 Bastide spoke with great restraint to the Austrian chargé, Thom, about the German parliament. Thom recorded:

   . He only told me that the fermentation of opinion and communistic tendencies rendered necessary the creation of a strong, energetic, and powerful executive extending to all parts of Germany, and that for this reason, the results which the deliberations of the national parliament in Frankfurt had brought to a head could have, for the moment at least, a practical utility.[41]

Bastide's July 24 conversation with Thom offers three points of interest. It reflects Bastide's sympathy for the Frankfurt assembly because of its "practical utility." Second, it demonstrates that his approval of that body was based on its ability to bring "strong, energetic, and powerful" leadership to Germany. Finally, it provides supporting evidence to Mikhail Pokrovsky's thesis that a major part of France's foreign policy was based on her primary domestic embarrassment, the "red menace." In the aftermath of the June Days, Bastide was worried about the communist threat, which could spill over from Baden and Württemberg into France. When, however, the Frankfurt assembly became the chief source of discord, undermining the united German front against "communist tendencies," Bastide sought allies elsewhere. At the end of July, Bastide complained to Thom that Archduke John seemed unable to control the Frankfurt parliament.[42]

The occasion for the final separation of Paris and Frankfurt was the Schleswig question. On July 24, as we have noted, Bastide was still friendly toward the German assembly and continued his policy of benign neglect of the Schleswig matter. Lord Normanby informed Hatzfeldt that the French government was "not in the least concerned by the affair of Schleswig and of the Danish-German strife."[43]

This rapid turn in attitudes toward the Frankfurt parliament transpired over the course of a few days. On July 28, the Prussian agent, Hatzfeldt, saw Bastide in a state of confusion. Bastide now felt that "everything happening at Frankfurt was incomprehensible."[44] That is, events in Germany did not correspond to Bastide's preconceived notions of ideological purity. Yet Bastide was still not a confirmed foe of the Frankfurt assembly. At least Hatzfeldt concluded that Bastide was "favorable rather than unfavorable" to that Frankfurt parliament, because the French minister regarded it as "representing the sovereignty of the German people."[45]

Renewed warnings flowed to Bastide from his special adviser on German affairs, Heinrich Börnstein, who cautioned him that while Frankfurt "placidly discussed the Germanization of part of

Poland storms were brewing. . . . Prussia was deeply wounded by the arrogant behavior of the 'writers and lawyers in Frankfurt,' " and a rupture might come at any time with Berlin. The last German note sent to the king of Sardinia threatened war because of the blockade of Trieste. The Germans clashed with the Swiss, refused an alliance with France, and before the menace of Russia they refused to ratify the armistice with Denmark and renewed the war. "In a word, the new Germany begins on bad terms with everyone."

Börnstein could find only one word to describe the condition of Germany—botched *(gâchis)*. In that situation, Börnstein saw hope only in the republican party, which was organizing and to whom "the future belongs." Its victory could only be held back by a reactionary alliance of the German princes with Russia and England in a war against France. This would result in a "true German revolution and the republic on both sides of the Rhine." "The only policy for France *vis-à-vis* Germany now," Börnstein advised, "is to withdraw as much as possible and not be drawn into any matter into the domestic and external struggles which menace Germany in the immediate future." Germany must turn toward France.[46]

Arago on July 20 likewise advised Bastide to watch and wait. France ought to avoid conflicts with Germany, which was on the verge of civil upheaval, dividing it north-south. The north would support the monarchy and separation, and the south, democracy and union. France should intervene late in the war to uphold the national principle against Russia. For the present, though, France must continue her policy of waiting.[47]

Bastide's attitude altered definitively with the military situation in northern Italy. With the Sardinian army endangered, France found itself having to reckon with a German assembly that had become frankly pro-Austrian. Facing the possibility of an immediate confrontation with Germany in Italy, Bastide for the first time showed an interest in the war in the Baltic duchies. He made his threat openly to the Austrian chargé. "If Archduke John is unable to make the Frankfurt parliament reasonable, then that affair in [Schleswig] could have incalculable results."[48]

The same day, July 31, Bastide vented his disgust with developments in Frankfurt to Arago, his envoy in Prussia. "This national assembly of Frankfurt is a very sorry spectacle of political morality in the questions of Schleswig and of the Grand Duchy of Posen." Bastide worried that "such a state of affairs assured the existence of discords and divisions dangerous for the creation of a unitary system in Germany and deadly for peace in that country." The conduct of the parliamentarians was leading Germany into a domestic turmoil that would destroy the national and liberal movements. Under the present leadership at Frankfurt, Bastide did not see it in the interest of France to support the Frankfurt assembly's concept of a German unity hostile to France.

Bastide made it clear that he now believed it inappropriate for France to centralize its diplomacy in Frankfurt in support of the national assembly. The men in Frankfurt were creating a situation conducive to "democratic anarchy and perhaps civil war," speculated Bastide.[49] "I do not see that we have an interest in desiring that unity and even less in pressing it," Bastide concluded. Thus the author of the French resolution of May 24 went on to declare bankruptcy. All of his efforts to weld together the national assemblies of the neighboring lands had been futile. German unity under the Frankfurt assembly would democratize the country, "but it will also make of that people of more than 40 million souls a power more dreadful for its neighbors than Germany is today."[50] In summary, unity under the Frankfurt assembly might bring democracy and unity in the short run, but ultimately this would lead to civil war and the destruction of the ephemeral fusion.

Historians have too quickly looked to events in succeeding decades to praise Bastide for his supposed foresight. More careful examination of the documents casts doubt on the hasty conclusion that Bastide recognized the danger that a united Germany would pose for France.[51]

Alarmed by the recent violence of the Paris "June Days," Bastide was terrified by the prospect of a communist victory in the German states. Thus he told German diplomats that both France and Germany "had a common enemy to combat, that which in the name of progress tends to deliver society to brutal force and brigandage."[52]

From the Frankfurt assembly, Palmerston learned that the French government:

> complains of the inactivity of the Central Power in putting down revolt and attributes the present inquiet state of public opinion in Germany to the encouragement given at Frankfurt to those ideas of Socialism and Communism which the French government is endeavouring to combat.[53]

The Württemberger chargé in Paris likewise reported the

French preoccupation with communism: "I know that Mr. Bastide is very preoccupied with the state of Germany. He spoke to me a short while ago, telling me that he feared that communism in a short time had taken even greater increase than in France," and that anarchy extended over the entire civilized world.[54] Bastide informed several other diplomats as well that he thought that a social revolution in Germany would lead to "an internal war whose disastrous consequences can only be compared to the Thirty Years' War."[55]

Yet none of this lends credence to Pokrovsky's speculation that the fear of communism caused Bastide to propose an alliance with the reactionary German princes and the tsar himself against German unity. This would hardly have been consistent with his concern that the Frankfurt parliament was sabotaging Germany's unification. Crucial to understanding Bastide's thinking during the previous week and for the rest of the year is awareness of his anxiety about a civil war in Germany. Bastide, who had collaborated with Philippe Buchez and Prosper-Charles Roux on their *Histoire parlementaire de la Révolution Française*, tended to look back to the eighteenth century. His analysis was in terms of the Great French Revolution. He was most concerned with a Babeuf or a Napoleon. He had very little knowledge of conditions abroad and made his decisions on the basis of his cognizance of France. Just a week earlier, Bastide had favored the Frankfurt government's consolidation of power over all Germany, because he thought that this would form the best dam against a new Thirty Years' War.

Such a conflict in central Europe could have vast domestic and international ramifications. France would necessarily be engaged against Russia, since the tsar would champion the monarchical ideal. The internal danger was that of the French Directory: the proletarian menace and a possible military dictatorship in the wake of this great war, which would release dangerous passions which the French government could only control with difficulty. The Frankfurt assembly's actions had increased the need for stability and consolidation in Germany. Bastide sought a strong sovereign to nullify the Frankfurt parliament and embrace the alliance with France. The assembly, Bastide now thought, was a "bunch of loudmouths," whose pretentions were exaggerated, particularly in Schleswig.[56]

Bastide's new caution was most likely effected by the disturbing news from Budapest. The Hungarian government had begun during June to entertain the illusion that the court, which had fled Vienna for Innsbruck, might move to Buda. In such a case it would be unnecessary to divide the diplomatic service into two halves. Meanwhile in Paris, the news of the possible diplomatic appointment of Pascal Duprat as French envoy to Budapest stirred up a hornet's nest. The Poles objected to Duprat because he was notoriously pro-Magyar and anti-Slav in his views. His appearance as French envoy would seem to endorse such anti-Slav opinions.[57]

The French cabinet decided instead once more to send Bernays to Budapest with new and far-reaching instructions that were denied him during his earlier mission. This time he was empowered to use extreme measures in Budapest to counter the seriously deteriorating situation. France had to adopt non-diplomatic means to save Italy.[58] It looked as though the present Hungarian cabinet was no longer interested in opening diplomatic relations with France. And French involvement in the war in Italy against Austria seemed imminent, just as the Magyars appeared to have lost interest in doing something for Italy.

The true nature of the "non-diplomatic" measures Bernays was authorized to utilize in Budapest immediately became known to the legation councillor of Baden, Baron F. A. von Schweitzer. A double agent in his employ informed him that Bernays had been sent to overturn the Batthyány-Kossuth cabinet.[59]

The crisis brought on by a possible Franco-Austrian conflict in northern Italy demanded an intense effort on all three levels of French diplomacy. The unanimous resolution of May 24 needed serious reconsideration, for instead of grasping the extended hand of the French assembly, the Frankfurt parliament appeared to be siding with Austria, France's potential enemy in northern Italy. If Bastide hoped to enfranchise Poland and Italy, he had to find an ally. Given that this task of liberating the sovereign peoples was utterly impossible without a German supporter, Bastide's task was to find an associate willing to unite the scattered Germans into a single state that would in turn free the other peoples of central Europe.

Yet the French must have been heartened by intelligence filtering back to Paris, via Czartoryski's well-informed Polish network of agents, of a spreading disillusionment of the south Slavs with Austria. The profundity of this growing estrangement is reflected in a letter written by Rajačić on August 1, which was quoted by Alan Sked. The Serb Patriarch complained of the Austrian failure to defend the population in southern Hungary while "its sons

[were] fighting like lions on the fields of Italy in support of the Emperor and in order to uphold the Empire as a whole." The letter ended with the menace that if matters did not improve:

> The first step will be to recall all its sons from the Italian army; the second will be to call on the help of all Slav nations; the third, that it will enter into an alliance with Charles Albert and the Italians; the fourth, that it will appeal to England, France, and the whole of Europe.[60]

At the most critical moment in Franco-Austrian relations, Bastide could only have been encouraged by hints of a fissure in the solid wall of the Austrian armed forces. But in order for the French to exploit the opportunity, Hungary needed a cabinet more sympathetic to the national aspirations of the struggling peoples. This explains the Bernays-Didier mission and their contacts with the Budapest radicals.

In summary, the French government used the victory over anarchy in the June Days as proof of French credentials to speak as moderates. This has misled historians to exaggerate the "conservative" conversion of the Cavaignac government and to overlook signs of an unbroken connection between foreign policies before and after the June rebellion against the French republic. By fixing their attention on Western Europe historians have overlooked the subversive activities of the secret agents of Prince Czartoryski's Polish underground among the southern Slavs. That Polish diligence appeared at last to bear fruit with Patriarch Rajačić's possible defection with the Serbic minority in southern Hungary. But the new front on the lower Danube in the universal war against autocracy was all for naught if it in turn gained new reinforcements from Germany. Bastide now had to deal with the growing probability of the Frankfurt assembly's defection to the enemy. If the Frankfurt assembly were to continue its defiantly aggressive attitude toward Germany's neighbors, the French had to reckon with a powerful adversary instead of the fraternal alliance envisioned in the May 24 unanimous resolution of the French assembly. Yet the military defeat of the Italians made a drawing together of the peoples to free Poland and Italy all the more urgent. France in turn was threatened because the defeat of the peoples meant the eventual demise of a republic in France. For the survival of this republic, the French government had to deal quickly with the Frankfurt assembly's treason to the cause of freedom for the oppressed peoples.

NOTES

1. Schweitzer to Dusch, Paris, July 18, 1848, BGLA, fz. 48/2037.

2. Election du Vicaire-général de l'Empire, July 15, 1848, Cav 1 Mi 2 R 24; the Cavaignac papers give an invaluable indication of the foreign minister's thinking. He summarized important incoming and outgoing correspondence. Cavaignac's annotations, frequent underlinings, and occasional deletions denoted an active interest in the German question in particular. Most important, the memoranda passed on to him by the foreign minister reveal a clear pattern of reinforcing a particular viewpoint and ignoring contrary opinion. In this sense, the greatest importance of the Cavaignac papers is what they lack: the singular failure to consider conflicting opinions, but a striking consistency in the judgements of the inner circle. Significantly, Cavaignac's intimate secretary during the June Days, signing orders in Cavaignac's name, was Bastide's *chef de cabinet*, Hetzel. cf. Jennings, *France and Europe*, pp. 124n–25n.

3. Arago to Bastide, Berlin, July 4, 1848, AEF, Prusse 302, fo. 142, passage underlined twice in Paris.

4. *Ibid.*, July 6, 1848, fo. 143.

5. Bastide to Arago, Paris, July 11, 1848, AEF, Prusse 302, fo. 152.

6. Arago to Bastide, Berlin, July 15, 1848, AEF, Prusse 302, fo. 157.

7. Bastide to Savoye, Paris, July 21, 1848, AEF, Allemagne 805, fo. 223.

8. *Ibid.*

9. Hans Roth, "Die Linke in der Paulskirche und der Nationalismus," (doc. diss., University of Freiburg, 1950), pp. 31–33; Günter Hildebrandt, "Die Stellung der äussersten Linken in der Frankfurter Nationalversammlung zur Polenfrage in Sommer 1848," *Jahrbuch für Geschichte der sozialistischen Länder Europas* XVII (1973), 87–106, and *Opposition in der Paulskirche* (Berlin, 1981); Rolf Weber, *Die Revolution in Sachsen 1848/49: Entwicklung und Analyse ihrer Treibkräfte* (Berlin, 1970).

10. Roth, pp. 33–41; The problem of the Frankfurt parliament's nationalities policy was that the majority thought in terms of its own nationality, and in doubtful cases cast the balance egotistically; Namier, *1848*, p. 110, Börnstein, Bulletins, AEF, MD, Allemagne 129, fo. 45–49.

11. Thom to Wessenberg, Paris, July 12, 1848, HHSA, PA, IX, fo. 40–41.

12. Thom to Wessenberg, Paris, July 19 and 25, 1848, *Ibid.*, fo. 66–69.

13. Hatzfeldt to Foreign Minister, Paris, August 2, 1848, GSA, fz. 856, fo. 240.

14. Hatzfeldt to Foreign Minister, Paris, August 4, 1848, GSA, fz. 861, fo. 107.

15. A. J. P. Taylor, *Italian Problem*, pp. 149, 194.

16. Bastide, *La République française*, pp. 29–30.

17. *Ibid.*, p. 29.

18. Bastide to Bixio, Paris, June, 1848, and to Boislecomte, July 19, 1848, *Ibid.*, pp. 45–47; Bastide to Tallenay, Paris, July 18, 1848, AEF, Angleterre 670, fo. 249.

19. Schweitzer to Dusch, Paris, July 20, 1848, BGLA, fz. 48/2037, fo. 749–51.

20. Bastide to Tallenay, Paris, July 23, 1848, AEF, Angleterre 670, fo. 264.

21. Hatzfeldt to Foreign Minister, Paris, July 25, 1848, GSA, fz. 861, fo. 84; Procès-verbaux, Comité des affaires étrangères, July 12, 14, 17, 18, 20, and 22, 1848, Archives Nationales, C 926 [C277] 561, fo. 21–26.

22. Lefebvre to Bastide, Baden-Baden, Courier of July 17, 1848, Cav 1 Mi 2 R 26. Nowhere is the vast gulf separating the limited and realistic policy of Bismarck in greater contrast with the Frankfurt assembly's than in their attitudes toward Italian unification; Italy was the paramount concern of France in 1848 as in 1859 and 1866, which had enormous repercussions on France's disposition toward the Frankfurt parliament during July and August, as it threatened to make Austria's war against the Italians a cause of German nationalism.

23. Bastide to Tallenay, Paris, July 23, 1848, AEF, Angleterre 670, fo. 264.

24. *Ibid.*, July 31, 1848, fo. 291.

25. Bulletin, July 24, 1848, AEF, MD, Allemagne 129, fo. 52.

26. Rothan to Bastide, Kassel, July 14, 1848, AEF, Hesse 34, fo. 75; Tallenay to Bastide, London, July 6, 1848, AEF, Angleterre 670, fo. 209.

27. Bulletin, July 17, 1848, AEF, MD, Allemagne 129, fo. 44; Arago to Bastide, Berlin, July 7, 1848, AEF, Prusse 302, fo. 148.

28. Arago to Bastide, Berlin, August 2, 1848, *ibid.*, fo. 192.

29. Cowley to Palmerston, Frankfurt, August 7, 1848, PRO, FO 30/109.

30. Note sur la question du Schleswig et du Holstein, August 2, 1848, from the Minister des affaires étrangères, Cav 1 Mi 2 R 25; the Cavaignac papers include a number of memoranda and pamphlets on the Schleswig-Holstein question, *all* from the Danish perspective.

31. Bulletin, July 14, 20, and 26, 1848, AEF, MD, Allemagne 129, fo. 38, 47, and 55.

32. Normanby to Palmerston, Paris, August 1, 1848, PRO, FO 27/811.

33. Note sur le Limbourg, August, 1848, Cav 1 Mi 2 R 25; Hans-Georg Kraume, *Aussenpolitik 1848: Die holländische Provinz Limburg in der deutsche Revolution* (Düsseldorf, 1979); Wollstein, *Das Grossdeutschland der Paulskirche*.

34. Eyck, *Frankfurt Parliament*, pp. 254–68; Bastide's analysis of the ethnic character is problematic, but his criticism of the assembly's action emphasizes the difficulty of using language as a test of nationality in border areas. A recent assessment of the area: "The population . . . is cosmopolitan in outlook and has close ties with German and Belgian cities close to Limburg's borders. A high proportion of Limburgers speak both German and French, in addition to Dutch." John H. Paterson, "Limburg," *Encyclopedia Americana*, (New York, 1972) XVII, 486.

35. Börnstein, Bulletin, July 29, 1848, AEF, MD, Allemagne 129, fo. 59.

36. De la Cour to Bastide, Vienna, July 26, 1848, AEF, Autriche 436, fo. 34–35; cf. Paul Wentzcke, "Bayerische Stimmen aus der Paulskirche (Juni–Juli 1848)," *Archivalische Zeitschrift*, L/LI (1955), 493, and Heckscher to Oscar Parish, Frankfurt, March 30, 1849, in F. Heskel, "Hamburgische Stimmen aus der Paulskirche," *Mitteilungen der Verein für Hamburgische Geschichte*, XXVI (1906), 202–05. Heckscher placed a portion of the blame for the Frankfurt assembly's difficulties on "foreign intrigue" and charged that views of the "foreign powers" continued to play a role in German politics; Cowley judged that it was less treachery than "chaos and confusion which still reign paramount here." Cowley was pained by Heckscher's "public announcement on Limburg inconsistent with my dispatch No. 52 (August 21, 1848) that the government wishes to let the matter drop." Cowley to Palmerston, Frankfurt, September 9, 1848, PRO, FO 30/110.

37. Börnstein, Bulletin, July 5, 1848, AEF, MD, Allemagne 129, fo. 27; On June 4 there were already complaints in the committee that France was a "dangerous ally." Ley, p. 95.

38. Börnstein, Bulletin, July 25, 1848, fo. 53; Basserman and Beckrath charged during the debate that a desire for war existed in France. Ley, p. 95.

39. Hatzfeldt to Foreign Minister, Paris, July 25, 1848, GSA, fz. 856, fo. 224.

40. Mancler to Foreign Minister, Paris, August 21, 1848, Württemberg. Hauptstaatsarchiv (Stuttgart), E70a, fz. 19, No. 19 (hereafter WSA); Schweitzer to Dusch, Paris, August 5, 1848, BGLA, 48/2037.

41. Thom to Wessenberg, Paris, July 24, 1848, HHSA, PA, IX Frankreich, fo. 62.

42. *Ibid.*, July 31, 1848, fo. 80.

43. Hatzfeldt to Foreign Minister, Paris, July 24, 1848, GSA, fz. 861, fo. 83.

44. *Ibid.*, July 28, 1848, fo. 90.

45. *Ibid.*

46. Bulletin, July 28, 1848, AEF, MD, Allemagne 129, fo. 57–58.

47. Arago to Bastide, Berlin, July 20, 1848, AEF, Prusse 302, fo. 159–161.

48. Thom to Wessenberg, Paris, July 31, 1848, PA, IX Frankreich, HHSA, fo. 80.

49. Bastide to Arago, Paris, July 31, 1848, AEF, Prusse 302, fo. 187.

50. *Ibid.*

51. *cf.* Jennings, *France and Europe*; Pokrovsky, "Lamartine, Cavaignac und Nikolaus I"; Hahn, "The Attitude of the French"; and Paul Henry, "La France et les nationalités en 1848."

52. Schweitzer to Dusch, Paris, September 28, 1848, BGLA, fz. 48/2037.

53. Cowley to Palmerston, Frankfurt, September 25, 1848, PRO, FO 30/110.

54. Mancler to Foreign Minister, Paris, August 9, 1848, WSA, E70a, B19.

55. Hatzfeldt to Foreign Minister, Paris, August 10, 1848, GSA, fz. 861, fo. 132 and Rogier to Hoffschmidt, Paris, August 12, 1848, AEB, III, France, fo. 267, warning that a French armed intervention in Italy "strongly risks provoking a new civil war."

56. Hatzfeldt to Foreign Minister, Paris, July 31, 1848, GSA, fz. 861, fo. 98–99 and 856, fo. 229.

57. Hajnal corrects the misconception that the non-appointment of Duprat was due to French indifference or hostility to Hungary, *À Batthyány*, pp. 93, 108–09.

58. Bernays to Foreign Minister, St. Louis, Missouri, February 23, 1849, dossier personnel, AEF. This extensive report on Bernays' subversive activities as a French secret agent which was written to Drouyn de Lhuys was corroborated by the highest permanent officials in the French ministry; cf. other materials in this dossier personnel, AEF.

59. Schweitzer to Dusch (Foreign Minister), Paris, July 9, 1848, BGLA, fz. 48/2037, fo. 706.

60. Sked, *Survival of the Habsburg*, pp. 68–69.

Chapter Six
The Policy of Richelieu?

EARLY AUGUST 1848

*D*URING EARLY AUGUST, BASTIDE sought to evade his commitment to the democratic alliance with the Frankfurt assembly. Searching for an alternative strategy, he briefly considered encouraging Prussian particularism, until his chargé in Berlin, Arago, convinced him that a democratic link to the Prussian assembly was a preferable alternative. The essential objective remained the same throughout the revolutionary year: determined opposition to the house of Habsburg in order to free Italy and to resurrect Poland. As the Frankfurt assembly seemed to drift into the Habsburg camp, French policy shifted eastward, relying increasingly on Budapest and Berlin to counteract the danger posed by the strident tone heard in the Frankfurt parliament. However, we shall see the historic wisdom linking Bastide's change of heart to a supposed anti-German sentiment is fallacious, since Bastide considered Germany's unity an inevitable development. His primary frame of reference remained the Habsburg menace to the cause of free peoples as tensions mounted when France moved inexorably toward a showdown with Austria. With the increasing likelihood of a Franco-Austrian war, the French sought to pressure Austria to accept a proffered Anglo-French offer of mediation of the terms of peace between Austria and Sardinia.

France's frustration with the Frankfurt parliament's apparently pro-Austrian attitude increased, but strict neutrality was necessary to avoid affronting nationalist feelings among Germans. The French were committed to a fatherland for the Germans, but viewed this particular parliament as unrepresentative of the legitimate wishes of Germans for national unity.

The French could be more encouraged by talk in Budapest of a "Second Revolution" among Hungarian radicals, who were impatient with the unwillingness of the Batthyány cabinet to disengage Hungarian forces from Radetzky's army of conquest in Italy. The announcement on August 9 of the harsh terms imposed by the Austrians as the price of an Austrian-Italian armistice brought the possibility of a French military expedition south of the Alps nearer. This accelerated France's desire to settle the conflict in northern Europe quickly.

The French protest in Frankfurt and Berlin on August 20 was meant to speed up negotiations on an armistice with Denmark. The protest against the delay in ending hostilities between Prussia and Denmark came only three days before the final Prussian decision to accept the armistice at Malmö on August 26.

Meanwhile the French prepared Austria for the declaration of war by suggesting terms for a possible peace settlement. On August 23, France for a second time offered Vienna the Danubian principalities as compensation for her losses in Italy.

This diplomatic effort occurred against a background of radical activity. In addition to the growing radical rhetoric in Budapest, workers demonstrated in Vienna on August 23, and on the same day the First German Workers' Congress opened in Berlin.

The lack of Austrian response to the Franco-British mediation offer led to a new low in Franco-Austrian relations as the month closed. France and the Danubian monarchy appeared to be inching toward war. Increasingly the primary French concern was the possible military support that the Frankfurt parliament might give the Habsburgs, which would enable them to continue their domination of eastern and southern Europe.

Under the pressure of events, Bastide would briefly contemplate easing away from France's commitment to the German national movement because of the Frankfurt assembly's treacherous violation of the precept of liberation of all nations. But the exigencies of economic and military survival and France's future role in Europe inevitably drew Bastide back into the reaffirmation of close Franco-German cooperation, albeit with the Prussian government rather than the Frankfurt assembly.

During early August, Bastide reassessed his entire policy toward German unity and the Frankfurt assembly. On August 2, the resident minister of Baden informed his government that the *National* of that morning "perfectly translated the intimate thought of Bastide and the French government on German unity." The writer of the article assured readers that France was supportive of

German unity. This warm sympathy for Germany caused France to "notice with pain that [Germany] seemed to deviate from the principle that governs relations between peoples: the respect of nationalities." First the Poles were sacrificed in Posen, then Schleswig attacked, now it was Venetia and Limburg. The "policy of encroachment" gradually dominated in Germany, causing the Poles to rally to the tsar for concessions. Germany's real enemy was in St. Petersburg, the article stressed, not on the Adige. The writer speculated that the recent Polish debate was part of an attempt by the Frankfurt assembly to create a link with Russia at the expense of the Poles. Free Italy and Poland would be surer and more profitable allies than Nicholas I, the article noted.[1]

Seeking an agent to counter the Frankfurt assembly's "policy of encroachment," Bastide in desperation contemplated Prussian particularism, speculating that a "passionate reaction" against German unity might come from Prussia. He noted the sentiment in a pamphlet opposing the "idea of a system of fusion and absolute centralization as a chimera." Bastide suggested that France ought to encourage this viewpoint.[2] During the next several days, he indecisively attempted to construct a new policy replacing the May 24 resolution of a fraternal pact between the French and German parliaments.

The travail in Paris was reflected in France's attitude *vis-à-vis* the Frankfurt assembly as it debated the fate of Posen on July 24–26. Two days before the opening of discussion in Frankfurt, the French envoy in Berlin, Arago, warned Bastide that the Poles were alarmed and expected a debacle. They requested help and protection from France, regarding it as "their only support." A number of Poles wanted the French government to publish in the newspapers a protest over the division of Posen. Few believed that this would favorably influence opinion in Berlin and Frankfurt; the actual motivation was to "calm the Poles of Posen in their anguish."[3]

Bastide's response was negative, and history has charged that it indicated an indifference to Poland's fate. Across the top of Arago's dispatch Bastide wrote, "Do not publish anything in the newspapers and do not excite people."[4] He advised Arago that any remonstrance ought to be made privately to the cabinets, not in public. By the first of August, however, he believed that such an action was worse than futile, and observed:

Now that the matter is terminated, I see little timeliness in

publishing in the newspapers, as you recommended, the rep-
resentations of June 9. In the general situation of Europe and
relative to other questions, the Duchy of Posen is of secondary
interest.[5]

Poland was "secondary" in two respects. The immediate and
overwhelming French concern was the danger of a war in Italy.
Then there was the practical problem that General Pelet had pointed
out in his memorandum on a war in Poland: Without the complete
cooperation of the Germans it would be impossible to give Poland
any military assistance. Lamartine and Bastide repeatedly agreed
that the Poles depended on German largess for their freedom and
liberty. Bastide was shocked and dismayed by the disastrous outcome of the Frankfurt assembly's debate on Posen, especially as it
rejected a paragraph protecting the nationality of Poles living in
Prussia's eastern provinces. Until there was a change of heart in
Germany, there was little of a practical nature that the French
could do for Poland. On July 30 Bastide reported to Cavaignac
that Savoye had done "everything to avert the fatal decision. He
had sounded [minister in Central Power] Schmerling to inform the
assembly of the open and disinterested disposition of France and
its representative. Schmerling promised; he did not dare to keep
his word."[6] France had protested privately prior to the decision
on Posen, but the Germans had spurned France's advice.

France's attitude was clarified by Arago, who imposed his
analysis of the German question on Bastide and probably on Cavaignac as well. In a dispatch of August 1 (which Bastide showed to
Cavaignac on August 4), Arago advised that German unity was
inevitable and France had to adjust its policy to this certainty. In
spite of the mistakes of the Frankfurt parliament, Arago wrote,
the separatist reaction was making hardly any progress. The Prussian minister was using his influence to avoid an open rupture and
attempting to control the extreme Germanism prevailing in the
Frankfurt assembly. "The Berlin cabinet has just sent the imperial
vicar an energetic invitation to end the war in Italy soon." Arago
expressed a "firm hope" that the Berlin government would "persist
in a more just policy" toward Posen than the Frankfurt assembly.
If a public statement concerning Posen was not advisable, Arago
requested permission to send a precise note to the Prussian government conforming to the French protest of June 9.[7]

On August 4 Bastide abruptly dropped his objection to the
protest and completely subscribed to Arago's analysis of a generally

friendly attitude among Germans towards France's wishes. Fear of a Russo-German alliance apparently vanished under the weight of Arago's judgment. Bastide requested Cavaignac's permission to allow Arago to deliver a protest against the division of Poland. Bastide now believed that "there is in the German parliament a tolerably strong democratic party, and this party will welcome with pleasure our protest."[8] The policy of friendship with the German liberal movement was reaffirmed, and after four days as a "secondary interest" Poland was again a primary concern of the French.

Bastide apparently drew away from the idea of encouraging particularism among the German states and once again returned to the policy of the "democratic alliance" with the Frankfurt assembly. He assumed that the ultimate audience for a French protest was in Frankfurt, where a "democratic" faction was sympathetic to France and Poland. He had not yet been fully converted to Arago's heretical viewpoint that France should break with the entire Frankfurt assembly and seek a fraternal pact with Berlin. Most significantly, Bastide did not label the Frankfurt democrats as the enemy.

The next day in a private letter, Arago made the proposed policy explicit. France should "support Prussia against Frankfurt." The parliament had "cruelly sacrificed the Polish nationality." It had treated the Schleswig and Limburg matters unjustly, and "it seems disposed now to embrace Austria's quarrel with Italy." At Berlin, however, the rights of the Poles were not taken lightly, and they favored the reorganization of Posen. Prussia wished to terminate the Schleswig affair "on a honorable basis." Prussia's government protested vehemently against the idea of bringing Germany into a war in Italy. If Bastide were unwilling to send an official message to the Prussian cabinet concerning Posen, Arago suggested a verbal communication.[9]

Arago wrote two days later that Bastide was mistaken if he imagined that the Frankfurt parliament reflected the general sentiments of Germans. Public opinion, he assured, was not in accord with the "Frankfurt ideologues" any more than with the partisans of the old Prussian party, who rejected German unity and preferred absolute monarchy. Certainly, all German liberals wanted a central power, but one that took into account particular interests and needs. "The Prussian cabinet itself shares these ideas." It would resist the "mad exaggeration" of the Frankfurt parliament and rally the sympathies of those alienated by Frankfurt. Prussia would put itself peacefully at the head of the German union and "give the French republic serious guarantees of lasting friendship." Prussia could save Germany from the blind madness of the Frankfurt assembly. Arago reassured Bastide that he was mistaken in his belief that the division of Posen was final. Prussia would save Germany's honor. He noted:

> In your dispatch of August 1 on the subject of the vote in Frankfurt on the Posen question, you said "today all is consummated." I do not think this is so. From the decision to the execution is a long way, and the execution can only come from Prussia. This is more than uncertain. I believe firmly that the grand duchy will never be divided.[10]

Arago's next letter took issue with Bastide's speculation of August 1 that France might consider encouraging Prussian particularism as a reaction against German unity. France's advocacy of Prussia, Arago emphasized, ought in no way to be directed against Germany's union. A united Germany "rightly understood and intelligently organized will be favorable to us," Arago suggested. The folly of Frankfurt had not destroyed the principle of unity, and the Prussian cabinet could prevent the impending civil war which would be fatal to German liberty. A unitary power resting on a solid basis, recognizing the rights of neighboring nations, restricting itself to setting the interests of Germany in order, would be "sympathetic to the French republic." Germany would form "an insurmountable barrier between France and Russia." Opposition to German unity was not an available alternative for French policy, since it was "impossible now to root up the principle of union in Germany without a civil war." France need not impede German unification, "It is only necessary to arrange it," to prevent its extending too far. "That is Prussia's mission; it will not fail."[11] Arago believed that Bastide was mistaken in his August 1 judgment that France had no interest in contributing to the triumph of German unity.

Arago's efforts to delineate a strong contrast between Berlin and Frankfurt was strengthened by the Prussian government. During early August it assured the French that it in no way supported Frankfurt's imperialistic "policy of encroachment." The tone of the Prussian cabinet was in harmony with Lamartine's Manifesto and sympathetic to national self-determination, particularly in Italy. The Prussians opposed joining Lombardy or Venetia to Germany.

"I am completely unaware how such a rumor originated," the Prussian foreign minister confessed, "and I do not even recall that annexation was raised in the discussion of the Italian question at Frankfurt." He then dismissed the matter with a few words. German public opinion would oppose such a move. "Germany is strong enough and large enough to have no need for extending its territory, but in a period when nationalities everywhere seek recognition, Germany could not desire an aggrandizement in Italy which, without offering her more strategic advantages, would only be a new source of embarrassment for her."[12]

The Belgian ambassador in Berlin reported Prussia's absolute clarity on the Italian question. The Berlin cabinet insisted that "under no circumstances would it take up Austria's cause in Italy. Prussia has also advised the imperial vicar to terminate the Italian affair."[13]

During early August the Prussian government also disassociated itself from the continuation of the war in Schleswig, the actions of the Frankfurt parliament, and its minister of war, General Eduard von Peucker. Hatzfeldt was instructed on August 4 to tell Bastide:

> The minister of war in Frankfurt announced in the fifty-first meeting of the parliament at Frankfurt that troops would be increased to bring as speedy an end to the war as possible. That announcement being in direct contradiction with the pacific and conciliatory views that we have always professed and that we still profess, it cannot fail to produce a great sensation, and one could easily believe that, General Peucker being a Prussian general, Prussia approved in secret the measures and shared in that manner of opinion, although the government of the king holds to opposed language. To dispel the suspicion of duplicity, I think you ought to declare that since General Peucker has become a minister of the empire . . . we can no longer influence him.[14]

Thus, while Frankfurt appeared unreasonable and bellicose in Schleswig, Posen, and in Italy, Prussia presented itself as peaceful and supportive of the French position on these issues.

During 1848 Bastide carried out a single overt act of diplomatic support for Denmark, the protest of August 20. This brought the first serious conversations of the year on this matter with the Prussian chargé, who had to ask Berlin for instructions. The Prussian foreign minister sent Hatzfeldt three circular dispatches outlining the basic Prussian policy. Bastide informed the Prussian envoy,

Hatzfeldt, that France objected to the entry of German troops in Jutland "as an abuse of power and as an unjustifiable measure." Bastide, however, declined to comment on the matter, claiming weakly that it was something for powers having no direct interest to decide. When Hatzfeldt asked where the note was to be sent, Bastide replied, "to Berlin," then, after a short pause he added, "also to Frankfurt."[15]

On August 5 the Prussian foreign minister responded in a cipher dispatch to Bastide's planned protest, emphasizing the gap between Berlin and Frankfurt's attitudes toward Schleswig and France's interference in the affair:

> The government can only see with pleasure that the French government addresses its protest against the entry of German troops into Jutland to Frankfurt and not to Berlin. It sees it as a means of mitigating the bellicose ardor of the ministry and the national assembly of Frankfurt; and it engages you accordingly to seek to influence the situation in this sense.[16]

The French protest of August 20, 1848, was thus invited by the Prussian cabinet. It was encouraged by Berlin to improve Prussia's diplomatic situation and to quiet the heated Frankfurt assembly. France's action indicated no hostility toward Prussia nor even a great knowledge of the Schleswig question. Bastide continued to refuse detailed discussions with Hatzfeldt—most likely, as Hatzfeldt guessed, because Bastide failed to understand the Schleswig problem in depth.[17]

The results of Prussia's attempt to court France's favor were apparent by August 10. Bastide complained bitterly and candidly to Hatzfeldt of the Frankfurt assembly's Polish policy, contrasting it with Prussia's humanitarian attitude. "Do not worry," he assured Hatzfeldt, "we shall raise no objections to what you did in Posen."[18]

Taken out of context, this comment of August 11 has been widely misunderstood as evidence that Bastide was unconcerned with Poland. In fact, the entire conversation clearly signified the opposite; the Polish border question was one of the major reasons for the abrupt change in the official French attitude toward the Frankfurt assembly.[19] Lawrence C. Jennings has cautiously stated that "the Polish cause was seemingly being sacrificed because of France's overriding concern with the Italian question," but appears unaware of Bastide's decision on August 16 to authorize Arago to proceed with a formal protest in the Posen matter whenever he felt it efficacious.[20] Henryk Batowski concluded that France had increasingly turned into a conservative bourgeois republic, abandoning the revolution and refusing concrete aid to European liberation movements.[21] But these assessments are erroneous. Not only had France not abandoned Poland, but Bastide was in the process of forging that Franco-German alliance which alone, he believed, could save the Poles.

Hatzfeldt meanwhile insisted that Frankfurt was entirely responsible for the continued troubles in Schleswig. He concluded from conversations with Bastide that the French "understood that it is Frankfurt which France ought to influence and pressure to halt the war with Denmark" and its European ramifications.[22]

Bastide proceeded to replace his hostile tone toward Hatzfeldt at the beginning of August with "friendly and personal confidence." Hatzfeldt now speculated that Bastide's "mind was not made up" on the Schleswig matter, nor that he was particularly favorable to Denmark.[23]

By mid-August Bastide denied that his impending protest on Schleswig had any meaning for Prussia. In a mood of extreme intimacy, he insisted that France's move was not caused by "the duty imposed by treaties, but essentially by the conviction that it was time to impose limits on the execution of the Frankfurt assembly's projects." Bastide particularly objected to the assembly's attempts to annul the power of the German princes and its approval of annexations in Limburg, Schleswig, and Poland.[24] His protest was not anti-Prussian or anti-German. He reiterated that he was willing to examine and modify his position on the treaty of 1720, assuring Hatzfeldt that the French actually wanted to help the Germans by making the Danish less obdurate. If France gained a greater voice in Copenhagen, it could lead the Danes on a path of moderation and conciliation which would bring a "friendly arrangement" to the entire matter.[25]

Two articles that appeared at this juncture seem to have reflected accurately the French government's position. The *National*, which favored German unity, was troubled by events in Schleswig. The "general needs of Europe" demanded that Germany proceed by peaceful means. Its policy irritated Scandinavians, who turned to Russia. Germans had no right to interfere in Schleswig, which had never formed part of its territory. The *Moniteur* on August 12 expressed the hope that the German parliament would unite its efforts to those of France to conclude an accord in Schleswig-Holstein:

> *The struggle that has gone on in the duchies for relatively secondary interests ought to be halted.* The German parliament wishes, we do not doubt, that its first act will be an act of conciliation, and it will unite itself to our efforts to conclude an accord already long overdue. *It ought not to forget that the efficacy of its actions depends on its wisdom.* [26]

Historical evaluation of France's role in the Schleswig problem has been of uneven quality. In his *Die Europäische Grossmächte*, Alexander Scharff alleged that "France fought with all means of diplomacy and propaganda the German popular *(Volks)* and unitary ideas, above all the striving of the German national movement"; and "Since July 1848 France attacked Prussia with unfriendly notes in the Schleswig-Holstein question." As proof of "all means," Scharff cited Bastide's conversations with the Danish ambassador, dispatches to his own agents, and the single protest of August 20, which was not in the least directed against Prussia. [27]

Scharff's reproach that France's "clearly taking sides against Germany in Schleswig-Holstein" was evidence of a "dismantling of the 'fraternal union with Germany' "[28] is strained. The French always assumed that "a great majority of the population in Schleswig is Danish and wants to remain Danish," and that the war in Schleswig was ruinous for Germany economically and politically. [29] Börnstein assured Bastide that German public opinion was opposed "very vehemently" to an outbreak of hostilities between Denmark and Germany. [30] Bastide thought that the overwhelming majority in Schleswig and in Germany itself opposed the Schleswig war of the Frankfurt assembly. While the German masses wanted an end to the fighting, a few "loudmouths *(bavards)*" and a handful of fanatics in Frankfurt posed as defenders of Schleswig-Holstein-Mer-Umschlungen, protecting the interests of a feudal prince against a reforming Danish monarch.

For his part, Lawrence Jennings has claimed in "French Diplomacy and the First Schleswig-Holstein Crisis," that France played an important role in Schleswig, without investigating the Germany primary and secondary material on the subject. He is apparently unaware of the conversations Bastide had with Hatzfeldt in August, which take all the sting out of his protest of August 20. Jennings has relied on Bastide's correspondence with his chargés and his conversations with the Danish ambassador in Paris, but has never produced evidence that France played an important role in the actual outcome of the Schleswig question. [31] Friedrich Ley and

Alois Mertes noted that France did not participate in any manner in the armistice of Malmö. In his *Frankreich und die deutsche Revolution*, Ley speculated that France's attitude may have given Denmark some support in the negotiations.[32] Perhaps it would have, if Prussia had been pressured by France to back down. Instead, Bastide became increasingly friendly toward Prussia, which therefore did not need to take France's anger over the Schleswig negotiations seriously.

In his *Frankreichs Stellungnahme*, Mertes adjudged that France was "not of decisive weight." "The matter would have developed exactly as it did if France had withdrawn completely" and played no role at all, he asserts. Neither England nor Russia was interested in French intervention in the north. The French press, whose "propaganda" Scharff claimed was opposed to Germany, Mertes found "non-partisan, not seldom even favorable to Germany." A number of French newspapers were bribed by the Danes, who were busy in Paris, while the Germans did nothing until the end of July, which was too late. The French protest of August 20 was "no proof . . . that France actually had an influence in the negotiations."[33]

Writing in "The Attitude of the French Revolutionary Government Toward German Unification in 1848," Robert J. Hahn thought that Bastide's concern for Schleswig was limited to the possibility that a general war might grow out of this or the Italian situation. Hahn specifically took issue with S. A. Kähler's contention in "Die deutsche Revolution von 1848 und die europäischen Mächte," that France wanted to use the Schleswig situation to strike a blow at German unification.[34] Hahn believed that the primary motivation was the French government's wish to protect a weak, unoffending people against the expansionistic fever current in Germany. Although Hahn charged that France used three devices "to hinder" German unity, its policy in Schleswig was not among these.[35]

In any case, having been assured of the warm sympathy of Prussia and the German masses, Bastide reversed his original decision and withdrew his objection to having Arago deliver a renewed protest against the division of Posen and Frankfurt assembly's vote of July 26. Arago's generous explanation of the Prussian cabinet and assembly's disposition in the Posen question induced Bastide to authorize Arago to present the Prussian government with a note conforming to his dispatch of June 9. He left it to Arago's discretion to edit it "in the spirit and along the lines that you indicated."[36]

Bastide and Cavaignac's brief circumspection on the Polish

matter had come to an end. The object of France's primary concern remained an intimate relationship with Germany, which alone could bring the reconstruction of Poland. France's Trojan horse in central Europe was no longer the Frankfurt parliament but the Berlin assembly. Bastide's attitude toward Prussia had changed from hostility to cordiality.

Bastide's new-found preference for the Berlin over the Frankfurt parliament is not as absurd as it may appear at first glance. The Prussian national assembly that met in Berlin was far more liberal and representative than the better known Frankfurt assembly. Friedrich Meinecke stressed in *Cosmopolitanism and the National State* that Berlin and not Frankfurt was the "hope and the battleground of the democrats" during the latter part of 1848. And Bastide shared the contemporary assumption that the left would come to power momentarily in Berlin. He could not foresee that in 1849, William IV would triumph against the Berlin assembly.[37] It was thus from Berlin that the French expected assistance in solving the problems of central Europe.

WHEREAS SCHLESWIG WAS HARDLY EVEN a secondary interest for France, Italy was vital. During early August, the French received frequent warnings that the Frankfurt assembly was determined to reassert Austria's power over the peninsula. The new French ambassador in London, Gustave de Beaumont, cautioned that the Frankfurt parliament "unanimously" wanted to accord Austria the line of the Adige.[38] The Bavarian king was doubtful that he could withstand the strong impulse coming from Frankfurt that was forcing Bavaria to side with Austria in a war against France.[39]

In early August Cavaignac sent his friend Anselme Petetin on a special mission to Germany to learn two things. First, what was the real importance and the "probable future of that thought of German unity which at the moment characterized the Frankfurt assembly, presided over by Archduke John of Austria." Second, "what would Germany do if France went to the aid of Charles Albert in Italy." Petetin answered that German unity was absolutely inevitable and nothing France could do would prevent it. The Italian question brought together most Germans in sympathy for Austria, but their intervention was not certain.[40]

In his University of Freiburg dissertation on the left in the Frankfurt assembly, Hans Roth observed a transformation of the

Frankfurt assembly after the Polish debate in late July:

> A strong national striving for power and a conviction that
> Germany had a direction mission was expressed. As a result,
> a critical and finally hostile judgment was directed no longer
> against the "barbarian" states of the east, against the dynasties,
> rather also . . . against even England and France, the originally
> "allied" peoples.[41]

The Frankfurt assembly considered a new and alarming resolution on August 12, that the "central power in Germany should
protect the interests of the confederation in the Austro-Sardinian
war question."[42] Although the Prussian cabinet could not contemplate the possibility of intervention for Austria in Italy, the
Frankfurt assembly discussed precisely this eventuality. The debate
on the resolution demonstrated the practical political gulf between
the Berlin and Frankfurt assemblies.

The voice of reason was sounded by Dozent Karl Nauwerck
of Berlin, who opposed the bill in Frankfurt. He reviewed the
history of German insults to Italy, of earlier military expeditions
by German emperors which had impeded the growth of Italian
unity, calling this story a "thousand years of German injustice" to
Italians. The rule of the house of Habsburg had never been popular
in Italy, depending for its maintenance on what he ironically referred to as "violent conciliation." He affirmed the sympathy of the
Frankfurt left for the principle of national self-determination for
all peoples, asking the assembly to leave Italy alone, pleading for
the body to be consistent in its nationalistic outlook. The Italian
nation had the same rights as the German. "Every people must be
free and independent." All nations must win their freedom together
for the common goal of humanity to be advanced. He was the
moral and humane spokesman of Herder and Mazzini's views.
Nauwerck proclaimed to the body:

> I shall not go back into the Middle Ages to remind you what
> a misfortune the Germans themselves have brought back from
> Italy. You know the saying that "Italy is the graveyard of the
> Germans." Have we any interest in supporting Austria's
> tyranny in northern Italy? Austria has been the evil spirit in
> Italy.[43]

This impressive display of academic knowledge, typical of the
"revolution of intellectuals," was answered in a defense of historical
writing by his famous colleague, Friedrich von Raumer. Raumer,

who was later sent to Paris as a special envoy, defended the traditional civilizing mission of the Germans in Italy, and compared the alien rule over parts of Italy by Austria with the foreign royal houses in England, Sweden, Naples, and Spain. The English had rarely complained that their rulers were originally from Hanover, nor did the Swedes seem overly concerned that the House of Bernadotte came from France. Austria's domination had given northern Italians as good a "foreign" government as Sweden, England, Naples, and Spain, he conjectured.

"Alone, gentlemen, I have traveled throughout Italy," asserted Raumer, "where I observed the condition of the people," and how they were administered. He concluded that the "Austrian government seemed to be the best in all of Italy." If that regime had not pleased all shades of opinion, it was natural; this was a result of the conflict of nationalities. "As the Poles in Posen have a better administration under the Prussians than they ever had under Polish domination," the Austrian Empire had brought honest and efficient government to their provinces that was rare in Italy. Raumer denied the possibility of making a "present of freedom" to any country. "You can give a people its freedom as easily as you could give a man courage and a woman her chastity." He suggested that the Italians were not advanced enough yet for self-government. A few years later he clearly demurred at the "ability" of Italians to achieve political unity in his book, *Zur Politik des Tages.*[44]

Günther Kunde in his doctoral dissertation on the Italian question and the situation in Germany, defended Raumer's speech because of his realistic approach and his understanding of the importance to united Germany of protecting itself against a French attack from the south by dominating the passes of the Alps. Kunde praised him because "Raumer was far from sacrificing old lands of the *Reich* because of some doctrine" of unrealistic dreamers. While Germany was asked to cut off "with foolish magnanimity large stretches of land, no one gave Germany similar generosity." Raumer grasped the problem that united Germany would later face when "he stressed the importance of the strategic moment."[45]

The West German historian Theodor Schieder concluded that the bourgeois liberal nationalists, whom Bastide expected to aid France in expelling Austria from Italy, were persuaded in the Italian debate by strategic considerations. They put the needs of military frontiers above the principle of nationalism. General Joseph Maria von Radowitz maintained that the "hegemony" of France in northern Italy had to be resisted for the "safety of the German Confederation." His speech was greeted by "stormy applause from the right and center" of the Frankfurt parliament.[46]

The resolution of August 12, 1848, was passed by a large majority. Theodor Schieder contended that no clear decision opposing Italian freedom, *per se*, was taken, rather the left was sympathetic to the argument of defense; the conservative Roman Catholic-universalist party favored Austrian—or more a *Reich's*—traditionalism. Savoye, reporting to Bastide, concluded that the parliament was simply "very reactionary," and was using "all of its efforts to drag Germany into a war against republican France."[47]

Börnstein assured Bastide that the German parliament once again was proving "faithful to its mission of confusing the simplest questions, like those of Schleswig and Limburg."[48]

During the same session of August 12, the Frankfurt parliament considered the petition of the deputies from the Italian districts of southern Tyrol, who appealed in the name of their constituents that they *not* be part of Germany (although remaining united with Austria), and that their political and administrative organization be separate from that of German Tyrol. The German parliament rejected their request.[49] The wishes of the population of southern Tyrol were sacrificed to the ideal of the German nation. As Savoye had predicted a month earlier, because of its composition, the Frankfurt parliament could never represent the "true" aspirations of the German people.

Defense of Austria's claims across the Alps appeared even more vehemently in Frankfurt than in Vienna itself. De la Cour wrote to Bastide that a "powerful opinion" existed in the Austrian capital that numerous interests militated against all consideration of the complete re-establishment of the old Austrian order in Italy. The bourgeoisie in particular favored peace because of the enormous costs of the war.[50] Bastide answered that he realized that the party of progress was not France's enemy in the Italian question, even though he knew that ambition and Radetzky's success had excited some quarters in Vienna.[51]

By the first week in August, Bastide concluded that German unity was inevitable. The most that France could do was to try to shape it to conform with her interests and to negotiate a liberal treaty of commerce with united Germany. Discussion on a commercial treaty had begun towards the end of 1847, and Bastide had recently received a memorandum showing the possibilities and the advantages of the treaty from the French ministry of commerce. Bastide's lengthy dispatch to Savoye of August 5 examined the economic consequences of Germany's unity for France. Bastide, a man of the people and a Christian socialist, tended to think in economic terms, but these economic motivations of his German policy have hitherto escaped the attention of historians.

Bastide stressed the importance of Franco-German commerce, which was rapidly growing, as was apparent in the value of French trade with the *Zollverein*, Hanover, and Austria:

1841	149,500,000 francs
1845	171,000,000 francs
1846	168,500,000 francs (a depression year)[52]

Foundation of the customs union in Germany had led to an industrial boom, with benefits for France. Improved economic power and the need for increased outlets for trade resulted in German attempts to negotiate commercial treaties with various foreign powers. Egress to the coast had been an object of the *Zollverein's* navigational and commercial treaty with Belgium concluded September 1, 1844. Later there were negotiations with the United States and Brazil for the entry of German goods into those countries at reduced rates.[53] The north German states outside the *Zollverein* and the Baltic provinces of Prussia adamantly opposed any common system of "differential duties." The seaports of Bremen and Hamburg would have been seriously affected by American and British retaliation. Their wealth depended on shipping and commerce; higher German customs would have meant fewer imported British and American goods. The debate between proponents of differential duties and free trade became so acrimonious that the *Zollvereinblatt* expressed a wish that the port of Hamburg be silted over! Discussion in Germany before 1848 was far from a consensus on the future of economic unification.

Although Bastide anticipated the triumph of political unity in Germany, he did not assume that this would necessarily lead to a predictable economic policy. Victory in the debate between high and low tariffs would now depend on which states were included in the new order. The *Zollverein* owed its past success to an adherence to free trade. The inclusion of new states from southern Germany would upset the old balance of economic forces that had controlled the *Zollverein*. Bastide, who like so many idealists sobered suddenly at the mention of money, cautioned that the argument on economic policy would continue: "Interests do not in the least change for political sentiments, and one can predict that the struggle will be renewed with ardor when they proceed to organize the economic system of the great German union."[54] He exhorted his agents to carefully monitor the discussion of protection and free trade in Germany. "Above all," cautioned Bastide, "it is with respect to industry that the growth of productive forces in Germany demands our attention." The direction of a united Germany's industrial development was critical to French business interests.[55]

The contrast between the mercantile character of the Prussian-dominated *Zollverein* and Austria explained Bastide's attitude. A *kleindeutsch* policy, i.e., one excluding Austria from the economic as well as the political borders of the new German *Reich*, was preferable as far as French capitalists and merchants were concerned. Austrian control of the German economy would inevitably bring high tariffs against French merchandise.

The economic arrangement of the "vast Austrian Empire" caused profound anxiety in French quarters. Austria's protective policy had created a condition of virtual autarchy. Bastide noted that Bohemia, Moravia, Styria, the Archduchy of Austria, and Carinthia furnished manufactured finished goods for the rest of the empire without much outside competition. The high protective tariffs assured these Austrian businessmen—who were principally Germans—an outlet among the agricultural population of Polish Galicia, Hungary, and the rich northern Italian states of Lombardy and Venetia.

Bastide noted with dismay that the industrial areas in Austria were also within the borders of the German Confederation, and these could upset the old balance between industrial production and consumption that had existed in the *Zollverein*. The new German *Reich*, if it included Austria's German-speaking population, would have a surplus of industrial goods, whereas the *Zollverein* members, lacking this manufacturing capacity traditionally had been important consumers of French manufactured products. Bastide cautioned:

> Their [Austria's] accession to the *Zollverein* would greatly increase the element of production in the body, which would necessarily react on the commercial policy of the association. To assure an outlet for goods, they will naturally reserve more and more of the national market for German manufacturers by raising tariffs.[56]

Not only would France be cut out of German markets but it would also lose out on new markets Bastide anticipated in the provinces that were in revolt against Austrian domination. He expected the Hungarian revolution to end the German-Austrian industrialists' monopoly. Then France would be able to compete successfully in the Hungarian market. The revolts in Austria's Italian provinces of Lombardy and Venetia were equally important, since these constituted major markets for French goods, as well as serving as sources for vital raw materials for France's silk industry, one of the most important export industries.

Bastide further cautioned, "It is feared that German products will even be given a privileged position in Hungary and Italy,"[57] if Austria were absorbed into the new united Germany. This development disturbed Bastide as much as the prospect of Austria's revolutionizing the trade policy of the *Zollverein*, and led him to warn, "These measures would be particularly unfavorable to us."[58]

Equally detrimental for France would be Austria's influence on the navigational policy of the unified German state. The current figures were highly favorable to France:[59]

Total ships leaving France for		*Number under French flag*
Zollverein	213	12
Mecklenburg	37	1
Hanover	9	0
Schleswig-Holstein	7	1
	266	14

Total ships leaving France from		
Zollverein	336	15
Mecklenburg	18	1
Hanover	3	0
Schleswig-Holstein	8	0
	365	16

For Austria, Bastide had only the number entering and leaving Trieste, with 71 Austrian and 7 French ships coming from Trieste into French ports. Leaving French ports for Trieste were 148 ships, of which 9 were French. Among the Hanseatic cities, only Hamburg had a significant trade with France, but with a very different pattern for the French merchant navy. There were 141 ships leaving France for Hamburg, of which 73 were French and 4 from Hamburg; ships leaving Hamburg for France included 71 French and 7 from Hamburg. The reason for the disparity was that the Hanseatic cities were the only states in Germany where the French ships were treated as equals, suffering no special disadvantages. In their own ports the French ships profited from special legislation. Under a German navigation act which placed the Hanseatic ports under the same law as applied for Austria and the *Zollverein*, the 160 French ships that carried the French flag to the Hanseatic ports would be gravely endangered. A uniform code of navigation in a unified Germany would, in effect, act as a surtax on French shipping.[60]

In view of this disturbing possibility, the French diplomatic agents were counseled, not to "lose sight of any of our essential interests, and in the presence of attacks menacing them, it is a duty of the legation to redouble its watchfulness and the activity of its informants."[61]

Clearly it was vital for France's merchant navy to prevent Austrian domination of a united Germany. French shipping interests had much more to hope from Prussia, where the cabinet was known to oppose naval subsidies. Moreover, the Hanseatic cities would have a far greater relative importance and bargaining position in a smaller Germany that did not include Austria than in a larger one that did.[62]

While the needs of commerce undoubtedly exerted an effect on French policy, it is impossible to say to what degree. However, the fact that trade was a direct and personal concern of Bastide must have had some influence. In mid-August, disturbed by a *Zollverein* surtax which had offset the French export subsidy on manufactured articles, Bastide instructed Arago to proceed with discussions of a commercial treaty. The Prussian government exploited French interest in such a treaty to reinforce its own political position.

On August 14 Arago reported that the Prussian minister of commerce and former president of the assembly in Berlin had told him "that he would be disposed to conclude a great commercial treaty [embracing] all the objects of French and German factories, a treaty which, according to him, would be equally favorable to the industry of both countries."[63] But on the same occasion they also talked about Italy. The minister said that he hoped the Franco-English mediation would succeed, and he added explicitly that "Prussia would be pleased to cooperate in it."[64]

Thus Prussia asked to be brought actively into the mediation between Vienna and Turin while making overtures for a commercial

Charles Ludwig Bernays, French Secret Agent and Secretary to Legation in Vienna, photograph, Missouri Historical Society.

treaty, which, in effect, would have given France the advantages of membership in the *Zollverein*. Nevertheless, Arago cautioned against seeing economics as the sole factor governing Prussian politics:

> The legation of the republic has not . . . ignored all that could interest our commercial relations with Germany and particularly with Prussia. You know . . . that in the state of fermentation and travail which operates in Germany and the grave circumstances in Prussia, political interests dominate commercial questions.[65]

In summary, the economic composition of a united German state was a major concern of the French government. France's maritime, commercial, and industrial interests were all affected by any change in Germany. The French generally welcomed a Prussian victory over Austria in central Europe. Prussia reinforced this French sympathy be dangling the carrot of a possible trade treaty before France. Such a treaty would continue the traditional tendency of the *Zollverein* to grant the French generous terms of trade. The French now hoped that the inclusion of the old Hanseatic cities on the German coast in the new state would influence a common maritime policy that could extend the penetration of French ships into German ports. In contrast, matters would undoubtedly be far worse for the French if protectionist Austria dominated a common commercial regime. This would more likely exclude French goods because Austria, in direct contrast to Prussia, had little trade with France. Perhaps the most interesting point in Bastide's memorandum is a surprisingly contradictory assumption that somehow French manufacturers—who had hitherto carried on little exchange of goods with Austria—might under certain circumstances gain a place in this closed market of the old Danubian monarchy. Such an eventuality could only transpire if successful revolts in Budapest and in Italy reinforced the political and commercial consequences of a Prussian hegemony over Germany. Once more, the French turned their attention toward Budapest, where the fate of the European revolution hung in the balance. If the Magyars defeated the Habsburgs in Budapest, then a victory was possible in northern Italy and in Germany.

Meanwhile in Hungary the situation was critical for the French. The French sent an agent in Budapest to look over the situation first hand. The second mission of Carl Ludwig Bernays to Budapest led, once again, to a sudden flare-up of activity by the radicals and renewed threats to overthrow the Hungarian cabinet.[66] Upon his return to Vienna, Bernays sent another agent, Charles Didier, to inform Bastide of such matters that "one cannot put in writing." Bernays deeply regretted that the foreign minister had not allowed him to turn the Batthyány cabinet out in May. "If we had sent someone two months ago with more extensive powers, Hungary might have escaped the fate of Poland and Italy." Within a week he expected either a "revolution or an armed revolt of the peasants stirred up by Kossuth."[67]

On the exact date Bernays had predicted a week previously— on August 15—the Society for Equality began to "contemplate the overthrow of legitimate authority."

And apparently while Bernays was in Budapest, Kossuth abruptly shifted positions to oppose the cabinet's original bill and to side openly with France's policy of seeking free and constitutional institutions for Italy.[68] Again, Kossuth's change came precisely when the French believed armed conflict with Austria to be imminent.

On August 26–28, 1848, the French prepared their diplomatic corps in the Italian states for war against Austria.[69] At the same time, an extraordinary session of the Society for Equality in Budapest set September 8 as the date for a banquet which would signal the "Second Revolution" in Budapest. But this violence became unnecessary because the Batthyány government was already secretly drifting toward a military alliance with France.

On August 4, 1848—with Bernays already in Budapest—the Hungarian government had discussed sending Szalay to Paris.[70] The Magyar historian Hajnal writes that Batthyány inquired about opening diplomatic relations between Hungary and France sometime during the first half of August. Most likely, this was the message that Charles Didier took directly to Paris and that Bernays "dared" not mention in his written dispatch to the French government.[71] By August 21 Bastide believed that France needed to send an emissary to Hungary to reconcile the dangerous tension between the Magyars and the other nationalities in Hungary. The region appeared on the eve of civil war.[72]

And on August 25—while the French were preparing for a war against the Habsburgs and while the Hungarian radicals were calling for the overthrow of the Batthyány cabinet—the Hungarian Ministerial Council approved a diplomatic mission to France, because it had learned the day before that the French would give the envoy formal recognition.[73] For since August 18 Batthyány had been preparing Hungary for an armed struggle. "We have at the most three weeks," Batthyány wrote Szalay, and on August 19

Batthyány urged the Danubian Shipping Company not to delay unloading arms.[74]

France's new relationship with Hungary was a sign of the times. The increasing likelihood of a Franco-Austrian war made military alliances and the undermining of Austria's army a paramount interest. Bastide likewise saw German matters within this context. The French assembly's resolution of May 24 had anticipated an ideological alliance with the Frankfurt parliament, which would join in liberating Poles and Italians from their "oppressors." Some three months later this assumption of a union of free peoples flew in the face of actuality; the German assembly seemed bent on encroaching on the territory of the Danes and Poles. Instead of siding with the "oppressed" peoples, a number of delegates to the Frankfurt assembly appeared to be more sympathetic to their oppressors. Even worse, leaders of the German parliament came down on the Austrian side against the Italians, and hence might fight with Austria against France and the Italian peoples.

Under these circumstances, Bastide's new objective was to counter the "encroachments" of the Frankfurt assembly on Germany's neighbors. But Bastide made a clear distinction between the assembly and the "democratic party" in Frankfurt which recognized the legitimacy of the aspiration of other peoples for their freedom. Thus Bastide's protests concerning Schleswig and Poland were made to hearten the Danes and Poles and at the same time to encourage those Germans sympathetic to the cause of liberation of all mankind from tyranny. The historical wisdom that Bastide used Prussia to "decentralize" Germany must be examined in greater detail. The French did have a tradition of client states among the German princedoms, but it remains to be seen whether Bastide actually carried through on his threat to invoke the "policy of Richelieu," that is, an effort to divide and rule by the encouragement of small, weak neighbors by thwarting German efforts to unify themselves into a single state. What we can say with certainty is that Bastide had grave reservations concerning the Frankfurt parliament's expansion of German claims over peoples on its frontiers.

A word of caution is in order. Historians charging that Bastide acted as a "decentralizing agent" fail to explain Bastide's memorandum of August 5. That extremely significant document contained two important depositions. First, Bastide clearly realized the economic advantages of a united Germany for France, as long as Prussia dominated that state and excluded Austria. Secondly, Bastide assumed that Germans would inevitably overcome all obstacles to their unity. Thus he appears to have believed that France had a minimal influence on that future combination. Although Bastide had increasingly strong misgivings concerning the Frankfurt assembly, his preoccupation with liberating Italy and Poland necessitated having a German ally. The peoples of central Europe could break out of Habsburg domination only with external assistance. Bastide did briefly consider encouraging Prussian particularism to return to the old Richelieuist strategy of using German princes as clients because of their common enmity to the Habsburgs, but he abandoned that strategy after strong dissent from his chargé in Berlin, Arago. Bastide, at his urging, persevered with a revolutionary Girondist tactic, even while combining this with a close working relationship with the Prussian government. His synthesis of the revolutionary and traditional methods brought together (he thought) the powerful coalition of the Prussian Junkers and the new forces unleashed by the March revolutions in the German states, whose democratic nature was strongest in the Prussian assembly.

But the revolutionary nature of Bastide's machinations was clearest in the lower Danube. His secret agent Bernays was deeply involved in the politics of the democrats in Budapest. And once more Bastide followed Lamartine's lead in attempting to divert Austria to the east. Bastide offered Vienna territorial compensations on the lower Danube if she would cooperate with his schemes to free the Poles and Italians. This so-called Danubian confederation was Czartoryski's pet project.

NOTES

1. Schweizer to Dusch, Paris, August 2, 1848, BGLA, 48/2037 and *Le National*, August 2, 1848.

2. Bastide to Arago, Paris, August 1, 1848, AEF, Prusse 302, fo. 188.

3. Arago to Bastide, Berlin, July 22, 1848, AEF, Prusse 302, fo. 165.

4. *Ibid.* Taylor was confused by Bastide's answer to Arago's specific request for public protest after the Frankfurt assembly's Polish debate. Instead of indicating his policy since May, all Bastide actually meant was that, after the harm had been done in Frankfurt, the public protest of France would not help matters; *cf.*, Taylor, *Struggle*, p. 15.

5. Bastide to Arago, Paris, August 1, 1848, AEF, Prusse 302, fo. 188; Bastide was following Arago's own advice; France should avoid conflicts with Germany and wait on events, since German democrats were eager for an alliance with France to free Poland. Arago to Bastide, Berlin, July 20, 1848, *Ibid.*, fo. 160–61; Bastide to Arago, Paris, July 31, 1848, fo. 187.

6. Diplomatic courier of July 30, 1848, annotating Savoye's dispatch of July 27 from Frankfurt. Cav 1 Mi 2 R 26.

7. Arago to Bastide, Berlin, August 1, 1848, Prusse 302, fo. 189.

8. Diplomatic courier of August 4, 1848, Cav 1 Mi 2 R 26; Bastide considerably strengthened Arago's hopes for Posen: "The question of Posen continues on a good course." Cavaignac questioned in the margin, "What note?"

9. Arago to Bastide, Berlin, August 2, 1848, AEF, Prusse 302, fo. 192.

10. *Ibid.*, August 4, 1848, fo. 194.

11. *Ibid.*, August 6, 1848, fo. 196–98; diplomatic courier of August 9, 1848, Cav 1 Mi 2 R 26.

12. Foreign Minister to Hatzfeldt, Berlin, August 2, 1848, GSA, fz. 861, fo. 95; Hatzfeldt to Foreign Minister, Paris, August 7, 1848, GSA, fz. 861, fo. 120; Arago to Bastide, Berlin, September 3, 1848, AEF, Prusse 302, fo. 238.

13. Nothomb to Hoffschmidt, Berlin, August 7, 1848, AEB, Prusse, fo. 72.

14. Foreign Minister to Hatzfeldt, Berlin, August 4, 1848, GSA, fz. 861, fo. 101–02; similarly *ibid.*, August 5 and 8, 1848, fo. 105 and 113–14, emphasizing the Prussian desire to end the affair in Schleswig peacefully, "in pressing with vigor the negotiations for the conclusion of an armistice."

15. Hatzfeldt to Foreign Minister, August 1 and 2, 1848, GSA, fz. 856, fo. 230 and 239.

16. Foreign Minister to Hatzfeldt, Berlin, August 5, 1848, GSA, fz. 861, fo. 105.

17. Hatzfeldt to Foreign Minister, Paris, August 10 and 12, 1848, GSA, fz. 861, fo. 130, 135–36 and fz. 857, fo. 1.

18. Hatzfeldt to Foreign Minister, Paris, August 12, 1848, GSA, fz. 861, fo. 137.

19. Pfisterer, p. 74, Ley, p. 85, Mertes, p. 53.

20. Jennings, *France and Europe*, p. 134.

21. Henryk Batowski, *Legion Mickiewicza w Kampanni Wlosko-Aus-triackiej 1848 roku* (Warsaw, 1956), chapter IV.

22. Hatzfeldt to Foreign Minister, Paris, August 10, 1848, GSA, fz. 861, fo. 130; Arago to Bastide, Berlin, August 21, 1848, AEF, Prusse 302, fo. 219.

23. Hatzfeldt to Foreign Minister, Paris, August 12, 1848, GSA, fz. 861, fo. 135–36.

24. *Ibid.*

25. Hatzfeldt to Foreign Minister, Paris, August 17, 1848, GSA, fz. 861, fo. 148 and fz. 857, fo. 9.

26. *Le National*, August 9, 1848; *Moniteur*, August 12, 1848; also quoted by Hatzfeldt to Foreign Minister, Paris, August 12, 1848, GSA, fz. 857, fo. 3; emphasis made in Berlin.

27. Scharff, *Die europäische Grossmächte*, pp. 43–46.

28. "Schleswig-Holsteins Erhebung," p. 181. Scharff's misconception that a change of direction hostile to German unity came in May, 1848 is a result of his general confusion of the Schleswig-Holstein question with the German question.

29. Bernard des Essarts (Consul) to Bastide, Hamburg, September 8, 1848, Cav 1 Mi 2 R 25; the Consul in Mayence, August 12, 1848, assured that south Germans wanted peace; De la Cour, Vienna, July 26 and August 3, 1848 affirmed that public opinion in Austria "opposed invariably the Teutonist projects" of the Frankfurt assembly; Savoye agreed that in Frankfurt itself there was a general desire to end the war, Frankfurt, August 4, 1848, Cav 1 Mi 2 R 26; Anselme Petetin was surprised at the harm that the war was causing in northern Germany, where the Danish blockade was ruining commerce and causing "extreme suffering," Petetin to Cavaignac, Hamburg, August 24, 1848, Cav 1 Mi 2 R 25.

30. Bulletin, August 5, 1848, AEF, MD, Allemagne 129, fo. 73.

31. Jennings, *France and Europe*, and "French diplomacy and the first Schleswig-Holstein crisis," *French Historical Studies*, VII (1971), 204–25.

32. Ley, "Frankreich und die deutsche Revolution," p. 118.

33. Mertes, "Frankreichs Stellungnahme," pp. 58–80.

34. S. A. Kaehler, "Die deutsche Revolution von 1848 und die europäischen Mächte," in *Vorurteile und Tatsachen* (Hamlin, 1949).

35. Hahn, "Attitude of the French," pp. 150, 179, 266–68.

36. Bastide to Arago, Paris, August 16, 1848, AEF, Prusse 302, fo. 213.

37. Friedrich Meinecke, *Cosmopolitanism and the National State* (Princeton, 1970), pp. 266–67 and Theodore Hamerow, *Restoration, Revolution, Reaction* (Princeton, 1958).

38. Beaumont to Bastide, London, August 9, 1848, No. 1, Cav 1 Mi 2 R 26.

39. Klein to Bastide, Munich, August 4, 1848, Bavière 224, fo. 409–10.

40. Anselme Petetin, *L'Allemagne et l'Italie en 1848: dépêche adressée au Général Cavaignac* (Evian, 1871), Petetin to Cavaignac, Berlin, August 17, 1848 and Hanover, August 31, 1848, Cav 1 Mi 2 R 25; Niles to Buchanan, Turin, August 2, 1848, *L'Unificazione italiana vista dai diplomatici Statunitensi*, Howard R. Marraro ed. (Rome, 1964), II, 37; De Briey to Hoffschmidt, Frankfurt, August 7, 1848, AEB, Frankfurt IV, 148; Lefebvre to Bastide, Baden-Baden, August 15, 1848, AEF, Bade 34, fo. 198.

41. Roth, p. 43.

42. *Stenographischer Bericht*, II, 1568.

43. *Ibid.*, II, 1564.

44. *Ibid.*, II, 1567; Schieder, "Italienbild," pp. 148 and 151.

45. Günther Kunde, "Die deutsche Revolution von 1848 und die italienische Frage," excerpt of unpublished dissertation, (Saalfeld, privately published, 1938), p. 9.

46. *Stenographischer Bericht*, II, 1566–67; Schieder, "Italienbild," pp. 148–50.

47. Schieder, "Italienbild," p. 148; Savoye to Bastide, Frankfurt, August 12, 1848, Cav 1 Mi 2 R 26.

48. Börnstein, Bulletin, August 16, 1848, AEF, MD, Allemagne 129, fo. 88.

49. *Ibid*; Friedrich Raumer was among those opposing autonomy for Italian Tyrol, *Moniteur,* August 18, 1848, p. 2054.

50. De la Cour to Bastide, Vienna, August 11, 1848, AEF, Autriche 436, fo. 74.

51. Bastide to De la Cour, Paris, August 27, 1848, AEF, Autriche 436, fo. 119.

52. On the background of the memorandum see Petetin to Cavaignac, Berlin, August 17 and 24, 1848, Cav 1 Mi 2 R 26; Bastide to Savoye, Paris, August 5, 1848, AEF, cc. Frankfurt III, fo. 213; rough draft, July 1848, fo. 199ff.

53. *Ibid.*, fo. 217–219. Attempts to increase foreign commerce by diplomacy had caused a heated discussion in Germany between the proponents of free trade and the adherents of a system of variable duties. The goal of the latter was to gain most favored nation concessions for

German goods. Manufacturing states in Germany hoped to aid their industry and commerce by the threat of raising common German tariffs; this would have meant an end to the relatively low duties in the *Zollverein*, and Germany's important trading partners might retaliate, perhaps bringing on tariff wars; Heinrich Best, *Interessenpolitik und nationale Integration 1848/49: Handelspolitische Konflikte im frühindustriellen Deutschland*, "Kritische Studien zur Geschichtswissenschaft, Band 37" (Göttingen, 1980).

54. *Ibid.*, fo. 221–25; the language of the memorandum reflects Bastide's deterministic thinking; the analysis appeared to him absolutely necessary: "the inductions" were "fatally brought about." fo. 231–32.

55. *Ibid.*, fo. 227.

56. *Ibid.*, fo. 228–29.

57. *Ibid.*, fo. 229.

58. *Ibid.* Lombardy's economy rested on a "stream of silk" which was converted to a "stream of gold" during the first half of the nineteenth century, when the production of silk increased from 1,860,000 pounds (Milanese pounds of about 12 ounces) in 1800 to 4,710,000 pounds in 1841. The Milan Chamber of Commerce in 1848 reported that the silk crop had tripled since 1827. The market for raw Lombardy silk had also shifted during this period from London to Lyon. While Austria allowed crude silk to be sent freely to France, Piedmont prohibited export, so that the misgivings about Charles Albert could possibly have had some economic basis. If Sardinia absorbed Lombardy, its prohibition on vital crude silk exports might also be extended to Lombardy. The adhesion of Austria with Lombardy-Venetia to the new Germany would perhaps have removed a supply of vital raw materials, and, at the same time, decreased a large market for finished products. German imports of finished French silk amounted to a quarter of the total French exports to *Zollverein*. These silk imports were two and a half times as important as the next item, woolen cloth. If Venetia, Lombardy, as well as Hungary became independent with their own commercial legislation, there would have been a very large potential commercial market created for France, as French consuls there often pointed out; Sardinia itself was the third most important French trading partner in 1848; Kent R. Greenfield, *Economics and Liberalism in the Risorgimento: A Study of Nationalism in Lombardy, 1814–1848*, 2d. ed., (Baltimore, 1965), pp. 38–40; Rudiger Renzing, "Die Handelsbeziehungen zwischen Frankreich und Deutschland von der Gründung des Zollvereins bis zur Reichsgründung," (doc. diss., Frankfurt/M., 1959), pp. 161ff.

59. Bastide to Savoye, Paris, August 5, 1848, AEF, cc, Frankfurt III, 230–31.

60. *Ibid.*

61. *Ibid.*

62. *Ibid.*

63. Arago to Bastide, Berlin, August 14, 1848, AEF, cc, Berlin IX, fo. 117; Bastide to Arago, Paris, August 31, 1848, fo. 119–20; September 30, 1848, fo. 124; December 9, 1848, fo. 138–39; Renzing, p. 42.

64. Arago to Bastide, Berlin, August 14, 1848, AEF, Prusse 302, fo. 211.

65. Arago to Bastide, Berlin, October 4, 1848, AEF, cc, Berlin IX, fo. 127. The French thought that the German actions were economically motivated. During the most important crisis of the Frankfurt assembly, the September debate on the armistice of Malmö, Tallenay charged that the south Germans voted to continue the war because it was good for business, while the north Germans were for peace because war was damaging their commerce. Tallenay to Bastide, Frankfurt, September 14, 1848, AEF, Allemagne 806, fo. 23.

66. Deme, "Nationalism and Cosmopolitanism," pp. 42–44; "The Society for Equality in the Hungarian Revolution of 1848," Slavic Review, XXI (1972), pp. 73–77; Deak, pp. 145–57.

67. Bernays to Hetzel, Vienna, August 8, 1848, published in Chastain, "Iratok," document 3, pp. 291–92.

68. Deme, "Society for Equality," p. 77.

69. Jennings, France and Europe, pp. 171–90; Bastide to Harcourt (Rome), to Denois (Milan), to Favre (Genoa), to Boislecomte, Paris, August 25, 27, and 29, 1848, Cav 1 Mi 2 R 25.

70. Hajnal, p. 110.

71. Ibid.

72. Ibid.

73. Ibid.

74. Ibid., pp. 111–12 and 62.

Chapter Seven
The Danubian Confederation
AUGUST-SEPTEMBER 1848

*D*URING AUGUST AND EARLY SEPTEMBER, Bastide explicitly turned his back on the democratic alliance with the Frankfurt assembly, reverting to a close cooperation with the Prussian government. The German parliament had lost its elevated position as France's preferred collaborator in overthrowing the crowned heads of Europe because it sympathized with the Habsburgs, thereby joining forces with France's principal enemy. This treason to the cause of liberating peoples made matters increasingly serious for the French. A showdown on the battlefield with Austria seemed imminent since Radetzky's victory over the forces of King Charles Albert of Sardinia during late July had emboldened reactionaries throughout Europe. Thus, Bastide felt that the Germans had betrayed the French at a juncture when war might break out momentarily. But the Frankfurt assembly did not limit its treachery to Italy alone; the Germans disputed every border, quarrelling with the Poles and fighting with tiny Denmark.

The Frankfurt assembly, from a French perspective, was an irresponsible source of mischief. On September 5 the German constituent assembly rashly "rejected" the painfully negotiated armistice between Prussia and Denmark signed at Malmö. Within a fortnight, however, the parliament reconsidered its move and reversed this decision. Nevertheless the passions of Frankfurt's citizens had been dangerously aroused by the rhetoric of the debate, and a popular uprising on September 18 led to the brutal murder of two deputies who were closely associated with the forces of order. It took the entry of Austrian and Prussian troops to restore peace.

In contrast, the attitude of the Prussian elected assembly appeared to correspond more closely to France's hopes and wishes as democratic agitation in Berlin increased. The increasingly leftward drift of the Prussian revolution delighted the French at the very time that they began to fear that the Frankfurt assembly would have to be written off as pro-Habsburg.

News from Hungary was critical. On September 11, the Croat Ban Jellačić invaded Hungary, imperilling Magyar separatism. The possibility now loomed that national fervor in Budapest might undo the effect of Radetzky's military victory in northern Italy, and might draw troops away from Italy to fight under the Croat and Magyar banners. Such a development would greatly diminish the size of the Habsburg's armed forces in Italy and thus the direct danger that France would be forced to fight.

A further note of encouragement for the French was the promulgation of a new constitution in Switzerland on September 12, strengthening the neutral government. This lessened the possibility that the powers could use "disorder" as an excuse to occupy Switzerland.

Meanwhile, the formation of a Committee of National Defense in Budapest silenced radical talk of a "Second Revolution." The radicals' darling, Lajos Kossuth, organized a vigorous mass arming of Hungarians to counter the Croat threat. This people's army defeated Jellačić near Budapest on September 29. Two days earlier, however, Russian troops had invaded Wallachia in support of the Croats, thus posing a further threat to Magyar aims.

The general predicament had advanced to a critical phase. During September France was closest to actual war. And Bastide had to recognize that some things had failed to work out as he had hoped. No democratic alliance existed with the German parliament; instead, Germans bickered with the Danes over insignificant Schleswig. A conflict between the south Slavs and Magyars erupted, a battle whose significance could be crucial because it could draw in the tsar. By the end of September the long awaited arrival of Russian troops to suppress revolt in Europe appeared on the horizon. At any moment the tsar might intervene in Hungary and decide the destiny of all of the revolutions of 1848—including France's. Thus the problems of Schleswig, Croatia, Italy, and Poland were more than ever intimately entwined. France confronted a possible battle with the united reactionary forces of the Habsburgs and Romanovs.

To counteract the danger, Bastide moved once more on several fronts. First, he sent a special envoy to St. Petersburg to sound out the possibility of developing a direct understanding with the tsar. Second, more than ever he needed assurances that Prussia would not side with her old allies, the three northern courts. Third, Bastide once more attempted direct negotiations with the Habsburgs in a renewed effort to split the Austrians from their alliance with the tsar. To pressure the Habsburgs, Bastide used Czartoryski's military adviser to launch a desperate bid to unite the Magyars, Italians, and south Slavs.

Bastide's response to this complex situation was broad in scope because the challenges were so widespread. First, there was her hereditary enemy, Austria; second, as a legacy of the French Revolution, there was her ideological enemy, Russia. In addition, there was the ripening issue of restive nationalities calling for recognition and not only Germans, Poles, and Italians, but also Czechs, Croats, Magyars, and Rumanians. And finally there was the "eastern question," posed by the progressive weakening of the Ottoman Empire. Austria, kingpin of the anti-French coalition, was central in all four cases.

Early August brought Bastide the intriguing news via Heinrich Börnstein, his special adviser on German affairs, that Vienna was on the verge of a crisis. Within a month, he predicted, the political complexion of Austria would change completely.[1] "The monarchy is lost in Austria," Börnstein wrote, "and the unitary republic is impossible. There will be a dismemberment of old Austria, perhaps a federative republic."[2] The Hungarian Diet took a step toward federalism on August 3 by approving an intimate alliance with Germany and refusing its aid to Austria in a struggle with Germany.[3] Public opinion in Vienna energetically opposed any continuation of the Italian war, and "all of the newspapers demand a prompt pacification." Even the reactionary camarilla in Austria wanted "to terminate the war promptly."[4] Vienna was a powder keg threatening to go off at any moment with a "war between the throne and democracy."[5] Austria would then have to negotiate the reconstruction of its entire empire on France's terms.

The core of France's grand design remained Lamartine's proposal in late April to compensate Austria with the Danubian principalities for its sacrifices in northern Italy. The situation at the mouth of the Danube had become acute with the Russian occupation of Moldavia in June. Soon after this date, two undated and unsigned memoranda in the Cavaignac Papers proposed in detail what would in effect be an upheaval in France's foreign policy.

Bastide's proposed "Danubian confederation" demonstrated clearly the shortcomings in his diplomatic style. The plan was basically Adam Czartoryski's scheme to create a strong south Slav and Magyar bloc that would force Russia to free Poland. Gabriac was intimately associated with Czartoryski's secret agents, who more than likely wrote the lengthy memorandum outlining the policy.

To an amateur diplomat with no experience in foreign affairs, like Bastide, the proposal probably sounded heaven-sent. Its weaknesses, though, were symptomatic of the problem of all French policy during the revolutionary year. Bastide's source of information was his parallel system of confidential agents, who inherently exaggerated the revolutionary potential of the situation while simultaneously underestimating the strength of the dynastic loyalties. Eventually this allegiance to the Habsburgs restored the Danubian monarchy. Bastide failed to heed the many caveats in Gabriac's memorandum and thereby ignored the antagonisms between peoples; the entire policy of liberation of peoples was founded on the unproved assumption that the peoples of Europe could somehow come together under French auspices to cooperate in liberating one another. Bastide's utter ignorance of geography and lack of first-hand knowledge of European peoples were further weaknesses in his handling of foreign affairs. He was at the mercy of his advisers and his essentially ideological world view.

Bastide's starting point was never "realism" or "prudence" but romantic idealism. A true believer in the republican cause, Bastide was an idealist, committed to the belief that historic events could be motivated by the pure idea. For example, he thought that Austria's "terrible arm," which could bring tsarism to its knees, was "Catholic Slavism." Austria's idea of "Slavism" could supposedly neutralize another idea, Russia's "Greek Slavism." Bastide, like Lamartine, lived in an age of romatic zeal, which *Realpolitikers* like Bismarck and Cavour derided. The post-1848 generation ridiculed such ideologues as Bastide because they were victims of their emotions, incapable of framing policy by the cool light of logic. Supposedly, the realist at least attempts to overcome sentimental concerns in an effort to frame policies strictly according to national interests. In Palmerston's dictum: "Great Britain has no permanent friends and no permanent enemies, only permanent interests." In contrast, Bastide was a cosmopolitan advocate of universal revolution, assuming that the reactionary powers were enemies and the peoples were friends, dividing Europe along ideological lines. He risked involving France in Italy for the sake of ideological consistency—for King Charles Albert. Yet despite the king, France would battle for the Italian people.

Bastide took as the starting point for a "Danubian confederation" the treaty of Adrianople of September 14, 1829, which gave the Ottoman Empire and Russia a protectorate in the Danubian principalities, "but truthfully, because of the inequality of forces of the two courts more than particular clauses of the arrangements, the sovereignty of the Porte is only nominal."[6] A "national and liberal" constitution for the people of the region was prevented by the "culpable and barbarous" intervention of the protecting power.

Until the dismemberment of the Ottoman Empire, however, the maintenance of the present state was "preferable in the general interest to a partial revolution." The limitations on the control of the Porte and Russia's protectorate constituted a "sort of rights of man" giving the other powers a prerogative to intervene. Though this was no shield against all acts of oppression, it offered a "barrier to Russian ambition." If the principalities were "decimated by an unforeseen coup," they would be "independent but necessarily weak," and with the first shock "pass under Russian domination."[7]

The author of the memorandum was unconvinced that a breakup of the Ottoman Empire was imminent or that it would benefit France. The French ought to prolong the existence of the empire, not because of an expectation of a "faithful ally," but because "unlike Russia, Austria, and even England, we have little chance to gain anything by the fall of the empire, unless it is tied to one of the great European upheavals." If a dissolution of the state did occur, "we ought, contrary to the policy of the last centuries, to work with all of our efforts to obtain for Austria the largest portion possible." There were two advantages for France. By gaining a "large interest in the east," Austria could more easily resign itself to the "results of the revolutions" in Italy and Germany, "and will cease to be our natural adversary." Secondly, the "antagonism of hostile contact" with Russia would render "impossible the renewal of an intimate alliance between the two courts."[8]

The underlying reasoning behind the diplomatic revolution is to be found in two memoranda by Viscount Jean Alexis de Gabriac, secretary of the French legation in Vienna. It was based on the following assumptions: (1) The traditional principles under which Austria operated, peace and the division of races, had been upset by the March revolution; (2) The Viennese national assembly now had a Slavic majority; (3) Opinion in the provinces was agitated, but "profoundly dynastic"; (4) The Czechs, though Panslavists, were "devoted to the emperor and to his family"; (5) The various nations wanted separate governments and administrations. The new element, one necessitating a complete reevaluation of French assumptions about the situation in eastern Europe, was the emergence of Russian Panslavism. "Gold and the Russian Bible" were making "incessant and formidable propaganda" from Bohemia to Serbia. The Russian intrigue, wrote Gabriac, was carried on with the knowledge of Nesselrode, Russia's chancellor. These efforts extended through the Balkans to Athens, where the "Greek cross" was a "powerful auxiliary."[9]

Austria's forces for survival were formidable; a population of 35 million, including 19 million Slavs, 6.5 million Germans, 5 million Italians, and 2.5 million Rumanians; an army of 436,000, not including the *Landwehr*. In case of a war with Austria, Gabriac warned that France could expect "all of the races, divided in peace, united as a single man against us," for two reasons. An ancient jealousy led them to detest France and to believe that that country secretly entertained a continuous thirst for conquests. And "all of the races prefer the paternal scepter of the house of Austria, which they assume alone offers a chance to be administered according to their traditions and their desire for independence." Russia and Germany would offer Austria assistance. Even the Lombards had "little true sympathy" for "our arms."[10]

Gabriac asserted that Paris should press Austria along the road it had been taking since March 14, 1848, toward a "federative monarchy." "Thus constituted," he continued, "it is no longer a cause of concern for us." Austria would become a "mass of small states separating us from Russia." If the French exacted an Italian administration, institutions, and army for Lombardy, they would accomplish more than they possibly could in war. "We shall cause Austria, by the very force of its old internal political system, to direct itself by the Danube towards the east; we shall prevent the Black Sea from becoming a Russian lake; and *we shall conserve excellent rapports with England*."[11]

Gabriac echoed Czartoryski's argument for an Austrian mission in the Balkans; only Austria could prevent Russian domination of all of eastern Europe. Austria, he wrote:

> has in its hands a terrible arm to oppose Russia, this is Slavic

Catholicism, sworn enemy of Greek Slavism; it has, among others, the Magyars, the Rumanians, and the Porte to second it. As for France, it should frankly forget the past and offer its hand, recognizing the regime founded on the March reforms.[12]

The main opposition to France's Austroslav policy came from the German nationalists in Austria. The secretary of the French legation in Vienna warned that the adherents of German unity "struggle against the tendency of Austria to become Slavic, an irresistible trend, since the German nation only constitutes a small, weak minority in the [Austrian] empire." But a complete division of the "races" in Austria would "throw towards Frankfurt the German portion of the monarchy."[13] Bastide wanted to avoid at all costs a complete division of Austria that would result in a *Grossdeutschland*.

The French proposed an interesting variant to Austria's own traditional basis of rule: a division of the national communities of the empire, but with control now vested in the former subjects. The antagonisms between the various nationalities would sap their strength, as far as France was concerned, since each nation would form a completely autonomous power base. The federal structure of the multi-monarchy would be held together only by the person of the monarch. The common antagonism to Russia would bring the various nations together, opposing Russia's Panslavism with Austria's own variety of Austroslavism, Bastide assumed.[14]

Following Gabriac's advice, Bastide first sounded out the English on his change in policy toward Austria. He deplored the war in Italy as a "hopeless struggle for Austria," which was weakening it. This gave France and England "serious ground for reflection on a barrier between Russia and the complete domination of East Europe." He did not doubt that England and France "both wish to support Austria in the East and to shield the Sultan at Constantinople." Since Austria's defeat was "certain," it ought to be given "compensation for losses in Italy," which would be of a nature to "concentrate her strength in that portion of her dominions" which was not "so seriously threatened." Cavaignac agreed, and asked Normanby to write Palmerston that "some means might be considered of giving practical effect" to Bastide's suggestion.[15]

Bastide next repeated Lamartine's offer to Austria of compensation in the Danubian principalities for the loss of its Italian provinces. He told the Austria chargé in Paris, Ritter Ludwig von

Thom, "We hope above all that Austria should be strong . . . in the east. . . . It is on this border that we wish it to roll back its frontiers, rendering itself mistress of all the lower course of the Danube and extending its possessions to the Black Sea."[16] Similarly, Bastide reiterated: "The French republic does not have the slightest interest in weakening the house of Austria; the losses of that house in Italy would be compensated elsewhere."[17]

France's overriding immediate concern was possible war in Italy. Bastide still hoped to "enfranchise" Italy peacefully, but France was committed to fight as an "extreme measure and a regrettable necessity." But first the Italians themselves must request French intervention. In this case, France would look to her own interests, but make no annexations.

Bastide was not pleased at the prospect of a strong state like united Italy on France's border, yet "if that is the wish of that population, the republic has neither the desire nor the right to oppose it; however, no one can impose on it the duty to contribute to this." France would exhibit an even handed prudence because of the mistrust of the Turin court. If the Turin cabinet wanted Austria's possessions "enfranchised" while respecting their independence, the French would help.[18] They desired the "enfranchisement" of Italy but "not the establishment of a domination more disturbing than Austria's." "We will admit," Bastide assured, "Italian unity, but as a federation."[19] The republic was never interested in remaining an "indifferent spectator to the ambition and the unlimited aggrandizement of Piedmont."[20]

Bastide understood that the goal of the Franco-British mediation was to construct the united states of Italy to the advantage of the French, not merely to arrange an end to the fighting in the north and to settle the relationship between Austria and its revolting provinces, Lombardy and Venetia.[21] He repeatedly accused Palmerston of wanting only a greater Sardinia, an unfriendly state on France's border. "England negotiates for Sardinia, and we for the peninsula."[22]

By the later part of August, however, it looked as though there would be no mediation, as Vienna stalled in accepting the Franco-English offices. France threatened an "armed mediation" of three to four thousand troops and a fleet in the Adriatic to warn Vienna that France was serious.[23]

The French consul general in Milan was informed that the proclamation of the French assembly of May 24 for the "enfranchisement of Italy" must be respected. "Do not allow anyone to imagine for an instant that the peaceful solution of Italian affairs is the only possibility for us."[24] Bastide doubted, he told his ministers in Naples, that Italian or German unity would be carried out, "but we are determined that Italy will be liberated from Austrian domination."[25] "We shall not draw back," he assured Léon Favre, the consul general in Genoa, "before the *casus belli*."[26] Bastide asserted to his envoy in Baden, Armand Lefebvre:

> The liberation of Italy is the fundamental basis of the co-mediation. Austria must understand that the spirit of nationality, more tenacious than ever, perpetuates in reconquered Lombardy an imperishable element of resistance. Would it not be better [for Austria to] renounce [Lombardy] on reasonable conditions than obstinately to hold on to it despite its wishes? Venice moreover resists and we support it; public spirit awakens in Piedmont; Tuscany and the Roman states await only backing. We wish the enfranchisement of Italy, and we seek it by peaceful means. But if we are forced, we shall go to war without fear of Germany any more than Austria.[27]

Bastide assured Sardinia's minister, Brignole de Sales, that it was without a doubt an affair of honor as much as in the interest of France to help the cause of the "enfranchisement" of Italy with all its strength. They were pledged by the solemn resolution adopted unanimously by the French assembly on May 24.[28] Bastide was hardly pleased by the prospect of war, but the "honor of the country" was involved by the declarations of France's assembly and the Provisional Government.[29] Paris wanted a peace which was "honorable for France" and for Sardinia.[30]

If France fought, Bastide warned Hatzfeldt, it would not be an "ordinary war." The French would use "ultra-democratic and revolutionary propaganda abroad." A general mobilization would necessitate issuing paper money. He would reestablish the controlled economy *(cours forcé et le maximum)*, and step by step a "reign of terror" would become inevitable. France had reached the point that it might be obliged "to set fire to its own house to burn down its neighbors."[31]

At times it seems difficult to take Bastide's bluster seriously, yet he spoke as the foreign minister. Any evaluation of such excessive and violent rhetoric must surely begin by reviewing it within the context of the crucial components of a revolutionary policy; the quintessence of that program was set in stone in the French assembly's unanimous resolution of May 24, which was little more than a more explicit rendering of Lamartine's promises made in the Manifesto to Europe of March 4. The French republic was committed to joining with the Germans in freeing Poland and Italy. And this liberating sentiment was not limited to governmental circles; the periodical press also reflected a widespread support for the basic concept of enlarging the circle of free peoples. Within the context of this general accord on the substance of a revolutionary plan to free all Europeans from oppression, only the means was at issue. Vocal and politically active Frenchmen supported an anti-Habsburg policy. At this point in time only an insignificant realistic and conservative minority dissented from a virtually unanimous support of Frenchmen for a legacy of enmity toward the Habsburgs. The Duc de Broglie's article in the *Revue des deux mondes* and Thiers's protest in the French assembly's foreign policy committee against Bastide's "disloyal" employment of secret agents in Italy to undermine King Charles Albert expressed dissent. But Thiers and Broglie were thoroughly discredited by their close association with the old regime, so their criticism was scarcely a detraction from the consensus backing the revolutionary strategy. Bastide was thus articulating the view of the ascendant faction, and the real question was the most efficacious method for displacing the house of Habsburg. Tradition argued for a system of client peoples organized from Paris.

We may surmise that foreign diplomatic agents and Thiers were hardly alone in grasping the importance of Bastide's secret agents for spreading revolt and aiding in the overthrow of foreign monarchs. It therefore follows that a common antipathy for the house of Habsburg led the government and the majority of public opinion to tolerate some use of revolutionary methods to ensure French domination of central Europe and to welcome the encouragement of friendly states on France's borders. If we can assume that weakening the Habsburg domination over central Europe was generally endorsed, then the issue becomes how much the cabinet as a whole knew of Bastide's politics.

From the scant documentation available, it appears that the Cavaignac cabinet and the public as a whole was reasonably well informed of Bastide's intention to liberate oppressed Poles and Italians. Although the entire cabinet was probably poorly briefed on some of the finer points, Cavaignac was provided summaries of incoming and outgoing dispatches. More importantly, the Prussian chargé indicated that Cavaignac's language closely paralleled Bastide's bombastic outbursts. Beyond this, we are left with the fact that no member of the cabinet felt strongly enough about the conduct of foreign affairs to resign in protest. France's confrontation with Austria could hardly have been a mystery to anyone in informed circles.

Thus Cavaignac, supposedly more reasonable than Bastide, joined him in threatening war if Austria rejected the Franco-British offer of mediation. Cavaignac suggested that England and France send their fleets to Venice and land some troops. Then Austria would settle the whole matter, he believed. If the English had another suggestion for a demonstration, he was willing to adopt it. Should Austria refuse mediation and the English withdraw their cooperation, "He must at once march into Italy." "The war," he predicted, "from its nature must be one of propagandism." France would "use the weapons that the disposition of the people throughout Europe placed in their power." Without British cooperation in an "intermediate step," the French "would be obliged three weeks hence to appear in the plains of Milan backed by the Piedmontese." He expected Austria to withdraw beyond the Minico, and France would again ask them to accept the original terms of the mediation.[32]

Was this a gigantic bluff? Was France at this moment really willing to accept peace at any price? In his *France and Europe*, Jennings concluded that armed action seemed imminent and inevitable until Wessenberg gave in and accepted the mediation on September 3, 1848. After this, Bastide reduced French policy to "peace at all costs," believing that France "would not have gone to war," and preferred to limit itself to diplomatic means.[33] A. J. P. Taylor in the *Italian Problem* surmised that:

> Cavaignac and Bastide were very unwilling to go to war, but had committed themselves so far—and relied so much on foreign affairs to enhance their prestige—that in certain circumstances it would have been very difficult for them to have avoided intervention.[34]

Jennings and Taylor are representative spokesmen for the accepted historical wisdom that France was unwilling to use military force in support of its diplomacy in 1848. Both contemporaries and modern historians almost without exception agree that the French would not have fought because France was supposedly too weak militarily to act. The treasury was so close to bankruptcy that France's government theoretically did not have the economic means to support any extended armed struggles beyond her borders. Based largely on the printed record, most observers are in accord with the general view that France was more concerned with her own interests than with the formation of nation states along her borders. Thus the French government of 1848, by general consensus, has been labeled as a practitioner of *Realpolitik* and operating according to the precepts of Cardinal Richelieu—divide and rule— and presumably was quite content to have small, weak neighbors. Yet these arguments do not stand close scrutiny.

One historian, however, who has looked into the politics of the French army in 1848 has questioned the prevailing perception of France's strategic impotence. Witold Zaniewicki found that France for a number of years had not had so many men under arms as she did in the latter half of the year 1848. By the simple expedient of keeping the old troops under the colors, rather than giving them the usual furlough when new conscripts arrived in July, the French considerably increased the strength of the permanent army.[35]

The army of 370,000 men in the spring months grew to around 500,000 after August 1, when the military threat loomed.[36] Thus Zaniewicki concluded, "Until the closing of the Alpine passes in the winter, the army was ready in terms of morale and materiel to intervene" in Italy.[37]

An even more important factor than the actual number of men under arms was the perception of this army among the highest military and governmental circles. The minister of war, General Lamoricière, in his budget presentation to the French assembly of November 28, 1848 gave the strength of the French army in 1849 as the normal 320,000 men and 70,000 horses of peacetime. Yet he counted on an additional 280,000 men and 110,000 horses from the reserve army as well as a "mobilizable" national guard of 450,000 men in case of war. Thus Lamoricière concluded that the strength of the French army was "more than a million." His budget in fact proposed to use a third battalion to instruct the reserve of each canton.[38] Thus Lamoricière shared an optimism that is implicitly reflected throughout the contemporary French military and diplomatic record of France's military potential in 1848. The British foreign secretary, Lord Palmerston, agreed that the French had "never been more formidable."[39] Yet the real problem for France was that Austria's 567,346 soldiers might be supplemented by several hundreds of thousands in reinforcements from Germany.[40] France had to rely on Prussia's aspiration to dominate Germany to counter the threat of the Austrian legions to France. Thus France's envoy in Berlin, Emmanuel Arago, told the British resident minister in that city, John Fane, eleventh Earl of Westmorland, that France and Prussia "were on terms of alliance."[41] Bastide similarly wrote to Arago, "our natural ally in Germany is Prussia. It is she who, it seems to me, ought to be at the head of the German Confederation."[42] "Prussia and public opinion in England," Bastide wrote to Boislecomte, "are for us."[43] Generally the French continued to believe that with Prussia as an ally they were invincible; without Prussia, the situation was hopeless. The all-important factor for the French was the ideological bond between Paris and Berlin.

France above all depended on a successful revolution in Prussia to draw her to take up the Girondist cry of "liberation to the people!" As Bastide wrote to his ambassador in London, Gustave-Auguste de Beaumont de la Bonninière, France anticipated rallying "under the same flag, the diverse elements presently scattered in the Slavic and German world."[44]

The solid phalanx of sympathizers to republican France was to be organized by the French military command. A proposal for a military convention between France and the king of Piedmont-Sardinia required that "at all times the co-allied Franco-Italian army will be under the orders and command of a general of the Republic." The operations would be submitted for the "examination and approval of the king in person and without any intermediary."[45] Thus the author of the draft treaty perceived the united peoples of Europe as appendages of the French military machine—and by the same token, very likely saw that relationship as essential to the French commitment of its own soldiers in any armed intervention.

The same caution extended to the financial arrangements for a coalition army that would fight against the crowned kings of Europe. In his first dispatch to his political agents stationed abroad, Bastide saw advantages for the French exchequer in a foreign war. Such a conflict could be advantageous for France financially if it were to "nourish" the unemployed masses in the French capital; that army of the destitute could be mobilized and sent abroad, relieving the French government of the necessity of paying for the upkeep of hundreds of unemployed artisans who were a drain on the French economy.[46] Such an arrangement was written into the proposed military convention drawn up for a joint Franco-Sardinian army that would have fought the Habsburg forces in northern Italy. That French draft stated that "the maintenance, nourishment and pay of the French army shall be charged to Piedmont's treasury."[47] The French cabinet was acutely aware of the enormous costs of keeping an army in the field and set out to carefully compose the right arrangements before the French army took the field. With such planning, France's potential allies might make a war profitable for the French republic.

The charge that France had little interest in increasing the strength of her neighbors cannot be dismissed so quickly. This rhetoric of French egotism, or the French claim that the leaders of 1848 were more far-sighted in sensing the danger of strong neighbors on France's borders, has been politically motivated reproach for more than a century. The real problems for France in 1848 centered on the uncertainty concerning the sovereign of Piedmont-Sardinia and the Frankfurt assembly. In the cases of Italy and Germany, Bastide envisaged states that would be "federal," but in both Italy and Germany the primary concern for France was Austria.

Bastide's Italian policy was predicated on the existence of the old Austrian system. By directly controlling the two most important Italian provinces, Lombardy and Venetia, and by a series of alliances with the rulers of the other states, Vienna had exercised absolute mastery over the peninsula. The rich provinces provided a large portion of Austria's revenues, along with important troops that were central to the Habsburg policy of divide and rule. By garrisoning the various parts of their domain with soldiers from other regions, Austria ensured that each nation was held in check by the others. A federal monarchy in Austria—dominated by the Slavic peoples in cooperation with the Hungarians—and a united German state, under strong Prussian direction, would have radically altered the entire nature of the Danubian monarchy. Austria would no longer have been a natural enemy of the French. In this case, it did not matter whether an Austrian viceroy had nominal sovereignty in Lombardy and Venetia, as long as actual power was in Italian hands.

Under a "Hungarian solution" for the provinces, the army would be completely Italian and could only be stationed in the Italian region of Austria. Its administration would be entirely separate from the rest of the empire and would be staffed exclusively by Italians.[48] All the political institutions in the federal Austrian Empire would be on a national basis, and the central executive would be reduced to a figurehead. The proud house of Austria would be transformed into a constitutional monarchy unable to exert its will outside of Vienna. Bastide would have "enfranchised" the Italians by giving them total dominion over Lombardy and Venetia as well as over the other Italian states, which no longer needed to fear the interference of the Austrian army in their internal affairs. This would have left the way open for national revolutions liberating all of the peninsula, eventually achieving a unity of the peoples, as the Italian people matured politically and sought their own liberty. Repeatedly, Lamartine and Bastide warned that the revolution had to develop from below and promised that the French would never intervene in Italian affairs against the wishes of the population. It seems likely that Bastide never envisaged the mediated settlement with Austria as more than a transitional stage in the independence of the Italian peninsula.

If the Austrian government was unwilling to give in peacefully, the military convention between France and Piedmont proposed the "complete evacuation of northern Italy by Austrian troops to the line of the Isonzo in the east and the Brenner in the north, including the route of the fortress of Brixen and Italian Tyrol."[49]

Bastide and Cavaignac, like most leaders, were not anxious to fight if they could achieve their objectives peacefully. In this case, Bastide had "no taste" for an intervention in Italy if there was the least possibility of receiving Italian "enfranchisement" as a gift from Austria. There were more serious problems as well. Besides the inherent difficulty of having as an ally Charles Albert of Sardinia, whom Bastide considered treacherous, deceitful, and francophobic, there was little indication that the Italian masses were anxious to see a French army cross the Alps, or that they even preferred the French to the Austrians. "The defiance shown us by the population imposes on us the duty to examine thoroughly that question" of military involvement.[50]

The French invasion of Italy might threaten the entire fabric of Bastide's diplomatic revolution in Franco-Austrian, Franco-Prussian, and perhaps, as an outside possibility, Franco-Russian relations. Gabriac cautioned that a war with Austria would unite the various races of the monarchy against France "like a single man"—including the Lombards. The Frankfurt assembly made its intention to aid Austria clear (which could immobilize Prussia), and Russia was at best doubtfully neutral.[51] Certainly the semi-peaceful conquest of the Austrian state by the Slavic majority in cooperation with the Hungarians was predicated on Austria's inability to mobilize its strength against a foreign aggression by the French.

The French assumed that time was on their side, and if they waited, Austria would be weakened by the revolutionary evolution of Europe. "When the crisis had passed," Bastide surmised, "the advantages will be for those who have the wisdom to wait, because in war the victory always comes to the last fresh troops. I desire that our country possess fresh troops when the rest are exhausted."[52]

But all this caution was for nought if Austria did not allow the French an opportunity to wait out the degeneration of Austria's fortunes and inevitable collapse. The resolution of May 24 promising "enfranchisement" of Italy was a moral commitment, and France was in the position of an "affair of honor," like the man "obliged to fight a duel for which he has not the slightest inclination."[53] On receiving the news of the Austrian blockade of the port of Venice, Bastide, "extremely irritated," told Hatzfeldt, "If Austria wants war, they will have it; if they have the intention of humiliating France in Vienna, [the French] will not stand for it."[54] Bastide wanted "an honorable means to release us from the engagements that we have taken."[55]

Bastide and Cavaignac repeatedly spoke of a conference or a congress to discuss "all the presently pending European questions," including the Schleswig, Sicilian, and other pressing problems, "containing the germs of discord," and review the entire European structure of 1815.[56] Bastide saw his role as a new Metternich of the nationalities, destroying the superannuated structure left by the Congress of Vienna—not a Chamberlain sliding out from under his responsibilities at Munich. He always imagined that he was negotiating from a position of overwhelming strength.

Confidence in France's military potential was reflected in the instructions for the diplomatic mission to St. Petersburg of General Adolphe Emmanuel Charles Le Flô. The tone of these instructions were assertive, even threatening and belligerent, rather than diplomatically appeasing. From the beginning he struck a defiant posture toward tsarist Russia that reflected Lamartine's Manifesto to Europe of March 4.

Le Flô was ordered to seek the recognition of the French republic not as a request, but as a right. The French "completely refuse to admit one could hesitate to recognize the republic. It must be recognized. . . . We do not ask for recognition like Louis Philippe." Russia had instigated his mission; the tsar's diplomats in Naples and in Paris had taken the first steps. Bastide expected official recognition to take place soon after Le Flô's arrival in St. Petersburg.[57] But Bastide rejected the condition placed by Russia on recognition. France was unable to consider giving the tsar a free hand in Poland, since this was not within the power of any government. No person could impede the dissemination of revolutionary and republican ideas among the Poles any more than the rest of Europe. Bastide refused to "pardon the powerful action of [the republic's] ideas abroad," which responded to a particular "state of thought" and the "needs of society." Bastide would go no further than Lamartine, promising that France's army would not directly intervene in the internal affairs of other states.[58] It could not, however, prevent her subversive ideas from spreading in Poland.

Bastide scorned Russia's offer of the Rhine. "We have no project, no desire for aggrandizement; our desire is very simply, on the contrary, to constitute our republic by peace and for peace." If the republic were forced into a war, he speculated, "it recognized that a natural alliance would be that of France and Russia, and in that case, [France] would be entirely prepared to determine the changes, the advantages, and the results." Bastide thus left the door ajar for a Franco-Russian alliance against Germany under certain circumstances.

Poland, Bastide made clear, was not to be sacrificed under any circumstances. As Lamartine explained to the French assembly in May, although the republic could not cross Germany to attack Russia in the name of Poland, "That cause is obviously dear to [France], and it will plead" Poland's case with all the insistence that friendly relations with Germans allowed. In case of a war against Russia, moreover, France, "finding a base in the sentiment of Polish nationality, will not hesitate to use it." The Polish question was for France "a defensive arm, but never a motive for aggression."[59] France thus continued the policy of ambiguity, threatening Russia in its most vital interest, Poland.

Bastide refused to allow discussions of the future of the Danubian principalities with Russia. France would hold to the "stipulations of the treaties and cannot desire that Turkey lose any part of its domination." The lower course of the Danube was reserved for a French understanding with Austria.[60]

France did bring up the question of the division of Europe on national lines, but the context of the discussion deepened the cleavage between Paris and St. Petersburg. The French attitude struck out not at the Germans, but at the Russians, and categorically rejected Russian Panslavism. France would never allow Russia's expansion into western Europe on the basis of a common Slavic affinity. The French maintained an attitude of reserve toward the principle of defining nationality by language.[61]

The most significant aspect of Le Flô's instructions was perhaps their failure to consider the German question in depth, or rather the manner in which it was to be discussed, namely, as an adjunct to the Italian question. While Russia's primary concern was Poland, France was interested in Italy, where it claimed "the right to intervene." France would not be indifferent to the expansion or to the destruction of Piedmont, nor did it wish German unity "enveloping it from Luxembourg to Nice. We shall fight for that question if we are forced, but we shall do everything honorably possible to maintain peace and the respect of our inconvertible interests."[62] France's disquietude about German unity was caused by Germany's tendency to expand in the direction of Switzerland and all of northern Italy all the way to France's Alpine and Mediterranean frontiers. This would have meant the resurrection of the Holy Roman Empire of the Middle Ages, extending across all of central Europe, including the Italian peninsula.

Thus the French confronted Germany with the Russian alliance only because of the remote possibility that the Frankfurt parliament might attempt to annex Italy and Switzerland, forming a mighty united state stretching from Nice to Luxembourg. As Tocqueville warned, German unity was "an immense extension of the *Zollverein,* a grand commercial and maritime establishment on the Mediterranean and Baltic Sea." The real danger for France was that "Austria and in her name German unity" would be "mistress of upper Italy."[63]

Otherwise, the only common bond between Russia and France was the Schleswig question, and this fragile link alone could never have created an alliance with Russia. The Germans, Bastide complained, were guilty of a "brutal usurpation" of Schleswig. France had a "personal interest," because of the apparent German intention to assimilate all those speaking the same language.[64] However, German unity within the geographical confines of the old German Confederation was explicitly approved by the French. France's reserve toward German unity was caused by a desire to avoid diplomatic difficulties, "but it would accept without hesitation any fact which was clearly defined."[65]

The only Franco-Russian alliance that the French contemplated, therefore, was not directed against united Germany, but only against German expansion that would absorb Italy and its other neighbors. Though France was only able to deliver ineffective protests against German encroachments on Denmark and Poland, Bastide was prepared to fight to protect the Italians against a Habsburg move to control all of northern Italy and threaten Switzerland. Thus Le Flô's instructions show no traces of *Realpolitik*. Rather than a prudent and realistic drawing together of the flanking powers, Le Flô's instructions reflect the ideological bias of romantic nationalists directing French affairs. This emphasizes once more Bastide's utter ignorance of Nicholas I's frame of reference.

Even before Le Flô's arrival in St. Petersburg, Nicholas I forestalled the attempted Franco-Russian rapprochement. Learning of the French threat to declare war to free Italy, Nicholas declared that he would immediately inform Paris "that he deprecated in the strongest manner the language . . . used by the French agent in Vienna, and that he could not recognize any right of France to interfere in the affairs of Italy." France was guilty of a "monstrous violation of treaties and international law, and a positive departure from the principles the French government had declared its policy." France's threat was a "violation of the assurances" that had been given when he consented to receive Le Flô. The tsar warned that he would "cease to hold relations with the French government if it persists . . . to interfere by force of arms in the affairs of Austrian Italy."[66] Bastide's confidence in Russian assistance to pacify the Italian question was an illusion. Better relations between France and Russia still remained on the plane of diplomatic speculation.

The failure of the Le Flô mission raises a serious question concerning Bastide's method of operations. His misdirected enthusiasm in an attempt to interest the Habsburgs in an exchange of territories (a "Danubian confederation"), without a major military defeat, reflects his ignorance of practical politics and historical realities. The documents quoted above time and again reflect an ideological shortsightedness that exaggerated the revolutionary situation at the very moment when the tide of revolt was receding.

Perhaps the greatest mistake of historians is to exaggerate the rationality of historical figures while denigrating or even ignoring the importance of their emotional reactions. Particularly when one is dealing with romantics like Lamartine and Bastide, the emotional factor seems to have been misunderstood. An old carbonarist conspirator, Jules Bastide mistrusted King Charles Albert of Sardinia. And this mistrust was an essential element of Bastide's attitude toward the remaking of the map of Italy. Certainly attributing Bastide's puzzling remarks concerning a "federal" Italian state, which would offset the power of Sardinia's monarch, cannot be attributed to "realism." Rather, his native element was a deluded optimism. The accepted wisdom that Jules Bastide was a realistic practitioner of *Realpolitik* is particularly belied by the story of his misdirected relations with Prussia.

NOTES

1. Börnstein, Bulletin de l'Allemagne, August 7, 1848, AEF, MD, Allemagne 129, fo. 76; August 8, 1848; "all the letters, written by impartial men, announce the republic, as the catastrophe in the great drama," fo. 78.

2. *Ibid.*, August 10, 1848, fo. 82.

3. *Ibid.*, August 12, 1848, fo. 84.

4. *Ibid.*, August 16, 1848, fo. 88.

5. *Ibid.*, August 17 and 19, 1848, fo. 90 and 92ff.

6. Cav 1 Mi 2 R 24.

7. *Ibid.*

8. *Ibid.*; Caution was exhorted in initiating the radical change of course; France, because of its "topographical position," could not act alone in the "Constantinople theater." Before doing anything, it must first learn the sentiments of England and Austria. In addition, France was "very closely tied to the principles of the rights of man," and any public knowledge of such a policy would be a major embarrassment. As a result, Bastide inconsistently appeared to oppose Austria's ambitions in Italy, while at the same time showing an interest in close relations with Vienna.

9. "Situation de l'Autriche au mois de septembre," note by M. de Gabriac and "Note succincte sur la situation de la Hongrie," September, 1848, by M. de Gabriac. Cav 1 Mi 2 R 24.

10. "Situation de l'Autriche," *Ibid.*

11. *Ibid.* underlined by Cavaignac.

12. *Ibid.*

13. C. G. Boilleau to Bastide, Vienna, November 4, 1848, AEF, Autriche 435, fo. 57.

14. "Aperçu succinct des négociations relatives aux affaires de la Haute Italie," No. 1, Cav 1 Mi 2 R 25; Bastide to Tallenay, Paris, November 2, 1848, AEF, Allemagne 806, fo. 174; Hatzfeldt to Foreign Minister, Paris, November 22, 1848, GSA, fz. 863, fo. 126; Arago to Bastide, Berlin, October 17, 1848, AEF, Prusse 303, fo. 33–34; Bastide concurred completely with this analysis October 20, 1848, *Ibid.*, fo. 38.

15. Normanby to Palmerston, Paris, July 14, 1848, PRO, FO 27/810; Bastide repeated a week later that "Austria should get some compensation" for its sacrifices in northern Italy, *Ibid.*, July 22, 1848.

16. Ritter Ludwig von Thom to Graf Karl Ludwig von Ficquelmont, Paris, August 23, 1848, HHSA, Frankreich, fo. 183. Bastide to De la Cour, Paris, October 13, 1848, AEF, Autriche 436, fo. 280.

17. "Instructions à donner à l'envoyé près du roi de Sardaigne," No. 3, Cav 1 Mi 2 R 25.

18. *Ibid.;* Bastide's draft of a military convention with the king of Piedmont, which was a precondition to French intervention, provided that after Lombardy and Venetia were liberated, the people would elect whether to become part of Piedmont or to remain separate. Moderna, Tuscany, and the Papal States were to have "absolute independence"; "Convention entre la République française et le Roi de Piémont," Cav 1 Mi 2 R 25.

19. Bastide to Boislecomte, Paris, July 19, 1848, accrediting him as extraordinary envoy and minister plenipotentiary by the king of Sardinia, instructions, Cav 1 Mi 2 R 25.

20. Bastide to Tallenay, Paris, July 19, 1848, Cav 1 Mi 2 R 25. There is an apparent contradiction between Bastide's statements. He told General Thiard, "We would prefer, without a doubt, the triumph across the Alps of a democracy like ours," but did not see how France could possibly "openly oppose what northern Italy demands today." He concluded that monarchy founded on democratic institutions "seems destined to serve as the transition to the pure republic." He wrote Harcourt that France was prepared to support Italy if it were powerless to bring its own "enfranchisement." "The government of the republic," he assured, "wants the independence of Italy." Yet he instructed Bixio that France's "principles and interests command us to be on guard against" the foundation of an Italian monarchy, which would be an "easy prey for Austria" and a "source of hostilities against France." France "favored" all those who wanted a republic in Italy. "We are willing to admit Italian unity," Bastide asserted, but as a "federation between independent states." The ambiguity is resolved by the explicit instructions drawn up with the military convention. France did not want a strong state on its border like united Italy; however, "If that were wish of people, the republic has neither the will nor the right to oppose it." France would accept a *fait accompli* of united Italy, as it eventually did under Louis Napoleon, but it refused to fight to help Sardinia conquer the other Italian states. Bastide to Thiard, Paris, May 23, 1848, DDF, II, 427; Bastide to Harcourt, Paris, May 26, 1848, DDF, II, 472; Bastide to Bixio, Paris, June 1848, and Bastide to Boislecomte, Paris, July 19, 1848, *République française*, pp. 45–47; Instructions à donner à l'envoyé près du Roi de Sardaigne, Cav 1 Mi 2 R 25.

21. "Aperçu succinct des négociations relatives aux affaires de la Haute Italie," Cav 1 Mi 2 R 25.

22. *Ibid.*

23. Hatzfeldt to Foreign Minister, Paris, September 1, 3, and 4, 1848, GSA, fz. 861, fo. 168–70, 174, 181; Börnstein disclosed "general opinion in Germany (frankly expressed by the reactionary press) is that the mediation of the French cabinet is ridiculed in Vienna, that M. Delacour is the dupe of Wessenberg, changing every day the pretexts,

going from one subterfuge to another. . . . If Austria finishes with her democrats, she will be able to count on Russia." Bulletin, September 25, 1848, AEF, MD, Allemagne 129, fo. 153; De la Cour accurately warned that the Viennese cabinet would never agree to the pretention of the mediators and was not willing to consider giving up Lombardy and Venetia without fighting. "Public opinion is entirely of the same disposition." De la Cour to Bastide, Vienna, September 19 and 26, 1848, Cav 1 Mi 2 R 25.

24. Bastide to Denois, Paris, August 27, 1848, Cav 1 Mi 2 R 25.

25. Bastide to Rayneval, Paris, August 28, 1848, Cav 1 Mi 2 R 25.

26. Bastide to Léon Favre, Paris, August 29, 1848; to De la Cour, Paris August 28, 1848; to Boislecomte, Paris, August 29, 1848, Cav 1 Mi 2 R 25; and September 4, 1848, AEF, Sarde 322, fo. 27.

27. Bastide to Armand Lefebvre (in Baden) Paris, August 31, 1848, Cav 1 Mi 2 R 25; When Normanby learned of Bastide's ultimatum to Austria, Bastide ineptly attempted to retreat back to Lamartine's policy of ambiguity, claiming weakly that it was meant "to open the eyes of the Austrian government to the truth, that if they pressed them beyond the point at which a government in the crisis of a revolution with an excitable population could maintain itself," General Cavaignac and he would be "driven from power and be succeeded by" the radicals, including Ledru-Rollin. Bastide assured that he would be the "victim" and "never the accomplice"; Normanby to Palmerston, Paris, September 28, 1848, PRO, FO 27/813. The diplomatic record, however, is overwhelming: Memorandum remis à Lord Palmerston par M. Gustave de Beaumont, August 25, 1848, AEF, Angleterre 671, fo. 97–99, "France could and perhaps ought not to intervene for Poland which was too distant; Italy was too near not to aid her. France resolved to intervene in Italy if the terms of the common mediation of England and France were refused by Austria." Hatzfeldt to Foreign Minister, Paris, September 26, 27, and October 4, 1848, GSA, fz. 861, fo. 216, 225 and 245; Bastide to Beaumont, Paris, September 26 and October 20, 1848, AEF, Angleterre 671, fo. 185 and 265; Bastide to De la Cour, Paris, September 26, 1848, Autriche 436, fo. 229 bis; Bastide to Arago, Paris, October 7, 17, and 20, 1848, Prusse 303, fo. 15, 32, and 38; Bastide to Boislecomte, Paris, September 4 and 6, 1848, Sarde 322, fo. 27 and 34. All make it perfectly clear that Bastide expected to do the fighting, not Ledru-Rollin. Beaumont and De la Cour even assured that the English would join the French as allies in the war against Austria; Beaumont to Bastide, London, August 31, 1848, Angleterre 671, fo. 124–25; De la Cour to Bastide, Vienna, October 9, 1848, Autriche 436, fo. 271.

28. Brignole de Sales to Pareto, Paris, August 22, 1848, AST, fz. 277.

29. Ibid., August 23, 1848.

30. Brignole to Perrone, Paris, September 6, 1848, Ibid.; cf. Bastide's promise read in the Turin assembly, October 21, 1848, that France "will not fail to honor the debt that she voluntarily contracted when she herself promised the enfranchisement of Italy." Moniteur, October 30, 1848.

31. Hatzfeldt to Foreign Minister, Paris, September 7, 1848, GSA, fz. 861, fo. 191–92.

32. Normanby to Palmerston, Paris, August 29, 1848, PRO, FO 27/812; Bastide to Harcourt (in Rome), Léon Favre (Genoa), to Boislecomte, Paris, August 25 and 29, 1848, Cav 1 Mi 2 R 25.

33. Jennings, *France and Europe*, pp. 172–90.

34. Taylor, *Italian Problem*, p. 196; cf. Ley, p. 141.

35. Zaniewicki, 127; Situation générale par ordre numérique des divers corps de Troupes composant l'armée, 1er janvier au 1er décembre, 1848, SHA.

36. *Ibid.*

37. *Ibid.*, p. 169, quoting *Moniteur de l'armée*, October 8 and November 19, 1848.

38. *Moniteur*, November 29, 1848.

39. Beaumont to Alexis de Tocqueville, London, August 31/September 2, 1848, Alexis de Tocqueville, *Oeuvres complètes: Correspondance d'Alexis de Tocqueville et de Gustave de Beaumont* (Paris, 1966–67), VIII², 34.

40. Tableaux statistiques des forces militaires et maritimes des puissances de l'Europe, MAE, statistique, Cav 1 Mi 2 R 20.

41. Reported by Westmorland to Palmerston, Berlin, September 4, 1848, PRO, FO 64/289.

42. Bastide to Arago, Paris, October 7, 1848, AEF, Prusse 303, fo. 15; October 17, 1848, fo. 32; October 20, 1848, fo. 38.

43. Bastide to Boislecomte, Paris, October 1, 1848, Cav 1 Mi 2 R 25.

44. Bastide to Beaumont, Paris, October 20, 1848, AEF, Angleterre 671, fo. 266 and September 26, 1848, fo. 185.

45. Convention entre la République française et le Roi de Piémont, Cav 1 Mi 2 R 25.

46. Le Ministre des Affaires Etrangères a MM. Les Agents politiques de la République, Paris, May 12, 1848, DDF, II, 186.

47. Convention entre la République française et le Roi de Piémont, Cav 1 Mi 2 R 25.

48. Hatzfeldt to Foreign Minister, September 9, 16, and 18, 1848, GSA, fz. 863, fo. 22, 35, and 40. Hatzfeldt correctly objected that Bastide inaccurately used the term "Hungarian solution." Hungarian troops had been sent to Italy, Bohemia, etc., and the Italian regiments into Bohemia and Hungary. "It was the only means for her to retain her possessions in Italy." Bastide understood that he actually proposed the destruction of the entire Austrian system of control by divide and rule.

49. Convention entre le République française et le Roi de Piémont, Cav 1 Mi R 25.

50. Bastide to Tallenay, Paris, July 23, 1848, Cav 1 Mi 2 R 26; Bastide, *La République française*, pp. 29–30.

51. Gabriac, Situation de l'Autriche au mois de septembre, Cav 1 Mi 2 R 24.

52. Bastide to Boislecomte, Paris, October 18, 1848, Bastide, *République française*, p. 113. By spring (1849) Bastide believed that the French would not need to use a large portion of its army to keep internal order. This underlined Bastide's illusion that time was operating in France's favor, cf., Jennings, *France and Europe*, pp. 201–03. On Bastide's confidence that the French would be stronger with time, Brignole to Perrone, Paris, September 6, 1848, No. 8 and 8A, AST, Mz. 277; The greatest difficulty that Bastide was having with the Parisian radicals was caused by their objection that the French government was doing nothing to free the Italians; a war could have strengthened the domestic position of the Cavaignac cabinet against pressure from the domestic political Left.

53. Hatzfeldt to Foreign Minister, Paris, September 1, 1848, GSA, fz. 861, fo. 168.

54. *Ibid.*, September 26, 1848, fo. 216.

55. *Ibid.*, September 1, 1848, fo. 168.

56. Hatzfeldt to Bülow, Paris, September 30, 1848, GSA, fz. 863, fo. 67; Hatzfeldt to Foreign Minister, September 9, 1848, fz. 861, fo. 194.

57. Instructions pour le Général Le Flô, Paris, September 9, 1848, Cav 1 Mi 2 R 24; Schweitzer to Dusch, Paris, July 31 and September 9, 1848, BGLA, Fz. 48/2037; Wendland to King, Paris, August 10 and 17 and September 9, 1848, BGStA, MA 2105.

58. Le Flô instructions, Cav 1 Mi 2 R 24.

59. *Ibid.*

60. *Ibid.*

61. The French received warnings from their Balkan diplomats of the menace of Russian Panslavism. Limpérani wrote from Belgrade June 16: "The struggle between the Slavs and the Magyars took a very serious character. From the two sides, the struggle will be very intense and the Slavs will throw themselves, if necessary, into the arms of Russia." He predicted, "The domination of the Black Sea, the Danube, and the Save to the Adriatic, that is Russia's goal." Serbia would be "an easy prey." Courier, July 11, 1848, Cav 1 Mi 2 R 26, DDF, II, 955. July 21 he warned "the reconciliation of the Austrian Slavs with the Hungarians alone can stop the progress of Russian Panslavism. Austria's situation on the Danube is deplorable." Courier, August 4, 1848, *ibid.* France's willingness to contemplate the remote possibility of seizing the Rhine frontier in some future war was not recognized as an attack on the German nation. Bastide—and apparently Cavaignac and Le Flô since no annotation or protest appears on the document—naively believed that French was the spoken language of the foreign lands, including "the provinces of the Rhine." Le Flô instructions, Cav 1 Mi 2 R 24.

62. Le Flô instructions, Cav 1 Mi 2 R 24.

63. Tocqueville to Beaumont, Paris, August 27, 1848, *Oeuvres complètes*, VIII^2, 29.

64. Le Flô instructions, Cav 1 Mi 2 R 24.

65. *Ibid.*, Stadelmann's conclusion stands: "Everything remained on the plane of diplomatic conjecture; nowhere is it possible to discover the proven fact of an anti-German coalition of the flanking powers." *Social and Political History*, p. 117; likewise, A. J. P. Taylor, *The Struggle for Mastery*, p. 15; France demanded that Russia give independence to Poland in exchange for détente; obviously Nesselrode created the myth of a Franco-Russian alliance in order to frighten Germans; Le Flô's instructions prove that no basis for a Franco-Russian understanding ever existed.

66. Bloomfield to Palmerston, St. Petersburg, September 12, 1848, PRO, FO 65/345.

Part Three

VENDEMIAIRE

LATE SEPTEMBER-DECEMBER 1848

Chapter Eight
The Prussian Entente

SEPTEMBER 1848

*M*AJOR CRISES OF THE GREAT REVOLUTION occurred during September, or the month Vendémiaire of the revolutionary calendar. So also in 1848, after the summer's distractions, the travail of revolution entered a new round of violence. According to the reports of France's secret agents, street fighting appeared imminent in Berlin, Budapest, and above all in Vienna. Armed clashes on the lower Danube between the Magyars and the Croats signaled a vigorous showdown between the forces of revolution and reaction. Symbolic of the new situation was the appearance in Paris of envoys from Turin and Budapest imploring military assistance from the French republic. Now, more than ever, Paris looked like the diplomatic hub of revolutionary Europe. And the French seemed more prepared to deal with the international situation, since the domestic position of the Cavaignac government was more secure after the June days. But before going to war, France needed two things: domestic solidarity and a favorable diplomatic constellation. Internal unity necessitated a popularly elected president, which meant quickly winding up the framing of a new constitution that would allow election of an executive. And to explore peaceful alternatives to an overthrow of the Habsburgs and Romanovs, the French would send feelers to Vienna and St. Petersburg seeking a negotiated settlement of the Polish situation. Above all, Bastide needed a foreign ally and could not allow a reemergence of the old alliance of the three northern powers. Now, more than ever, a close relationship between Paris and Berlin troubled him. Thus he began serious discussions with the Prussian chargé in Paris.

Bastide's fanciful grand design to alter the pattern of European diplomacy ultimately depended on a close relationship between

Chez Aubert, H. de la Bourse.

Imp. Aubert & Cᵉ

EMMANUEL ARAGO.

Montagnard farouche, mais trop gras.

Emmanuel Arago, French Envoy in Berlin, by Honoré Daumier, Bibliothèque
Nationale (Paris).

France and Prussia. It also assumed popular control of the formerly
subject nations, as well as of a united Germany. Austria's center
of gravity would be shifted to the east by the absorption of additional
territory, and, as a consequence, the Danubian monarchy would
lose its German character. Austria's new eastern orientation would
cause clashes with Russia; the tsar would be forced to turn to
France or Prussia for diplomatic support. Particularly if the new
Austrian state were "liberal" (as Bastide supposed), Russia would
face a united front of ideological enemies to its west. Thus Bastide
assumed that "the closest possible union with Prussia" would form
an "intermediary link *(Zwischenkette)* in France's relationship with
Russia."[1] France's vacuous diplomatic plans turned on her relationship with Prussia. If a solid phalanx of liberal states were formed
between Paris and Berlin, the decay of Austrian and Russian autocracy was only a matter of waiting.

Bastide's strategy was imperiled by the Frankfurt assembly.
It offered Austria military assistance to reconquer its Italian provinces. Once the imperial army was victorious in Italy, Vienna could
move against the Hungarian and Slavic peoples. The same armies
that put down Italy could crush the other nations of the empire
in succession and reassert absolutist rule. Frankfurt's ascendancy
in Germany was incompatible with Bastide's entire world view.

The former policy of an alliance with the "democratic and
unitary tendencies" of the Frankfurt assembly, Bastide believed,
was "entirely false." Frankfurt posed the "greatest danger for
France." The Germans had restored a *Reich* under an Austrian
archduke. Bastide concluded that the "policy of Cardinal Richelieu," which was to use the German princes against the house of
Habsburg, was the best for France.[2] France should want to
strengthen Prussia, because it was clear that Frankfurt aspired to
absolute supremacy in central Europe.[3] In view of this, Bastide
promised real support for only two German monarchies, Prussia
and Bavaria—"the states capable of having an independent policy
in Germany."[4] Austria, in Bastide's estimation, was no longer capable of exerting any force whatsoever in German politics—except
through the Frankfurt assembly. The diplomatic archives of such
stalwart former clients of France as Baden and Württemberg contain
no evidence of French interest in their independence. As far as
France was concerned, all except Bavaria were expendable in return
for a Franco-Prussian rapprochement that might serve as *"Zwischenkette"* to Russia. Thus Bastide explained his German policy to the
new French chargé in Frankfurt as follows:

Without exaggerating the importance of German unity, the
reconstruction of a German Empire, reestablishing Austria's
supremacy over 45 millions, an empire much more compact
than the old German Empire or German Confederation, is a
grave fact that ought to draw our attention, to say nothing of
the invading tendency of Germany, based on unity of race
and language, to absorb part of the Grand Duchy of Posen,
Schleswig, and Limburg, and menacing us in Alsace—these
tendencies . . . ought to render us circumspect and unhurried
to recognize *a priori* a German Empire.[5]

Bastide's summary of these instructions for Cavaignac identified the truly significant passages. He left out as inconsequential
to the main thrust of the document the phrase that France should
support Prussia "in the spirit of divide and balance," which France
had traditionally exerted in Germany.[6] In contrast, Cavaignac underlined Bastide's charge:

M. de Tallenay ought to present himself at Frankfurt as the
organ of a power friendly to Germany, to combat the evil
prejudices existing against France, the sentiments of hostility
with regard to the Italian nation. Study the travail of German
unity, avoiding any manifestation of compromising opinion.[7]

Bastide explained that his goal was "to detach Prussia from
Germany, where she was the greatest force." Without Prussia,
"that German Empire" in Frankfurt would be "reduced to the
proportions of a poorly united confederation and without serious
danger for France."[8]

Bastide's statements concerning the future shape of a united
Germany are, at first reading, hopelessly contradictory. On the
one hand, he spoke of the tradition of divide and balance and the
policy of Richelieu. On the other, he told the Bavarian envoy that
only Bavaria and Prussia could have an "independent" *(eignen)*
policy in Germany. At the same time, there runs through his
dispatches the impression that France sided with the German democrats, who were the strongest advocates of a unitary force in Germany! Then his memorandum of August 5 concluded that German
unity was "inevitable." The perplexing discord seems beyond simple analysis. How can one square his statement that Prussia should
be detached from Germany with the remark that Prussia and
Bavaria should share hegemony in Germany? And what could he
have meant by his suggestion that France return to Richelieu's
system of divide and rule?

The starting point must be the Second Republic's continuation of the tradition of countering Habsburg hegemony in Europe. That explains his rejection of the German Empire under "reconstruction" in Frankfurt, which would "reestablish Austria's supremacy over 45 million more compactly than the old German Empire."

Jules Bastide was the author of a history of the Reformation; the extremely devout Bastide perhaps identified closely with Richelieu's attempts to prevent a "universal monarchy" of the Habsburgs. The primary objective of Richelieu was to thwart a Habsburg dominion over all of Germany. That hostility to a "universal monarchy" was shared by a succession of French monarchs from Francis I to Louis XIV. This suggests that Bastide's aim was not to block German unity *per se*; rather he hoped to voice opposition to a particular variety of German unity that had developed in the Frankfurt assembly. Bastide voiced two very specific objections to the designs of this parliament's orators. First, he was alarmed by the "invading tendency," of their threat to expand Germany's borders at the expense of surrounding states. Secondly, he saw them working for "Austria's supremacy." Neither of these objections touched on the matter of German unity as such. And there is certainly no inconsistency between favoring German unity under Prussia and opposing that unity if it strengthened Austria's position. We shall see later that Bastide assumed that the cost of a Prussian entente for France must be to allow Prussia to dominate a united German state. If Bastide were willing to allow German unity under the dominion of Prussia, then his ill-concealed hostility to the Frankfurt assembly takes on new meaning. We must shift our attention to Bastide's overt acts of resistance to the efforts of the Frankfurt parliament to create a united German state. Did these efforts of the parliamentarians miscarry because of France's machinations?

Alexander Scharff's claim that the French acted as a "decentralizing agent" in German affairs rests largely on five overt acts of hostility to German unity. First, French diplomatic agents sympathetic to Germany's unity were purged from the diplomatic corps. Second, the French dispatch of General Le Flô to St. Petersburg was offered as proof that a Franco-Russian alliance of the "enveloping powers" joined to head off German prospects for unity. Third, the French failed to recognize the special envoy of the Frankfurt assembly to Paris, Dr. Friedrich von Raumer. Fourth, and for Scharff the quintessential proof, was France's protest of August 20 over the delay in concluding a peace treaty in Schleswig. Finally, the refusal of the French to protest publicly over the Polish question in late July was perceived as a sacrifice of the Poles for the greater French interest of an entente with Prussia.[9] All of these deeds have been offered as evidence that France's diplomatic efforts influenced the course of the German revolution and must be examined in turn.

We have discussed already three of France's supposed efforts to block German unity: the Le Flô mission to St. Petersburg, the Schleswig protest of August 20, and the failure to register an immediate objection to the Frankfurt assembly's seating of delegates from Posen. These efforts showed no hostility to German unity, but a French preference for Berlin over Frankfurt as a better negotiating partner in dealing with these thorny Polish and Schleswig questions. As for Le Flô's instructions for his mission to Russia, there are no expressed or implied threats to either German or Polish unity. That leaves as evidence of France's efforts to block German unity, Bastide's changes in the diplomatic corps and his reception of the Raumer mission from the Frankfurt assembly.

Bastide did promise the Prussian chargé Hatzfeldt that he would "replace diplomatic agents in Germany who did not follow the exact line of conduct that he had traced for them."[10] He elaborated later to Hatzfeldt that he would remove even his friends if they did not follow his lead in opposing the "democratic and unitary tendencies personified in the Frankfurt assembly."[11] When we examine the actual firings, Bastide's statement loses its force. In fact, Bastide made only a single change, and that was to replace Savoye, the French envoy in Frankfurt, who was outspokenly hostile to a Prussian-led unification of Germany. Thus it is erroneous for historians to cite the removal of Savoye as "proof" of Bastide's opposition to German unity.[12] As Bastide wrote to Arago, that replacement of Savoye came "for various reasons."[13]

There is considerable evidence that the decision to replace Savoye predated Bastide's change of attitude toward the Frankfurt assembly, and was instead a response to complaints from the government in Frankfurt itself that Savoye lacked judgment. The diplomatic envoy of the Central Power sent to Paris, Ölsner-Monmerqué, bitterly complained to Bastide's *chef du cabinet*, Hetzel, of Savoye's most undiplomatic behavior and requested the replacement because of Savoye's "inopportune zeal."[14]

An example of Savoye's misplaced enthusiasm was his letter published in the *Augsburger Allgemeine Zeitung* of August 21 denying that he had been responsible for unfavorable attitudes toward Germany expressed in the French newspaper *Le National*.[15] On August

26 the Belgian chargé in Frankfurt had informed his government that "for more than three weeks" Savoye's replacement, Auguste Bonaventure Marquis de Tallenay, had been discussed in Frankfurt, and "one generally desires his arrival."[16]

Bastide's instructions to Tallenay confirmed the French foreign minister's anxiety to avoid a repetition of the problems created by Savoye's unguarded expressions of opinion. Urging Tallenay to "study with care the labor of German unity," Bastide asked his envoy to keep him informed but to "refrain, with your habitual prudence, from any manifestation of untimely and compromising opinion."[17]

The last of the charges of French "decentralization" of Germany rests on the reception given the Frankfurt parliament's special envoy to Paris. The objective of the Berlin professor of history, Friedrich von Raumer, was to seek official diplomatic recognition of the Frankfurt assembly as the sole voice of united Germany. Bastide took great care in all of his meetings with Raumer, using precisely the same terms as those used by the British government for Baron von Andrian on a similar mission to London. Raumer would be "greeted in a manner that would not in the least offend Messieurs the professors of Frankfurt," Bastide promised.[18]

Bastide's most specific worry concerned the geographical limits of the new German state envisioned by the Frankfurt assembly. He was apprehensive about the use of the term "German Empire" no fewer than three times in an official letter that Raumer was to present to the French chief executive, Cavaignac. Before accepting the dispatch, the French wished to know the exact boundaries of that empire.[19]

Raumer's official purpose was to present the French government with that letter, which announced Archduke John's election as imperial vicar and the Frankfurt parliament's assumption of the powers previously exercised by the Diet of the old German Confederation. His mission was part of a general policy of bolstering the assembly's claim to serve as the single spokesman for united Germany. Raumer also hoped to convince the French to include Frankfurt in the joint Franco-British mediation between Sardinia and Austria.

The instructions drawn up by the foreign minister in the central power of Archduke John, the Hamburg lawyer Johann Gustav Heckscher, stressed to Raumer that the most important objective of his mission was to secure diplomatic recognition of the

Frankfurt assembly as representing the German nation. "I ask you, please, to do everything possible to show the peaceful character of the German unification desires in the right light and to convince France that it should strengthen this."[20]

When Raumer was received by the French foreign minister on September 7, he was told that the Frankfurt parliament could not be officially recognized by France until the "exterior constitution" was in accord with the other German states. Bastide then asked Raumer about the "territorial circumscription" of the new empire, complaining that:

> The elevated pretensions of Frankfurt on Schleswig and Limburg caused us scruples in that regard, and it seemed to us that the principle of assimilation of all those who spoke German in the world would well one day cause the unitaries of Frankfurt to demand Alsace and Lorraine.[21]

Bastide's immediate concern, however, was northern Italy, not Alsace and Lorraine, as fighting threatened to break out at any moment between Austria and the French.

In the all-important question of northern Italy, Raumer failed to placate French fears; instead, Raumer told Bastide that "Germany will not see with indifference a French army advance over the Alps, and, in this case, it would probably not delay in pronouncing itself against France." Raumer assured the Austrian chargé, "These words made a strong impression on M. Bastide."[22]

Rather than convince the French of the peaceful character of the Frankfurt *Zentralgewalt*, Raumer threatened the French with an invasion on the Rhine! The Saxon chargé perceived that Raumer's problems in Paris had little to do with the question of German unity as such. "The principal difficulty that the Raumer mission is experiencing results from the threat of seeing Germany take an active part in the war that could arise between France and Austria over Italy."[23] Cavaignac was outraged by Raumer's statements. Frankfurt wanted German unity but denied the same right to Italy. Frankfurt claimed to speak for all of Germany, but what of Austria and Prussia? Which authority was in the position to negotiate on the Italian question, Vienna or Frankfurt?[24]

Raumer had confirmed the worst fears of Bastide's special advisor on German affairs, Heinrich Börnstein. Börnstein had warned Bastide that a confidential source was "astounded by the lack of tact shown at Frankfurt in sending Raumer to Paris." In his lectures at the University of Berlin, Raumer's sentiments were "always most hostile toward France." After the February Revolution he hardly took note of the object of the course, and instead delivered a diatribe on the political events of the day, "amusing his audience with a war of epigrams and most severe criticisms of the men and acts of the French Provisional Government." Börnstein added that Raumer belonged to the "ultra-Teuton" party, which Bastide recognized as his archenemy at Frankfurt.[25]

Historians have been hasty in concluding that Bastide's reception of Raumer was proof of France's "earnest resistance" to German unity.[26] The evidence does not prove that France's policy was "hidden diplomatic sabotage of Germany's unification" or was meant to discourage by "any diplomatic means . . . all forms of Germany, a policy of divide and rule in the tradition of Richelieu."[27] Instead of universally opposing all efforts to unify Germany, Raumer's reception reflected the ambiguities in Bastide's attitude toward the Frankfurt assembly. Even as Bastide feared the exaggerated nationalism of some members of that body, at the same time he respected the legitimate aspirations of the German people for national unity. The opposition that the Frankfurt assembly encountered originated in the French fears that the assembly would be an instrument of Habsburg imperial aspirations to reassert its power over Italy and Hungary.

Bastide's anxiety that the Frankfurt assembly might prove to be a standard bearer for the Viennese reactionary party seemed confirmed when the new foreign minister of the Frankfurt central power was named in September. Anton Ritter von Schmerling, the former president of the old German Diet, according to an internal memorandum drawn up in the French foreign ministry, "seems determined to represent the principles of Austria and the old Diet in the central power."[28] As minister of interior and foreign minister, Schmerling, an Austrian nobleman, was an "absolute opponent of [Heinrich von] Gagern's program" of Prussian supremacy over a *Kleindeutschland*, which necessarily excluded the German-speaking parts of Austria. Schmerling "believed that the German people would be satisfied with a new federal state, and [that] a reform of the confederation would achieve their wishes."[29]

If Austria rejected the mediation of the Italian problem proposed by England and France, as now appeared likely, Bastide feared that:

We shall be forced, despite ourselves, to give the signal for a general war. It is evident that Germany will make a common cause with Austria and that the Frankfurt unitarians, in spite of their pretended respect for nationalities, will send German contingents to aid the oppressors of the Italian nation. At the same time, Germany refused to ratify the armistice of Malmö, and from that side we are exposed to be drawn into an unpleasant struggle.[30]

Schmerling instructed Raumer to make clear to Bastide that "Austria's interests are to a great extent Germany's interests. It must therefore be supported with the full strength of Germany. Through Austria, Germany must retain a strong position between the Alps and the Po."[31] This was in Germany's military, mercantile, and financial interests. Bastide was most struck by Schmerling's claim that, "A great portion of the Austrian troops in Italy are now troops of the *Reich*, under the control of the *Reichsverweser*."[32]

This complete identification of Austria's interests with those of the German national assembly in Frankfurt horrified the French, who assumed that the masses of Germans were ready to follow France and Prussia in a holy crusade against tyranny. Thus Bastide dismissed the voices friendly toward Austria in the Frankfurt assembly as "deaf" to the real sentiments of Germany's overwhelming majority, which Bastide believed he knew better than did the ultra-nationalists in the Frankfurt assembly. He informed Tallenay that the situation in Germany was very uncertain. France must at all costs remain a spectator in Frankfurt until the situation was more stable. Bastide reaffirmed France's support for German unification, which Germany's "civilization" demanded.[33]

Bastide was confident that the national party in Germany would be friendly to France. While Austria only invoked "the right of property" in Italy, "we are the representatives of the opposed principle of the sovereignty of peoples."[34] He believed, moreover, that if the war came, the struggle in Italy would find Germans and French fighting together. Should this occur, then the treaties of Vienna would be:

resolutely torn up, and we shall call all the peoples who only wait for the signal given by us for a war against the thrones. . . . It will be easy for us to find allies not only in all of Italy . . . but also in Germany and even among the states submitting today, after a fashion, to Austrian domination.[35]

The Frankfurt assembly, Bastide thought, was out of touch with "public opinion" and "deaf." The "dangerous party of German tailors and professors" in Frankfurt "wished to reestablish the old supremacy of Austria" in Germany.[36]

"If it is necessary," Bastide assured Arago, "to fight a war in Germany, to attack simultaneously in Holstein and the Tyrol while we support the revolutionary demons along the Rhine, then I think France will not be the worst off, if all the German statesmen are not as deaf as those at Frankfurt."[37] The French assumed that they were in control of the popular nationalistic forces in Italy, Germany, and elsewhere, because they were the natural spokesmen for the masses' aspiration for liberty and national freedom, while the Frankfurt assembly had become the instrument of reactionary Austrian supremacy.

Bastide's assumption that France commanded an international front of friends who would follow France into war was based on faulty intelligence. Such a misconception undoubtedly was a result of Bastide's over-reliance on the reports of his secret agents. The true believers in the republican cause reinforced Bastide's ideological predilections. The foreign minister and his agents were ideologues who perceived the dawn of the millenium approaching. And the agents were hardly content to wait on the sidelines for revolutionary conditions to develop abroad without outside interference. Matters had not changed materially since May 3 when the legation councillor of Baden had warned his government that "every day new agents leave here to make contact with foreign democrats, to stimulate the revolutionary spirit which one says here has begun to lie dormant in Germany." On September 18 he now informed his foreign minister that preparatory work by French agents in Italy and Germany had advanced to the degree that the French government was poised to set Europe on fire and these secret agents "only awaited a signal from the outside to proclaim the republic at several points."[38]

Such a strong commitment to take sides in domestic affairs of foreign states inevitably had major drawbacks. Bastide's ideological engagement blinded him to a realistic assessment of the international situation. He allowed his subjective prejudice to influence his valuation of matters instead of relying on the surer standard of assuring the long-range survival of the nation. Thus Bastide seemed blindly confident that France would lead those committed to the "principle of sovereignty of the peoples" against Austria, who could invoke only "the right of property." His myopic view of French interests was neither consistently prudent nor realistic, but more often biased by his abstract mindset. Perhaps the best illustration of Bastide's dependence on like-minded advisers who reinforced his suppositions is offered by his chargé in Berlin, Emmanuel Arago.

Bastide's dealings with Prussia turned on his assumption—derived largely from Arago's dispatches—that the old Junker-dominated Prussian monarchy was a permanent victim of the revolution. Ignoring all warnings to the contrary, Bastide believed that the Prussian assembly and government wanted a solid bond with Paris to free the Poles. Bastide must be censured for over-reliance on his spiritual kinsman and the nephew of a member of the French Provisional Government, Emmanuel Arago, his chargé in Berlin. Arago consistently praised the conduct of the Berlin assembly, contrasting the reason and moderation of the members of that Berlin assembly with the Frankfurt parliament. For example, whereas the Frankfurt assembly provoked an internal crisis by rejecting the treaty of Malmö on September 8, Arago wrote that the Berlin assembly had approved the peace in Schleswig the previous day. Arago had spent that morning talking with members of the opposition. He reported that he had told the deputies "with careful reserve" of his fears from the "European point of view," and had indicated that the policy of the present Prussian government of Auerswald was "preferable to Frankfurt." He had protested that Frankfurt's policy "menaced at the same time Poland and Italy." The reaction to this, as reported by Arago, was that:

> All cried out without exception. . . .They wished to do for Posen what France demanded; first, because it was just and right for the Poles, then because they wished to be friends of France. As for the war in Italy, in no case would they ever join Austria. They added that Frankfurt modified its policy daily. The national parliament would change from its errors, or it would again soon be under the influence of a frankly liberal Prussian cabinet.[39]

Not only was the majority of the liberal Berlin assembly favorable to France and Poland, Arago reported on September 19, but so was the king of Prussia. Arago had received this news in the course of a visit from General von Willisen, an intimate friend and aide-de-camp of Frederick William IV. Willisen had been charged to inform Bastide that the Prussian monarch would stand by the "solemn promises that he had made in the month of

March."⁴⁰ In September Frederick William IV repeated to France his support for the reconstitution of Poland.

In summary, Bastide disregarded a basic law of diplomacy by allowing his prejudices to stand in the way of a realistic appraisal of international conditions. A dilettante, inexperienced in foreign affairs, Bastide surrounded himself with committed republicans who reinforced his tendency to exaggerate prospects for foreign revolutionaries. Auguste Beaumont complained to Tocqueville of the deputies in the foreign ministry. "To keep inadequate agents," Beaumont charged was "not only a detriment *(tort)*," but a "sort of crime."⁴¹ Tocqueville likewise deprecated the "profound mediocrity" of the foreign ministry.⁴² The French ambassador in London, Beaumont, attempted to explain away Bastide's stupidities *(sottises)* to Lord Palmerston. "That poor Bastide," Beaumont lamented to Tocqueville. "How pitiful," replied Tocqueville as he recounted to his old friend yet another compromising stupidity of Bastide, the simpleton *(innocent)*. It was "frightening" to Tocqueville that "the direction of our foreign affairs was delivered into such hands!"⁴³

The exchange of correspondence between Tocqueville and Beaumont suggests that Bastide committed his worst indiscretions without the knowledge of his cabinet colleagues. It appears possible that the old conspirator hoped to present the world with a fait accompli of a solid alliance of free peoples as auxiliaries against Austria. Not the least of these allies were the Magyars, whom Bastide presumed would aid French penetration of east central Europe. But Bastide in turn was encouraged to believe this by the news coming out of Budapest.

Batthyány's government seemed ready to assure the French that the Magyars were prepared to support France against their nominal sovereign in Vienna. Even after the Austrian cabinet in early September indicated a willingness to allow negotiations over northern Italy, Batthyány did not alter his determination to seek a military showdown with the Habsburg cabinet. Meanwhile, on September 2, 1848, reacting to the combined pressure of Paris and Budapest, the Austrian chancellor agreed to accept the Franco-British proposal of mediation between Austria and the hopelessly defeated Sardinian army.⁴⁴ Hungary's opening of formal diplomatic relations with France—a direct challenge—became even more imperative now that the Habsburgs would be able to concentrate their entire army against the Hungarians instead of dividing it between Italy and Hungary.

László Teleki left Budapest on August 31 bound for his post as Hungarian diplomatic agent in Paris. He conferred with Batthyány and Deák, who were in Vienna, for one or two days before carrying the offer of a Franco-Hungarian military alliance to Paris. Teleki's mission was a direct defiance of Vienna. It coincided with the Austrian cabinet's notice of August 31, which categorically denied Hungary's right to independent military, financial, and foreign affairs and called into question the April laws themselves.[45] Despite the Habsburg objections, Teleki continued on his way to Paris, and on September 4, 1848, Batthyány called at the home of the French chargé in Vienna to request formally French military support for Hungarian separation from the Danubian monarchy.[46]

Teleki arrived in Paris on September 8 to negotiate the terms of a formal Franco-Hungarian military pact.[47] But his arrival also coincided with the news of the Austrian diplomatic surrender. The foreign minister of Austria, Wessenberg, gave in to the French demand for a negotiated mediation in Italy. Possibly Hungary's willingness to ally with France may have been a contributing factor in Austria's decision to accept the negotiations long sought by France and Great Britain.

On September 11, 1848 the Habsburgs allowed Ban Jellačić of Croatia to invade Hungary. This in turn coincided with a new suggestion by Wessenberg that he might renege on that promise to accept the Franco-British mediation in Italy.

Bastide responded to the increasingly desperate situation on September 26, 1848, with the threat that if France and Austria clashed, then Bastide expected the Hungarians to fight with France.[48] He sent Czartoryski's military adjutant, Count Ludwik Bystrzonowski, to Turin and Carlowitz. Bystrzonowski was to do two things: to coordinate the armed forces of Sardinia and Hungary, and to negotiate a truce between the Magyars and the southern Slavs by splitting off the Serbs from Jellačić's forces.[49] But once again, direct French military involvement proved unnecessary. Jellačić was thrown back near Budapest on September 29, 1848, and two days later began to make his way to Austria. The attempt to send troops from Vienna to fight the Magyars touched off a revolt in Vienna. Bastide's long-awaited rising in central Europe appeared to be on the horizon.

Thus, in the revolutionary month of Vendémiaire, the final phase of a worldwide struggle of the peoples seemed imminent in Budapest, Berlin, and Vienna. In retrospect, we can fault Bastide for overestimating the revolutionary potential of the Berlin democrats. However, if Bastide mistakenly assumed the inevitability of democratic momentum, he was not alone in that delusion. After all, supreme optimism had to be second nature to an old street revolutionary. Yet as a statesman Bastide bears the heavy responsibility for the frustration of French aspirations to liberate European peoples.

NOTES

1. Hatzfeldt to Auerswald, Paris, September 1, 1848, GSA, fz. 863, fo. 15–16.

2. *Ibid.*

3. Wendland to King, Paris, August 27, 1848, BGStA, MA 2105.

4. *Ibid.;* Hatzfeldt to Auerswald, Paris, September 1, 1848, GSA, fz. 863, fo. 15. Bastide had shortened his list of German states tolerated by France from a week earlier, when he assured that France wished Prussia, Saxony, and Bavaria to continue to exist beside Austria, "strong not only in Germany, but more towards the east, where it is called to develop its riches and its strength"; Thom to Wessenberg, Paris, August 23, 1848, HHSA, IX; the difference is the term "independent" or "separate" *(eignen)* for Prussia and Bavaria, and his very clear admonition that Prussia should spread its domination over southern as well as northern Germany. Bastide apparently assumed that Austria and Saxony would survive in Germany, as the latter actually did in Bismarck's *Reich*, with its foreign policy controlled by Prussia.

5. Bastide to Tallenay, Paris, September 5, 1848, analyse, Cav 1 Mi 2 R 25.

6. *Ibid.*, AEF, Allemagne 806, fo. 8 (complete text of instructions).

7. *Ibid.*, analyse, Cav 1 Mi 2 R 25.

8. Bastide to Beaumont, Paris, September 20, 1848, Bastide, *La République française*, pp. 116–17; Bastide to Arago, Paris, September 13, 1848, Prusse 302, fo. 271.

9. Scharff, *Europäischen Grossmächte*.

10. Hatzfeldt to Foreign Minister, Paris, August 10, 1848, GSA, fz. 861, fo. 130.

11. Hatzfeldt to Foreign Minister, Paris, August 12, 1848, GSA, fz. 861, fo. 137.

12. cf. Pfisterer, p. 102, Hahn, pp. 234–35, Scharff, "Schleswig-Holstein," pp. 180–81, Valentin, II, 113.

13. Bastide to Arago, Paris, September 9, 1848, AEF, Prusse 302, fo. 264.

14. Ölsner to Heckscher, Paris, August 17 and 18, 1848, Bundesarchiv Zweigstelle Frankfurt/Main, Ölsner-Monmerqué Papers.

15. Börnstein, Bulletin, AEF, MD, Allemagne 129, fo. 101.

16. Briey to Hoffschmidt, Frankfurt, August 26, 1848, AEB, Frankfurt IV, fo. 164.

17. Bastide to Tallenay, Paris, September 5, 1848, AEF, Allemagne 806, fo. 10.

18. Bastide to Arago, Paris, September 6, 1848, AEF, Prusse 302, fo. 247; Tallenay to Bastide, Frankfurt, September 11, 1848, Allemagne 806, fo. 12; Hatzfeldt to Foreign Minister, Paris, August 19, 1848, GSA, fz. 861, fo. 151.

19. Hatzfeldt to Auerswald, Paris, August 25, 1848, GSA, fz. 863, fo. 8. "France did not know what the German *Reich* was, where its borders began, where they ended," Bastide told the Bavarian minister, Wendland to King, Paris, August 27, 1848, BGStA, MA 2105.

20. Heckscher to Raumer, Frankfurt, August 20, 1848, Bundesarchiv Zweigstelle Frankfurt/Main, Raumer Papers.

21. Bastide to Arago, Paris, September 7, 1848, AEF, Prusse 302, fo. 250.

22. Thom to Wessenberg, Paris, September 6, 1848, HHSA, PA, IX Frankreich, fo. 36.

23. Bose to Foreign Minister, Paris, September 7, 1848, Kretzschmar and Schlechte, *Gesandtschaftsberichte*, p. 171; Bastide wrote Arago that Vienna expected help from Frankfurt if fighting broke out between Austria and France, September 6, 1848, AEF, Prusse 302, fo. 247.

24. Könneritz to Foreign Minister, Paris, September 11, 1848, Kretzschmar and Schlechte, *Gesandtschaftsberichte*, p. 176.

25. Börnstein, on a separate sheet, undated, between Bulletins, September 1 and 2, 1848, AEF, MD, Allemagne 129, fo. 113.

26. Hahn, pp. 232–48, Ley, 125, 133, Scharff, "König Friedrich Wilhelm," p. 160.

27. Scharff, *Europäischen Grossmächte*, pp. 77 and 82, "deutsche Einheit," p. 152, Jennings, *France and Europe*, pp. 207, 210, and Pfisterer, 102–07.

28. Ministres nommés par l'Archiduc Jean, Vicaire général de l'Empire, Cav 1 Mi 2 R 24.

29. *Allgemeine Deutsche Biographie*, LIV, 61.

30. Bastide to Beaumont, Paris, September 20, 1848, in Bastide, *La République française*, p. 116.

31. Schmerling to Raumer, Frankfurt, September 18, 1848, quoted in Hatzfeldt to Bülow (Prussian under-secretary of state), Paris, September 30, 1848, GSA, fz. 863, fo. 65–66; Bastide, *La République française*, pp. 51–56; Raumer conveniently allowed Hatzfeldt to install him in the same building *(Hôtel de Hollande)*, where Raumer permitted Hatzfeldt to copy his incoming and outgoing correspondence, Valentin, *Geschichte der deutschen Revolution*, II, 112; Hatzfeldt, GSA, *passim*. Andrian in London stressed to Beaumont the interest of the German empire that "Austria possess good frontiers in Italy; and he added an instant later with the same composure, that the German empire, being impartial and disinter-

ested in the Italian question, one could not refuse her participation in the mediation." Beaumont to Cavaignac, London, September 11, 1848, Cav 1 Mi 2 R 25.

32. Schmerling to Raumer, Frankfurt, September 18, 1848, GSA, fz. 863, fo. 65–66. Bastide concluded that, if the Frankfurt assembly took part in the mediation of the Italian affairs, "We would confront two Austrias in the place of one"; Bastide to Beaumont, Paris, September 20, 1848, *La République française*, pp. 51, 117.

33. Bastide to Tallenay, Paris, September 5, 1848, AEF, Allemagne 806, fo. 9–10.

34. Bastide to De la Cour, Paris, September 26, 1848, AEF, Autriche 436, fo. 229 bis; "We would be better disposed to recognize the Frankfurt government," Bastide assured, "if it posed as defender of nationalities instead of defending the pretentions of Austria in Italy and the treaties of 1815." Bastide to Tallenay, Paris, October 5, 1848, Cav 1 Mi 2 R 25.

35. Bastide to De la Cour, Paris, September 26, 1848, AEF, Autriche 436, fo. 229 bis.; De la Cour wrote that the "party of war" included "all the aristocracy" of Austria, Vienna, July 10, 1848; "public spirit and the interest of the peoples" were "invariably opposed to the Teutonist projects" of the "Frankfurt men." Vienna, July 26 and August 3, 1848, Cav 1 Mi 2 R 26; Beaumont believed that if France were forced into a war it would rally the sympathies of liberal Europe. English public opinion was pro-Italian, and if liberal England saw France fighting for the Italian independence, a rising in the land would demand that the British government support France in its efforts. Beaumont to Bastide, London, August 31, 1848, Angleterre 671, fo. 122–25; Beaumont welcomed "a war of a day to assure the world a half-century of peace." Beaumont to Tocqueville, London, August 31/September 2, 1848, *Oeuvres*, VIII^2, 34–35; Rothan assumed that the "reactionaries" hoped for "a struggle against France which would unite Germany and Russia; that is the goal of their policy. Only the republican party demonstrates a warm and sincere sympathy" for the French, Cassel, August 10, 1848, Cav 1 Mi 2 R 26. De la Cour repeated that "a powerful opinion" opposed a reestablishment of the old Austrian order in Italy. The bourgeoisie in particular wanted peace. De la Cour to Bastide, Vienna, August 11, 1848, Autriche 436, fo. 74.

36. Trauttmansdorff to Wessenberg, Berlin, September 21, 1848, HHSA, fo. 318; Bastide to Tallenay, Paris, September 5, 1848, AEF, Allemagne 806, fo. 8.

37. Bastide to Arago, Paris, September 9, 1848, AEF, Prusse 302, fo. 264.

38. Baron F. A. von Schweitzer to Dusch, Paris, May 3 and September 18, 1848, BGLA, fz. 48/2037.

39. Arago to Bastide, Berlin, September 8, 1848, AEF, Prusse 302, fo. 260–61.

40. *Ibid.*, September 19, 1848, fo. 289.

41. Beaumont to Tocqueville, London, October 10, 1848, Tocqueville, *Oeuvres*, VIII^2, 55–56.

42. Tocqueville to Beaumont, Paris, September 24, 1848, *Ibid.*, VIII^2, 52.

43. Tocqueville to Beaumont, Paris, December 1, 1848, *Ibid.*, VIII^2, 106.

44. A. J. P. Taylor, *The Italian Problem*, pp. 161–66.

45. Hajnal, pp. 114–15.

46. *Ibid.*, p. 117.

47. Teleki letter, Paris, October 6, 1848, abstract in Hajnal, pp. 103–06, 114; cf. Thomas Lengyel, "La mission parisienne du comte Ladislas Teleki," *Nouvelle Revue de Hongrie*, (1941), 109–17; Deak, pp. 294–95.

48. Bastide to De la Cour and Beaumont, Paris, September 26, 1848, AEF, Autriche 436, fo. 229 bis and Angleterre 671, fo. 185; Jennings is misinformed in his belief that France was unwilling to fight Austria after September 2, *France and Europe;* Taylor is uncharacteristically more cautious, *The Italian Problem*, p. 196.

49. Instructions for Bystrzonowski, in Chastain, "Iratok," pp. 280–82, 292–93.

Chapter Nine
The Emancipation of Enslaved Peoples

OCTOBER-DECEMBER 1848

A CRUSADE FOR THE LIBERATION of peoples depended upon external events, which more than ever dominated French policy during the last quarter of 1848. A rising tide of revolt in Vienna and in Berlin occasioned violence in both Germanic capitals. But the chief preoccupation of Europeans sympathetic to the revolutionary cause was with the continuing war in Hungary, unleashed by the Habsburg court's covert support of Ban Jellačić.

Following Jellačić's initial reverses on the battlefield in Hungary, the Croats withdrew across the Leithe into Austria, allowing the Magyars further time to organize their forces. On October 3, the Habsburg emperor finally took sides in the growing civil war by dissolving the Hungarian assembly and naming the rebel Jellačić as viceroy in Hungary. This action stunned partisans of the liberal cause throughout central Europe.

Meanwhile, during the last three weeks of October, Vienna revolted for the third time that year. The Austrian emperor fled to Olmütz, investing General Prince Alfred Windischgrätz with authority to retake Vienna by force. Thus Habsburg armies were diverted from Hungary by the necessity of suppressing the Viennese revolt.

On October 15 Berliners followed the example in Vienna, and violence broke out once again in the Prussian capital. Matters were complicated by a crisis within the Berlin assembly. The liberal majority was increasingly at odds with the king's cabinet. Thus a three-sided struggle ensued involving the people in the streets, the moderate liberals of the Prussian assembly, and the increasingly confident reactionary advisers surrounding the Prussian king.

One more reminder of the growing irrelevancy of the Frankfurt assembly was the opening of a Second Democratic Congress, which met not in Frankfurt, but in Berlin. The major decisions concerning Germany's future would be made in Berlin rather than in Frankfurt. An immediate issue needing resolution was the scope and method of bringing about the unification of Germany: Would German unity be bought at the cost of a military struggle or could it be received by parliamentary compromise without bloodshed?

As the month came to an end, the key issue as to the nature of leadership in Prussia remained open. The Prussian assembly took revenge on the reactionary clique around the Prussian king by abolishing the privileges of the aristocratic Prussian Junker class. Street disturbances in Berlin suggested that the time of compromises and half-measures might be drawing to a close.

In fact, the crisis of the Prussian revolution was only beginning. Even though contemporary observers could not make out the future form of the new Prussian state nor the role that this Prussian state might play in a united Germany, these speculations were temporarily pushed aside by a new concern, namely, fear of the "red" menace. Just as Bastide had drawn back before the "communist" menace of the June Days, so Berliners had to decide whether to continue the increasingly radical course of revolt, or to call in the army to restore "order." It was upon this issue that the course of the German revolution now turned.

In spite of Bastide's optimistic expectations, the revolutionary momentum in Vienna and Berlin began to falter. During November the authorities began to marshall their resources to regain their power base.

The victory of the Austrian army over the Viennese populace gave the Junker class in Berlin the telling argument in its struggle for the support of the Prussian monarch: The forces of disorder were in fact not invincible.

On November 9, King Frederick William IV of Prussia dissolved the Prussian assembly and ordered that parliament to meet in the small provincial town of Brandenburg. The resistance of liberals to royal fiat brought on a new crisis, which lasted throughout the month of November. General Wrangel entered Berlin on November 10 to follow the Austrian example of using brute force against the parliamentary government and street violence. The Prussian army chased the parliamentarians from one meeting place to another and finally out of the city limits.

In Austria a new era was inaugurated in Olmütz at the end of November, when Prince Felix von Schwarzenberg formed an imperial Austrian ministry committed to ending all half-measures and to excluding opposing liberal German nationalists. Schwarzenberg rejected any Austrian participation in the creation of a united Germany. In place of that ideal he offered the old call for the integrity of the Austrian Empire. The gathering of forces in Austria for the decisive blow against substantial change amassed new strength on December 2, when the Austrian Emperor Ferdinand abdicated in favor of his young nephew, Franz Joseph I.

King Frederick William IV of Prussia drew to his banner many of the liberals who had been ostracized in Austria. On December 5 he proposed a highly liberal constitution for Prussia and at the same time dissolved the assembly charged with writing the document, an ambiguous move characteristic of this monarch. The year closed with German liberals pinning their last hope on this frail reed—perhaps he would provide the national leadership that could unify Germany and close a millenium of division and discord.

From the end of October until December 10, the internal focus of French energies was the election of a French president by universal manhood suffrage. The elevation of Prince Louis Napoleon as president once more placed a Bonaparte in the highest post in France. And few contemporaries doubted that sooner or later this would lead to a fresh French attempt to avenge the disgrace of Waterloo.

Thus, when Austria opened her final offensive against the Hungarian rebels on December 13, a great number of the best informed Europeans thought that spring would see a French army fighting somewhere in Europe. Indeed the final weeks of the Cavaignac government in France were focused on negotiating a Franco-Ottoman alliance to preserve the "integrity" of the Ottoman Empire. The fighting in Hungary and the actions of the Russian army in the nominally Ottoman territories of the Danubian principalities brought France and the Ottoman sultan together.

The assumption that the Cavaignac government, during the autumn of 1848, seriously considered the possibility of a war was hotly disputed by Lawrence Jennings.[1] Jennings maintained that Bastide assessed France's situation realistically and sought "peace at all costs." A. J. P. Taylor more cautiously concluded that he was perplexed by the whole matter and doubted that he or anyone else would ever be able to sort out Bastide's real thoughts on the matter of a war.[2] New evidence unavailable to Taylor and Jennings enables us to examine the French policy within the wider context of secret agents sent "daily" into other countries to stir up revolt.[3] The vast archives of Prince Adam Czartoryski in Cracow, Poland (which formed the basis of Marceli Handelsman's masterful studies of Czartoryski) contain reports of the Polish contingent of the French foreign ministry's confidential agents. More recent works by István Hajnal, Cornelia Bodea, Aladár Urbán, and a number of other historians of east central Europe have greatly widened our understanding of the relations between France and that volatile area.[4] This superb scholarship has pushed our frame of reference toward the east. Their histories of Austria during 1848 emphasize that in spite of the war in Italy, Austria's attention could never be completely distracted from the stormy revolutions elsewhere in their empire, and eventually another war broke out against the Hungarian rebels. This was largely overlooked in the now very dated works of Taylor and Jennings because they focused almost entirely on Italy. In addition they overlooked France's underhanded operations. Neither remarked upon the activities of these wandering propagandists of the millenium sent out by the French government.

This new frame of reference permits us now to reexamine the old documents and gain insights that earlier researchers misunderstood. They certainly failed to appreciate the dominantly optimistic attitude in Bastide's public and private demeanor. Bastide really assumed that a great and secret revolutionary army awaited only a signal from France to spring into action. Thus he wrote to his ambassador in London, Gustave de Beaumont:

> If the kings are not wise enough to appreciate our moderation, if they wound our sentiments and honor, we shall be forced to pose clearly the question and to resolve it with arms in appealing to us all popular sentiments, however violent they might be.[5]

That optimism implies in turn that Bastide actually believed that he was in control of events, that he was the leader of that continent-wide coalition of sovereign peoples.

In addition to his optimism, the arrogance of his presumed power to mobilize the wretched of the earth implies a third characteristic of Bastide's mental framework: There were no material alterations of the assumptions contained in Lamartine's Manifesto to Europe on March 4. France was the protector of the oppressed peoples, or, as Bastide wrote in an extremely important document in the Cavaignac Papers, the French were "partisans of the sovereignty of peoples." Bastide contrasted this ideological bastion of protection of the downtrodden masses with Austria's role as the champion of the opposed "principle of the right of property of princes over states."[6] Bastide believed that France's mission was to overturn the entire state system to re-draw all borders to coincide with the ethnic make-up of central Europe. That was the ruling premise of Lamartine's Manifesto and the unanimous resolution of the French assembly on May 24.

What has caused real problems for historians is Lamartine's and Bastide's espousal of a "policy of peace." Even in instructions drawn up for an envoy to the king of Sardinia during October 1848, Bastide still maintained, "We are convinced that it is in the interest of the people that this transformation ought to take place peacefully."[7] Here we run into an absolute inconsistency. Not only does the document call for the "sovereignty of the peoples," but also the promise that "we know that the future of western Europe belongs to the purely democratic principle."[8] We shall have to deal with the problem of Bastide's view of the democratic future later; Bastide certainly was inconsistent in speaking about "democracy." And it is hard to take seriously anyone who speaks of overturning all established governments on the one hand and on the other hand claiming that this ought to be done peacefully!

It is evident that Jules Bastide was no realist; this "Forty-eighter" actually believed that these radical transformations of the European state system could materialize with no more violence than the small-scale street skirmishes on the level of the February Revolution. This romantic rebel shared this illusion of utopian transmutation with his intimate friend and chargé in Berlin, Emmanuel Arago. Arago wrote to Bastide from Berlin on November 25, 1848, when the utter failure of the 1848 revolutions ought to have been evident to anyone but the most starry-eyed, that the fate of Austria and Prussia was supposedly in the hands of the sovereign people. Arago mused that Germany was no longer a federation of kings, sovereigns, and absolute princes:

> It is the people who know and wish liberty, who will never allow a war of principle to be fought against France. So prudent, so restrained, so moderate until now, France would have an invincible force, the day when, declaring that she will not conquer a single province, that she would not augment her own territory with a single department, she could take in hand

the flag of propaganda and say to Europe that the French
armies have no other order of the day than the emancipation
of enslaved peoples.[9]

Bastide, as well, believed that France was invincible. Rather
than being reduced to despondent inaction by the belief that France
was powerless and had to seek "peace at all costs" (Jennings),
Bastide was confident that the disequilibrium caused by the European revolutions made it "now impossible to take an aggressive
attitude toward the [French] republic."[10]

To understand French foreign policy during the closing months
of 1848 we must look at events as contemporaries viewed them.
The expectation of a "final struggle" romanticized in the lyrics of
the *Internationale* strongly colored perceptions. Those expectations
we now know were unfulfilled; however, it was on the basis of
that vision that Bastide framed decisions on foreign policy in France.

In summary, new evidence, drawn from a wider range of
sources than was available to previous writers, indicates that
France's foreign minister was a perplexed daydreamer who optimis-
tically imagined that France held in her hands the strings to an
enormous net of secret agents who could carry off simultaneous
revolutions all over central Europe. He was restrained only by the
magnanimous hope that such a complete destruction of old
sovereignties would take place with as little bloodshed as possible.
Eventually all Europe would rise when the French chose to unfurl
the "flag of propaganda" and to emancipate the "enslaved" of the
earth. One of the decisive arenas of the final battle was east central
Europe, which the French hoped to reshape as a "Danubian confederation." And on September 30 Jules Bastide called in Prince Adam
Czartoryski, the chief conspirator in the Polish émigré network,
and the envoy of Sardinia-Piedmont, to discuss the top secret
mission of Czartoryski's adviser on military affairs, Count Ludwik
Bystrzonowski. The French had finally begun to contemplate seriously the possibility of a war by the spring of 1849. As a prelude
to that Franco-Austrian war, Bystrzonowski was to attempt to
divide the forces of the Austrian Empire. In expectation that the
Magyars would stand beside France and Sardinia-Piedmont, Bystrzonowski's mission was to negotiate a reconciliation between the
Magyars and the southern Slavs in preparation for a joint Franco-
Italian-Hungarian military action. The Sardinian envoy reported
to his government that Bastide, in his presence, instructed Bystrzonowski to advise the Patriarch of Carlowitz and other Serbian

and Croatian leaders to make their peace with the Hungarians as quickly as possible. Brignole reported that:

> In case (not improbable according to him [Bastide]) that a war broke out in spring between France and Austria, if they acted to separate themselves from her and to constitute one or several independent states which will form with Hungary, and later with the Principalities of Moldavia and Wallachia and other neighboring states, a confederation distinct from Germany and which one will call the Danubian Confederation, they will be able, he [Bastide] said, to count on the support and even on every sort of help on the part of the French government.[11]

In instructions for Count Bystrzonowski, Bastide termed the struggle between the Croats and the Magyars "deplorable," because "it is difficult for me to believe that the Magyar element and the Slavic element cannot be conciliated." "I told you," Bastide continued, "of our sympathies for the peoples that you will visit and our desire to see them fraternally reunited by the bonds of peace and concord." France wanted to foster such reconciliation as a bulwark against Austrian reactionary forces.[12] Thus Bastide's policy was founded on a profound ignorance of deepseated antagonisms that he expected to "conciliate" with a wave of the hand from Paris. It appears to us highly unlikely that the Magyar leadership could ever have brought themselves to accept the Serbs as equals without a major military setback, but such an interpretation in 1848 flew in the face of the French ideology of liberating all "oppressed peoples." Yet precisely that world view, which the French assembly's unanimous resolution of May 24 had embodied, now crumbled in the course of debates held in the German assembly in Frankfurt.

During August a decisive shift in the Frankfurt assembly's outlook had already become apparent. After encroaching on the territorial limits of the German Confederation with the Schleswig war and the Polish debates, new and even more violent rhetoric attacked Great Britain and France directly. From a criticism of France and England, the language soon became hostile, even from the political left, which before this time had exhibited political cosmopolitanism in the Polish debate of July. Now enmity was expressed toward the English and French, rather than toward the "barbarian" states of the east or the dynasties.

Günther Roth perceived this change in the Limburg debate in early September, and by the middle of the month it had reached its height. The entire assembly was angry and defiant, censuring the French heavily. The *Leitmotiv* of speeches was hostility toward the rest of Europe. The radicals preferred confrontation to conciliation and spoke of negotiation from strength. Basing relations on fear, rather than trust, the parliament rejected Bastide's whole conception of the revolutionary alliance among free peoples in the cause of the peaceful conquest of ideas. Instead of responding to the French assembly's resolution of May 24, members of the Frankfurt assembly glorified war as the ultimate reckoning. The democrat Heinrich Simon of Breslau fulminated against England, Russia, and France. Roth found that in the rejection of the armistice of Malmö the decisive theme in the speeches of the left was the honor of Germany.[13]

The British also questioned the possibility of working with the "crazy professors" at Frankfurt. Lord Cowley, British chargé at Frankfurt, wrote in vexation to Palmerston that Heckscher thought nothing of threatening both Britain and France with war to assist Austria:

> What answer can you make to a minister of foreign affairs who says, "What do you think we are afraid of—war? I am not sure that war is not the *best thing* for us. It must at all events settle the question of unity at once." In short, they are a parcel of children who want whipping and caressing alternately.[14]

"I grieve," Cowley complained, "to see how little repugnance there is here . . . to a war." German unity would come far more quickly by this means, the advocates of nationalism believed, while the "minor sovereigns, imagining that they cannot be worse off than they are, are willing to embrace this desperate chance" to recover their power. The republicans "rejoice in any necessity" to use troops and enable them "to pursue their plans."[15] Heckscher hoped that England "will not permit France and the northern Powers to coalesce against Germany" and the British would advise Denmark to accept any terms.[16]

Underlying the rancor against France was a new "strong national will for power and the conviction that Germany had a mission of leadership."[17] Even Karl Marx joined the chorus of angry agitators unable to understand the loyalty of the Czechs and other Slavs to the Habsburg monarchy. The attempt of the Frankfurt assembly to bring freedom to Europe seemed to the Germans to be doomed because the Slavs in the Austrian Empire rallied to the

Austrian emperor instead of to the Viennese revolution. The left in the Frankfurt assembly recognized the Italians, Hungarians, and especially the Poles as allies, but "under no circumstances could the Czechs and the Croats be considered friends."[18] As early as June, Venedey, in the discussion of the Czech question, reflected this hostility to the Slavs, characterizing them as the "greatest danger for Germany" because they served as allies of Russia.[19]

On every border, the Frankfurt assembly threatened its neighbors by basing its claim for inclusion of an area in unified Germany on the use of the German language by its people, rather than being content to consolidate within the historic frontiers of the Germany (German Confederation) recognized by the treaty of Vienna. Instead of quickly joining together Germany in its central core, the parliamentarians took their stand on strongly disputed areas like Posen, Tyrol, Limburg, and Schleswig. Some members of the Frankfurt parliament even advocated the annexation of Bohemia (with its Czech majority) into a united Germany. In this case, Bohemia was certainly part of the German Confederation but its inclusion violated the principle of national rights for the Czechs. Still, there is a distinction in this case. The real problem was in expanding beyond the borders of the old German Confederation. Europe placed only one condition on Germany, Stadelmann concluded, "Hands off the borders!"[20] Germany's tampering with her territorial limits constituted a cardinal sin in French eyes. Bastide was outraged by the moral and legal violations of both his principle of the rights of sovereign peoples and the letter of international treaties.

Thus Scharff's objection that the liberal powers used "other standards to measure the Schleswig-Holstein question than the Italian" is without foundation. Bastide consistently favored national liberation of all oppressed peoples throughout Europe, but he believed that the German assembly, by contrast, was guilty of using an extremely flexible standard to measure what was German.[21] Bastide believed that the Frankfurt assembly's support of the Austrian monarchy posed the greatest threat to his efforts to create sovereign nations in southern and eastern Europe and violated the French assembly's unanimous resolution of May 24. Yet Bastide did nothing to undermine that German assembly, because he believed that it was a spent force. He instead admonished Tallenay to speak to the parliamentarians with reserve since France must not insult a point of view that in Frankfurt attempted to unify Germany:

That opinion has some respectability in that it reposes, at least in part, in the interests of the people. On the other hand, we risk offending a force that does not concern the interests of France. We should leave Germany alone. . . . I believe, in effect, that Frankfurt has lost much of the force of initiative and centralization.[22]

Scharff misunderstood Bastide's hostility toward the Frankfurt assembly. First, Bastide rebuked parliament's support of Austrian ambitions in Italy and the German claims on the territory of surrounding states. Secondly, the French support for Prussia was equally unconnected with a disapprobation for the axiom of German unity. Bastide saw Prussia as the agent of his French design of united peoples on her frontiers. Thirdly, Scharff exaggerated the inconsequential (to the French) matter of Schleswig-Holstein, never realizing how trivial it seemed to Bastide. Finally, as we have emphasized above,[23] Bastide never understood the basic facts concerning Schleswig, mistakenly assuming that the province was overwhelmingly Danish and thereby that the Germans violated Danish rights. Thus Bastide was thoroughly consistent in seeking an associate in Germany to aid France in emancipating the peoples of Europe.

Bastide and Cavaignac assumed that Europe was on the eve of a new period of troubles in which Prussia would be France's "natural ally in Germany, . . . our best and surest ally" in the long period of European disturbances. Prussia would "progress without disorder" to "march at the head of liberal Germany and aid us in terminating the difficulties that the ambition of Vienna and Frankfurt opened up in Italy."[24]

Above all, Scharff misunderstood the trivial importance of Schleswig-Holstein within the larger framework of France's greater interests. Bastide made it clear that the Prussian foreign minister was "mistaken if he believed France entertained hostile sentiments toward Prussia" because of Schleswig. France's anger was only toward the Frankfurt unitarians.[25] He praised Prussia's "service to the maintenance of European peace by the conclusion of the armistice with Denmark."[26] It was "men like Heckscher and Dahlmann at Frankfurt," Bastide complained, who "can only envenom all questions placed in their hands."[27]

By mid-November, Bastide had backed away from his earlier support of Denmark under the treaty of 1720. Bastide now promised the Prussian Hatzfeldt that, "when a definitive arrangement between Germany and Denmark" came in question, it would be made "with regard to the dispositions and with the wishes of the population of Schleswig itself." Bastide admitted that basing negotiations on the treaty of 1720 instead of the principle of nationality was inconsistent with the basic axiom of France's policy, but he promised that the treaty would only serve as a point of departure in settling the matter of Schleswig. Bastide promised that he "reserved complete liberty for future judgement."[28] Thus the Schleswig question was never the touchstone for German unity that Alexander Scharff imagined it to be.

The French were pleased as well by Prussia's handling of the Polish question in the waning months of 1848. On October 23, Arago reported that the Prussian assembly refused to divide Posen. "The line of demarcation, the annexation, partition, all resolved and voted in so violent a fashion in the Frankfurt parliament," were rejected by Berlin. After repudiating the partition of Posen into German and Polish zones, the assembly voted on the Phillips amendment which, according to Arago, "solemnly guaranteed the rights of the inhabitants of the province of Posen. . . . These rights will be regulated in the future by an organic law that will be promulgated at the same time as the constitution."[29] Arago was ecstatic: "We have attained our goal. The victory is complete. . . . The Duchy of Posen will not be German; it will remain intact for Poland."[30] Bastide told the French assembly on November 8, 1848 that, "Prussia, following our friendly advice, just assured by a vote of the legislature the separate and independent existence of the Grand Duchy of Posen. . . . Never since the February Revolution have our foreign relations been more satisfactory."[31]

During the autumn, Bastide and Cavaignac repeatedly affirmed that France wanted a strong Prussia to unify Germany. Far from viewing the Berlin government as a "decentralizing force" standing in the way of a unified German Empire, Bastide assumed that it was destined to create national consolidation for the German people. "I certainly do not desire German unity like the ultra-unitarians of Frankfurt," Bastide admitted, but if that unity "were formed in a greater or lesser degree, I desire that it be for Prussia's gain and that Berlin and not Frankfurt dominate it."[32] "I shall always cooperate with you," Bastide remarked to Hatzfeldt, "to augment Prussia's position and influence, because I am convinced that this is in France's true interest." Hatzfeldt concluded that the French minister of foreign affairs "has the interests of Prussia at heart almost as much as a Prussian himself."[33]

Cavaignac on October 20 indicated that the French antipathy for Austria did not extend to the other German states. Prussia and the rest of Germany had often been allies of the former republic. The "complete unity of Germany" in a new German empire evoked little sympathy in France. Cavaignac added that this unity, "resulting in the total annihilation of Prussia and of Austria, seemed difficult to realize; but that, if nevertheless it were established, he believed then that France had no alternative but to form an entente at any price."[34]

Bastide was no less explicit, reassuring Hatzfeldt that the "enlargement of Prussia was not contrary to French interests, and [that] an intimate alliance between the two countries would bring reciprocal advantages."[35] In his report of the conversation with Bastide, Hatzfeldt recounted:

> As a Frenchman, you could not expect that he would applaud the creation of a new German empire based on a complete unity like that of France, but if that unlimited unity were nevertheless established in Germany, contrary to his wishes, he preferred that it would be for Berlin's benefit and not Frankfurt's.[36]

Bastide had added that "he was convinced that a much greater unity than in the past would be realized in Germany, and that it was in the natural order of things that Prussia was placed at the head of that moderate unity."

Deterministically, the French foreign minister asserted, "This protectorate over Germany could not escape the Prussian government if its conduct conformed to circumstances." He repeated that it "was not contrary to the true interests of France."[37]

How could Bastide and Cavaignac have been so blind? How could they have possibly believed that France ought to allow the reactionary, militaristic government of Frederick William IV to extend its "unlimited" control over Germany? And not as a federal state, of the kind advocated by Proudhon, but a completely centralized state like France! Thus the matter of German unity is intimately connected to the apparent inconsistency in Bastide's espousal of democracy in Germany, speaking often of the "democratic and unitary" tendency.

Ideological nationalists that they were, Bastide and Cavaignac envisaged no other possibility than respecting the will of the people.

Cavaignac told Hatzfeldt that while "it would be useless to hide the very natural desire of the French Republic to see other countries adopt the same form of government as it [had]," France also respected "the principle that the whole nation is the only judge" of what was right for it. Cavaignac "recognized that the state of Germany and the tendencies of the German people did not permit him to think that it could presently establish the republic in a manner beneficial for the country," although he thought that "the republic was the best form of government."[38] France was always willing to accept "moderate" German unity. It would apparently have fought German annexation of northern Italy, which would have created a state from Luxembourg to Nice on France's border, but Bastide did not oppose a united Germany as such. As for democracy, this was ultimately a matter for the German people to decide. Naturally, France would provide propaganda, underhandedly, but publicly could use only moral suasion to convince Germans to declare a "sister republic" across the Rhine.

Bastide's vision of Austria's future state was equally quixotic. The outbreak of the Viennese revolution in October, Bastide thought, assured that the house of Habsburg would have to allow a complete transformation of the Austrian Empire. His envoy in Berlin, Arago, wrote on October 17 that in the future Austria would be dominated by its provinces, because it had "ceased to be a united power." Prince Metternich's old system of "ruling over diverse nations, enemy races, under the same government" was now no longer possible. The Viennese revolution had terminated forever the "oppression of Slavs by Magyars, Czechs by Germans, Croats by Czechs, Italians by Croats." Instead of a German-dominated monarchy, there would be a "multi-monarchy."[39] Bastide concurred with this assessment in his reply three days later.[40]

Bastide's thinking was reflected in an article in the *National* of October 14, which claimed, "The Austrian Empire no longer exists!"[41] Bastide now believed that the revolution in Vienna would end Austrian influence over events in Italy, that the continuing dissensions among her subject nations meant that Austria's power to use Germany to dominate the Mediterranean peninsula had ended. Thus Jennings is clearly mistaken in his assessment that Bastide had no illusions about the October revolt in Vienna profoundly weakening Austria.[42]

Bastide was full of illusions. He mistakenly thought that the Slavs would dominate the empire, be "very liberal," and thereby constitute a strong threat at the borders of absolutist Russia. Ultimately, he saw Austria forced to seek a rapprochement with France because of an increase of tensions between Austria and Russia. This preoccupation in the east would necessarily weaken Austria's position in Germany, making it unable to "count on the aid of the German Confederation in Italy." The balance of power within the Austrian Empire, Bastide presumed, had decisively and permanently shifted, changing its entire character. "Austria has ceased forever to be able to be considered a German power. . . . Austria can only be a Slavic power, and it seems to me to have lost all chance to exercise the preponderance in Germany."[43]

Bastide emphasized two results of Austria's predicament: "First, this preponderance cannot fail to fall to Prussia, whose anxiety can vanish as it extends its domination over southern Germany; secondly, Austria by making itself an exclusively Slavic power will clash with Russia, that counted on using its Slavic affinities to expand its influence into western Europe."[44] Bastide concluded that these tendencies in Austria were "favorable to French policy."[45]

Bastide assured Hatzfeldt that he recognized the value of Austria's "Catholic Slavism" to form a "useful counterweight to the Greek Slavism of Russia."[46] Bohemian and Croatian control of the Habsburg monarchy was clearly preferable to German domination. Bastide and Arago approved Gabriac's program of new institutions for the Danubian monarchy. The Viennese revolution, Bastide thought, would "facilitate solution of the difficulties presented in Italian affairs." Lombardy-Venetia would gain a "degree of independence" whereby the population could "enjoy an unconstrained political existence of its own." On the other hand, Bastide observed, France had no interest in Austria's being "completely smothered by the Slavic element." Her government ought to "conserve a strong existence between Slavism and Germanism." To do this, Austria had to disengage herself completely from the source of her troubles, Italy.[47]

The transformation of Italy took on a new dimension in Bastide's thinking with the Viennese revolution. He falsely hypothesized that the Austrian court had lost its traditional allies. Once again his confidential advisers stimulated his quixotry. Heinrich Börnstein reported that German public opinion was unsympathetic to the Danubian monarchy and that there were demonstrations throughout Germany against the Habsburg ruler. Emperor

Ferdinand's victory over the Viennese democratic revolution would be hollow, because "it will be the beginning of the end of the Austrian monarchy, and true difficulties will take root in the burning debris of the capital." Even the conservative *Augsburger Allgemeine Zeitung* was indignant at the "stupidity and blindness of the court."[48]

Insulated from reality by the enraptured bombast of his secret agents, Bastide imagined that something called "German public opinion" stood by France against the Austrian monarch. Moreover, he really believed that Austria would disintegrate into her component national provinces, making the monarch a captive to a supposedly liberal and Slavic majority. These utterly false assumptions strongly colored his expectations. Before the Viennese October revolution, Bastide and Cavaignac believed that France might have to fight to protect the Venetian Republic proclaimed by Manin. Cavaignac promised on September 27 that:

> If Venice were now taken by the Austrians, he would be forced to bring the question before the National Assembly to know if the moment had arrived where it was necessary to go to war, a question which the National Assembly would have to decide.[49]

Bastide repeatedly mentioned to Hatzfeldt the unanimous resolution of May 24 committing the French assembly to enfranchising Venetia. After the supposed shift in the power balance within the Danubian monarchy Bastide assured Hatzfeldt that "all of his efforts tended to procure for Lombardy as well as Venetia the most independence possible *vis-à-vis* the Austrian government, but not to destroy all ties between the provinces and the sovereign of the Austrian monarchy."[50]

Bastide's wrongheadedness explains the seemingly glaring contradictions between his promises of support to Lombardo-Venetia for liberation and his belief that they should remain part of the Austrian monarchy. Bastide pledged on October 10: "We are certain to place Lombardo-Venetia in a situation so that the Italian nationality will be able to develop itself and establish itself in peace."[51] And as late as November 17, Bastide could assure Manin that the French would never abandon Venice, never accept another Campo Formio, and that the Venetians would be "liberated."[52] Jennings's misconception that this formal assurance by Bastide to Manin was "perhaps tongue-in-cheek"[53] reflects the degree that these documents are superficially contradictory. It is only when viewed from Bastide's frame of reference that such glaring inconsistencies are resolved. Within the so-called Danubian confederation, which Bystrzonowski was sent to bring together in Carlowitz, the Venetians could have been simultaneously free and independent and still within the structure of the Austrian Empire. Bastide would never have exposed himself to ridicule with a public document addressed to Manin that mocked the sense of honor of the French republic. Jennings most certainly misunderstood Bastide's sense of humor. The French foreign minister's official statement was a sincere expression of his sentiments, however poor his judgement might have been.

Nowhere was Bastide's complete misunderstanding of basic diplomatic reality more striking than in the stillborn entente with Russia. The Le Flô mission to St. Petersburg foundered on Bastide's misperception of Russia's attitude toward Austria. On September 8 Bastide told Hatzfeldt that he believed that Russia was prepared to associate herself with Prussia, England, and France in a conference to mediate the Austro-Sardinian peace.[54] Even in mid-November 1848 Bastide, after many warnings from his own diplomats and Hatzfeldt, clung to his completely unfounded notion that the tsar had advised Austria to accept the Franco-English mediation. This he thought was "an indication that even the Russian government made some concessions to the changes that had taken place in Europe."[55]

Despite Scharff's claim of the "alliance of the flanking powers," no close relations ever materialized between France and Russia. Instead, the Russians allowed reports to circulate back to Paris that Le Flô's reception in the Russian capital was "merely such as would have been given any other soldier of distinction." Le Flô told the British Buchanan on November 11 that he had confronted Nesselrode to demand an official Russian denial of the statement, but instead got a confirmation that this information of Le Flô's reception having no political significance was quite correct: "merely a statement of facts."[56] The much-advertised Franco-Russian détente never transpired because there was no community of interests between the republic and the tsar.

Previous accounts commonly suffer from a misuse of history. First, the age-old attempt to learn lessons from the past leads to a search for the causes of later cataclysms at their root. A second distortion is the rationalist bias of diplomatic historians who assume that governmental leaders, by their very nature, seek to maximize national self-interest and to use words to mask *Realpolitik*. Unfortunately, later writers too often read their contemporary conditions back into those of an earlier age to make the story "relevant." But the rationalist propensity is the more pernicious because it misleads historians to overlook evidence that fail to conform to the pre-arranged mold of "realism."[57]

The most pervasive prejudice is the national bias; historians choose devils and heroes, rarely criticizing their own nation and only in exceptional cases seeing anything to praise in "the enemy." Nationalistic passion inflames overwrought rhetoric, which all too often passes for historical narrative, and it is difficult to avoid allowing prejudices of another era to creep unawares into an account of the events.

Historical analysis of this period has suffered from political bias. The idealism of the men of 1848 has attracted a debate of partisan politicians. The cause of historical truth has hardly benefitted from the heated exchange of opinions. In addition to domestic critics a series of national historians has reproached the French for disloyalty to their stated objectives. The French republic's domestic opponents have complained that this program of national liberation in itself was blind to the long-range national interest of France. Caught between these camps, the defenders of the French Second Republic have too often been ineffectual, leaving historians with access to the diplomatic record the unenviable task of attempting to sort through the inconsistencies between a public republican defense of liberty and a secret diplomatic record denying the seriousness of that bombast.

The unfortunate result has been that historians have often failed to consider carefully a number of documents tending to support a conclusion that Lamartine and Bastide might have been duplicitous or that their words might have occasionally needed closer scrutiny than they have received.

The breakthrough to a new interpretation, which reevaluated the wide ranging diplomatic record of public and private documents, began with the shifting of the focus to central and east central Europe. The discovery of the network of secret agents has made such a reassessment possible. Highly colored accounts from the confidential agents overly stimulated the hyperactive imaginations of Lamartine and Bastide to the point that particularly the latter lost contact with the real nature of politics. We need to recall that

Bastide was a professional street revolutionary and a journalist in the interim between the overthrow of governments. Even Lamartine admitted, in his often neglected history of the revolution published soon after the events, that he and his assistant Jules Bastide chose an inner circle of close associates immediately following the February Revolution. Previous writers universally failed to break down the anonymity of that inner circle to discover who actually shaped that policy.

A second breakthrough was Charles Pouthas's observation that foreign policy was carried on personally by the foreign minister more than through the usual channels of his own diplomatic corps. This implied that important evidence lay in the diplomatic archives of the other great states of Europe. The largely unused diplomatic correspondence of the former state of Prussia permitted a reexamination of the old historical verity that the French were hostile to German unity in 1848 and that the French attempted to use Prussia as a "decentralizing agent" (Scharff).

The view that France sought to prevent German unity in 1848 arose after the events. It resulted from the realization within this century that the great issue of the latter portion of the nineteenth century was national consolidations of Germany and Italy. Yet that was not how Lamartine and Bastide viewed matters. They never saw national unity of these states as an end in itself but as a means to an end. The single-minded obsession of the French in 1848 was France's traditional "hereditary enemy," Austria. The liberation of all sovereign peoples was ultimately sought in order to weaken Austria. It is only with the benefit of hindsight that German unity now seems to us the overriding issue of the epoch. For contemporaries, the key document was the French assembly's unanimous resolution of May 24, 1848, calling for an alliance with the German parliament to enfranchise Italy and Poland.

Only after the wars of 1870–71, 1914–18, and 1939–45 was it clear that a unified Germany was the real danger in 1848; only after the Austrian Empire was weakened by wars in 1859–60 and 1866 and then dissolved in the aftermath of the war of 1914–18 could historians recognize that Berlin and not Vienna had been the greater threat to France. This understanding was unavailable to the French of 1848.

The central focus of French policy immediately following the Paris February Revolution of 1848 was national survival. After the March revolutions removed France's great anxiety, the French still feared war brought on by desperate reactionary princes who desired to regain popularity in a nationalistic war against a French republic.

To forestall the untoward possibility of a hostile coalition which might overthrow the French republic, France remained committed to seeking a military ally in Germany. The object of France's solicitations oscillated between Berlin and Frankfurt, as first one then the other seemed a more likely ideological partner to aid the French to restore Poland, unify Italy, thwart imperialistic ambitions of the Hapsburgs, and isolate Russia's tsar in eastern Europe. Through the twists and turns of French diplomacy, the objective remained the restoration of France to predominance in Europe by splitting the coalition of the three northern courts (Prussia, Russia, and Austria), driving a wedge between the members of the old coalition of 1815.

Increasingly, the Magyars gained importance in French diplomatic schemes—a fact suggested by the great Hungarian historian Hajnal. From the mouth of the Danube to the Adriatic, France clearly hoped for a reorganization of the Balkan peninsula, which would make Paris arbiter of affairs in the region.

Lamartine and Bastide later denied the actual crux of their diplomatic efforts to liberate the peoples of Europe. The French leaders of the year 1848 preferred to go down in history as scoundrels who abandoned these peoples for the exigencies of the survival of the French nation, but who remained peaceful. Lamartine boasted that he had kept the peace even when he promised liberation to the nations who were revolting against autocratic tyranny. Actually, Lamartine and Bastide were sincere if ineffectual leaders. The French in 1848 were blinded by ideologic optimism, confident of the inevitable victory of the revolution—a belief shared at the time by friend and foe of change alike—and naive spokesmen for international conspiracy and upheaval.

Lamartine, Bastide, and Cavaignac's diplomacy must be reevaluated in the light of new evidence. Historical wisdom has neglected several major aspects of French foreign policy. A primary oversight was the existence of Jacobinist secret agents, which caused previous writers to misunderstand the source of intelligence that so strongly reinforced Lamartine's and Bastide's fundamentally optimistic natures. The emissaries' descriptions of a rising tide of foreign revolt, which appeared destined to sweep away the last remnants of aristocratic Europe, strengthened an exaggerated conviction that a more radical worldwide revolution was inescapable.

A second misapprehension of historians has been their assumption that a conservative domestic policy carried over into foreign policy. But the June Days were not a fundamental dividing line in the realm of external affairs, separating a radical republic of the Provisional Government from a conservative Cavaignac republic allied with the old monarchs. This misconception was generated by a misunderstanding of such matters as the Le Flô mission to St. Petersburg and Bastide's loose talk of thwarting German unity in the spirit of Richelieu. In evaluating the evidence now available, we discover instead a strong political continuity from the February Revolution through the December presidential elections. The Cavaignac government's struggle against anarchy and communists within France did not materially influence relations with foreign states. A third cause of confusion was a failure to understand the priorities of the French leaders in 1848. The historic antagonism of France and the house of Habsburg was the crux of the republicans' concerns. Neither the February Revolution nor the June Days affected an old quarrel with Austria. Thus the nature of France's Rhine policy cannot be understood outside the context of a fundamental conflict between Paris and Vienna. Unable to appreciate Lamartine and Bastide's motivations, historians have failed to recognize their genuine commitment to a liberation of peoples from injustice and oppression. Moreover, France's policy, particularly after Bastide replaced Lamartine, has erroneously been characterized as conservative and realistic. Instead, we found no abrupt break between Lamartine and Bastide, who were both better and worse than their reputations in certain respects. Neither was a cold realist who solely considered French national interests; both were high-minded idealists who believed that the French had strong interests at stake in spreading their revolution abroad. Thus they based French aspirations to European hegemony on a Girondist revolutionary foundation. The republicans wished France to be the diplomatic center of a reconstructed world order. Even as they recalled some aspects of a Richelieu-Girondist legacy, their primary objective was to protect the rights of peoples to revolt against injustice and oppression. That ideological factor in French policy coexisted with territorial considerations. France always sought client states in peoples shielded by her, particularly Italians and Poles. As the year progressed, that zone of interest shifted eastward into the lower Danube valley. Always strongly swayed by the Polish Prince Adam Czartoryski, the French inheritors of Jacobin legacy of war to the castles and peace to the cabins sought to use revolutionary means to transform Europe by ending all oppression of sovereign peoples.

NOTES

1. Jennings, *France and Europe*, pp. 191–96.

2. Taylor, *The Italian Question*.

3. Schweitzer to Dusch, Paris, May 3, July 18, and September 18, 1848, BGLA, fz. 48/2037.

4. István Hajnal, *op. cit.*, Aladár Urbán, *op. cit.*, and Cornelia Bodea, *The Roumanians' Struggle for Unification, 1834–1849*, Liliana Teodoreanu, trans. (Bucharest, 1970).

5. Bastide to Beaumont, Paris, September 26, 1848, AEF, Angleterre 671, fo. 185.

6. Bastide to Le Flô, Paris, October 5, 1848, AEF, Russie 202, fo. 107.

7. *Ibid.*

8. *Ibid.*

9. Arago to Bastide, Berlin, November 25, 1848, AEF, Prusse 303, fo. 123.

10. Instructions à donner à l'envoyé près du Roi de Sardaigne, No. 3, October 1848, Cav 1 Mi 2 R 25.

11. Brignole de Sales to Peronne, Paris, September 30, 1848, AST, 277/34.

12. Bastide to Count Bystrzonowski, Paris, September 30, 1848, AEF. Autriche 436, fo. 237.

13. Roth, "Die Linke in der Paulskirche," pp. 43–48; Stadelmann, *Social and Political History*, pp. 108–14.

14. Cowley to Palmerston, Frankfurt, August 21 and 27, 1848, as quoted in Mosse, *The European Powers*, p. 24.

15. Cowley to Palmerston, Frankfurt, August 28, 1848, PRO, FO 30/109.

16. *Ibid.*

17. Roth, p. 43.

18. *Ibid.*, pp. 59–60.

19. *Ibid.*, pp. 60–65.

20. Stadelmann, p. 114.

21. Scharff, "deutsche Einheit," p. 154.

22. Bastide to Tallenay, Paris, November 2, 1848, AEF, Allemagne 806, fo. 174; Bastide to Fontenilliat, Paris, [October 19, 1848], Hanovre 68, fo. 202.

23. See above, p. 89.

24. Bastide to Arago, Paris, October 7, 17 and 20, 1848, AEF, Prusse 303, fo. 15, 32, 38.

25. Bastide to Arago, Paris, September 7, 1848, AEF, Prusse 302, fo. 251; Bülow assured Arago that if Frankfurt had not intervened, the armistice would have long ago been signed and a peace concluded. Arago to Bastide, Berlin, August 20, 1848, fo. 217.

26. Hatzfeldt to Bülow, Paris, September 21, 1848, GSA, fz. 863, fo. 45; Arago charged, "The parliament is the cause of the disorder and the instrument of anarchy which reigns today in Schleswig and Holstein." Arago to Bastide, Berlin, September 27, 1848 , AEF, Prusse 302, fo. 301.

27. Hatzfeldt to Foreign Minister, Paris, September 13, 1848, GSA, fz. 863, fo. 28.

28. Hatzfeldt to Dönhoff, Paris, November 13, 1848, GSA, fz. 863, fo. 101–104; and November 8, 1848, fz. 861, fo. 348.

29. Arago to Bastide, Berlin, October 23, 1848, AEF, Prusse 303, fo. 44–45.

30. *Ibid.;* Feldman credited the vote for the rejection of the partition of Posen on "the intervention of the new French Ambassador E. Arago." *Cambridge History of Poland* (London, 1941), II, 360.

31. *Moniteur,* November 8, 1848.

32. Hatzfeldt to Foreign Minister, Paris, September 21, 1848, GSA, fz. 863, fo. 46–48.

33. *Ibid.*

34. *Ibid.,* October 21, 1848, GSA, fz. 861, fo. 292–95.

35. *Ibid.,* November 3 and 22, 1848, GSA, fz. 863, fo. 96–97 and 125–26.

36. Hatzfeldt to Dönhoff, Paris, October 25, 1848, GSA, fz. 863, fo. 81.

37. *Ibid.*

38. Hatzfeldt to Foreign Minister, Paris, November 23, 1848, GSA, fz. 863, fo. 133–34.

39. Arago to Bastide, Berlin, October 17, 1848, AEF, Prusse 303, fo. 33–34.

40. Bastide to Arago, Paris, October 20, 1848, AEF, Prusse 303, fo. 38.

41. *Le National,* October 14, 1848.

42. Jennings, *France and Europe,* p. 239.

43. Bastide to Tallenay, Paris, November 2, 1848, AEF, Allemagne 806, fo. 174.

44. Hatzfeldt to Dönhoff, Paris, November 3, 1848, GSA, fz. 863, fo. 96.

45. *Ibid.;* cf. Jennings's confused analysis, *France and Europe,* p. 215.

46. Hatzfeldt to Foreign Minister, Paris, November 22, 1848, GSA,

258 The Liberation of Sovereign Peoples

fz. 863, fo. 126; Hatzfeldt's conclusion that increased Slavic strength in Austria added proportionally to Russia's influence on them failed to impress Cavaignac, *ibid.*, October 21, 1848, fz. 861, fo. 294.

47. Bastide to Thiard, Paris, October 14, 1848, AEF, Suisse 562, fo. 257.

48. Bulletin, AEF, MD, Allemagne 129, fo. 228 (early November, 1848).

49. Hatzfeldt to Foreign Minister, Paris, September 27, 1848, GSA, fz. 861, fo. 225–26.

50. Hatzfeldt to Dönhoff, November 18, 1848, GSA, fz. 863, fo. 113–15.

51. Bastide to Boislecomte, Paris, October 10, 1848, in Bastide, *La République française*, p. 121.

52. Quoted in Jennings, *France and Europe*, p. 241.

53. *Ibid.*

54. Hatzfeldt to Foreign Minister, Paris, September 9, 1848, GSA, fz. 861, fo. 194.

55. *Ibid.*, September 18 and November 18, 1848, fz. 863, fo. 40 and 110–14.

56. Buchanan to Palmerston, St. Petersburg, November 11, 1848, PRO, FO 65/346.

57. Charles Lucet, "Lamartine, Tocqueville, Gobineau, les Ministres des Affaires Etrangères de la Seconde République et leurs cabinets," *Revue d'histoire diplomatique* XCIII (1979) no. 3–4, 247–77.

BIBLIOGRAPHY

Archival Materials

Austria. Haus-, Hof, und Staatsarchiv, (HHSA). Vienna.
Politisches Archiv.
IX Frankreich, 1848, Karton 29–30, Berichte, Weisung, Varia.
III Preussen, 1848, Berichte, Weisung, Varia.
Deutscher Bund, 1848, Berichte, Weisung, Varia.
Frankreich, Korrespondenz, Karton 337–38.

Belgium. Archives des Affaires Etrangères, (AEB). Brussels.
Correspondance politique: Légations.
Allemagne,   1848.   IV.
France,   1848.   XII.
Prusse,   1848.   IX.

France. Archives des Affaires Etrangères, (AEF). Paris.
Correspondance politique.
Allemagne,   805–06.
Angleterre,   669–672.
Autriche,   435–37.
Bade,   34.
Bavière,   224.
Belgique,   30.
Brunswick-Hanovre,   68.
Danemark,   210–12.
Hambourg,   149.
Hesse-Cassel,   34.
Hesse-Darmstadt,   22.
Prusse,   301–03.
Russie,   201–02.
Sardaigne,   321–22.
Saxe-Ducale,   4 bis.
Wurtemberg,   72.
Correspondance commerciale.
Berlin,   9.
Frankfort,   3.
Londres,   32–33.
St. Petersbourg,   26.
Vienne,   3.
Mémoires et Documents.
Allemagne,   125, 127, 129, 130, 162, 163, 170, 171.

Autriche,   52.
France,   731, 2125.
Russie,   43.
Dossiers personnels.

France. Archives Nationales. Paris.
Procès-verbaux, l'Assemblée constituente, comité des affaires
étrangères, C926 [C277] 561.

France. Archives départmentales de la Sarthe. Le Mans.
Fonds Cavaignac   1 Mi 2 R 19–28.

France. Bibliothèque Nationale. Manuscrits. Paris.
Fonds Bixio.
Fonds Circourt.
Fonds Hetzel.

France. Bibliotheki Polskiej iv Paryzu. Paris.
Ludwik Bystrzonowski Papers.

France. Service Historique de l'Armée (SHA). Paris.
F 16–17 Rapports de Cent jours Divisions Militaires 1848–49.
F 79 République de 1848 Donation Pillas.
Mémoires et Reconnaissances (MR).
823 Mémoires Historiques
825 Pelet Papers
1370 Sardaigne, 1841–61.
1385 Italie 1811–57.
1411–12 Suisse 1846–50.
1478 Danemark, 1753–1873
1495 Russie
1511–14 Confédération germanique
1531–33 Prusse 1833–59
1601 Autriche-Hongrie, 1843–52
1634 Europe dans son ensemble 1839–74.
1894 Notes Rumigny
1941 Divers
2068–71, 2075–77 Fond Pelet
2110–2111 Commission de la défense
2112 Collection de mémoires du Général Pelet
2141 Projets et mémoires 1830–1851.
2156 Fond Pelet
Situation générale par l'ordre numérique des divers corps de troupes
composant l'armée au 1er janvier–1er décembre 1848.
dossiers du personnel

Germany (Baden) Generallandesarchiv (BGLA), Karlsruhe.
Abt. 48/1974 Gesandtschaftsberichte aus Paris.
Abt. 48/2036–37. Correspondenz mit dem Minister von Dusch.
Abt. 48/2891 Die bei den Pariser Juni-Aufständen verhafteten

Deutschen betreffend Correspondenzen mit de Grossherzoglich. Gesandten in Frankfurt und Paris.

Germany (Bavaria) Geheimes Staatsarchiv (BGStA), Munich.
1511 Die bayerische Gesandtschaft in Paris, Politische Schriftwechsel.
MA 2105 Gesandtschaftsberichte aus Paris.

Germany. Bundesarchiv Zweigstelle Frankfurt/Main.
Friedrich von Raumer Papers.
Ölsner-Monmerqué Papers.

Germany (Prussia) Stiftung Preussicher Kulturbesitz, Geheimes Staatsarchiv (GSA). Berlin.
III. Hauptabteilung.
I AAa fz. 6–7 Generalia.
I AAb Deutschland
fz. 44–48 Frankfurt am main Schriftwechsel.
fz. 62–67 Deutsche Angelegenheiten
I AAc fz. 271–73 Baden. Schriftwechsel.
I AAd. fz. 292–95, 301–06 Bayern. Schriftwechsel.
I AAe fz. 356–65 Danemark. Schleswig-Holsteinische Frage.
I AAg fz. 552–53 Hannover. Schriftwechsel.
I AAh fz. 585–86 Freie Hansestädte. Schriftwechsel.
I AAk fz. 672–74 Holland. Schriftwechsel.
I AAl fz. 691–704 Österreich. Schriftwechsel.
I AAm fz. 747–48 Sachsen. Schriftwechsel.
I ABa fz. 804–08 Belgien. Schriftwechsel.
I ABa fz. 825–34 England. Schriftwechsel.
I ABc fz. 855–65 Frankreich. Schriftwechsel.

Germany (Prussia) Zentrales Staatsarchiv–Historische
Abteilung II Merseburg (ZSA)
(old classifications)
Auslandsamt
I AAB. Deutschland 13, Frankfurt/Main. Schriftwechsel
A. A. ZB. 168–74 Paris. Schriftwechsel.
Rep. 81. Paris II. 32–39, 44–46, 49, 53, 85–86. Gesandtschaft zu Paris. Concepte.
Rep. 81. Wien I. 169–73, 176, 180–82. Gesandtschaft zu Wien. Schriftwechsel.
Rep. 81. 167–72, 177. Gesandschaft zu St. Petersburg I. Concepte von politische Berichte von Rochow aus Petersburg.
Ministerium des Innern
Rep 77. Tit. 343a. Nr. 72.
Rep 77. Tit. 343a. Nr. 72II.
Rep 77. Tit. 343a. Nr. 90.
Rep 77. Tit. 343a. Nr. 91.
Rep 77. Tit. 500. Nr. 36.
Rep 77. Tit. 509. Nr. 2.

(new classifications)
2.2.1. Geheimes Zivilkabinett. Nr. 13242. Nachrichten über Frankreich und die Fonds zu deren Mitteilung, 1840–48.
2.4.1. 4973. Paris. Politische vertraulicher Scriftwechsel.
2.4.1. Abt. I Nr. 6067–70. Österreich. Schriftwechsel.
2.4.1. Nr. 6435–4 Russland. Schriftwechsel.
2.4.1. Nr. 6919, 6929, 6931, 6934, 6943. Schweiz. Schriftwechsel.
2.4.1. 8798. Turkei. Schriftwechsel.
2.4.1. 8048–53. Revolutionäre Bewegung in Deutschland.
Acta des Ministerium des Innern. Polizei.

Germany. Württembergisches Staatsarchiv (WSA) Stuttgart.
E 9 fz. 67–78 Revolutionäre Bewegung
E 9 Kabinettsakten III fz. 106 Berlin Schriftwechsel.
E 70a. Buschel 23 Akten der Gesandtschaft in Paris.
    Bu. 19 Gesandtschaftsberichte nach Stuttgart.
E 70b. Bu. 20–26 Akten der Gesandtschaft in Wien.
    Bu. 63 Gesandtschaftsberichte nach Stuttgart.
E 72 Bu. 116–18 Gesandtschaft zu St. Petersburg. Konzepte.
E 73 Bu. 6–7 Gesandtschaftsakten Berlin. Berichte.
E 73 Bu. 29–31 Gesandtschaftsakten München. Berichte.
E 73 Bu. 82–83 Gesandtschaftsakten St. Petersburg. Berichte.
E 74 Bu. 81–83 Gesandtschaftsakten Berlin.

Great Britain. Public Record Office (PRO) London.
Austria   F. O. 7/343–353.
France   F. O. 27/797–816.
Germany   F. O. 30/103–116.
Prussia   F. O. 103–116.
Russia   F. O. 65/343–352.

Italy (Sardinia-Piedmont) Archivio di Stato (AST) Turin.

Archivio del Ministero per gli Affari Esteri.
Lettere Ministri. Allemagne Mazzo 6 (1848).
Legazione in Francoforte e piccoli Stati di Allemagna Mazzo 6 (1848).
Lettere di Ministri Francia Mazzo 277–78 (1848–49).
Legazione di Parigi. Mazzo 10 (1848).
    fagli 72 Lettere particulari al Ministro Marchese Brignole de Sale
    fagli 73 Missione Marchese Alberto Ricci
Lettere di Ministri. Legazione di Prussia. Mazzo 31–32 (1848–50).
Legazione in Prussia. cart. 3. Missione del Conte Rossi 1844–49.

Poland (Cracow) Czartoryski Museum.
Rps Czart. 440a List Bystrzonowski
Rps Czart. 441–42 Papiery gen. Ludwika Bystrzonowskiego
Rps Czart. 5369–72, 5398–5451 Ludwik Bystrzonowski. Correspondence with Adam Czartoryski, 1848–49.
Rps Czart. 5394 Serbie. Żach 1847–48.

Published Government Documents

Austria. Angelo Filipuzzi, ed. *Le relazioni diplomatiche fra l'Austria e il Regno di Sardegna e la Guerra del 1848–1849.* III serie: 1848–60. Rome: Instituto storico italiano per l'età moderna e contemporanea, 1961.

Austria. Johann A. Rantzau, ed. *Europäische Quellen zur schleswig-holsteinischen Geschichte im 19. Jahrhundert: Akten aus dem Wiener Haus-, Hof- und Staatsarchiv, 1818–1852.* (Baltische Kommission. Kiel. Schriften. XXIII) Breslau: Ferdinand Hirt, 1934.

Belgium. Alfred de Ridder, ed. *La crise de la neutralité belge en 1848: le dossier diplomatique.* 2 vols. Brussels: Weissenbruch, 1928.

France. Charles H. Pouthas, ed. *Documents diplomatiques du gouvernement provisoire et de la commission du Pouvoir exécutif.* 2 vols. Paris: Imprimerie Nationale, 1953–54.

France. Armando Saitta, ed. *Le relazioni diplomatiche fra la Francia et il Granducato di Toscana.* III. serie: 1848–60. Rome: Instituto storico italiano per l'età moderna e contemporanea, 1960.

France. Comité national du Centenaire de 1848. *Procès-verbaux du Governement provisoire et de la Commission du Pouvoir exécutif (24 février–22 juin 1848).* Introduction by Charles Pouthas. Paris: Imprimerie nationale, 1950.

Germany. Bavaria. Anton Choust, ed. *Gesandtschaftsberichte aus München, 1814–1848. III. Abteilung. Die Berichte der preussischen Gesandten.* vol. IV. Munich: Beiderstein, 1951.

Germany. Frankfurt. Franz Wigard, ed. *Stenographischer Bericht über der Verhandlungen der deutschen constituirenden Nationalversammlung zu Frankfurt am Main.* 9 vols. Frankfurt/Main: Sauerländer, 1848–49.

Germany. Saxony. Helmut Kretzschmar and Horst Schlechte, eds. *Französische und Sächsische Gesandtschaftsberichte aus Dresden und Paris, 1848–1849.* (Schriftenreihe des Sächsischen Landeshauptarchivs Dresden. Nr. 2–3) Berlin: Rütten und Loening, 1956.

Great Britain. Parliament. House of Commons. *Sessional Papers.* "Correspondence relative to the Affairs of Hungary" 1851, LXIII, 1–404.

Great Britain. Federico Curato, ed. *Le relazioni diplomatiche fra la Gran Bretagna e il Regno di Sardegna.* III: serie: 1840–60. vol. I. Rome: Instituto storico italiano per l'età moderna e contemporanea, 1961.

Naples. Giuseppe Coniglio, ed. *Le relazioni diplomatiche fra il Regno delle Due Sicilie e il Regno di Prussia.* III. serie: 1848–60. Rome: Instituto storico italiano per l'età moderna et contemporanea, 1964.

Papal states. Michele Fatica, ed. *Le relazioni diplomatiche fra lo Stato Pontificio e la Francia.* III. serie: 1848–60. Rome: Instituto storico italiano per l'età moderna e contemporanea, 1971.

Poland. d'Angeberg [Comte Leonard Chodzko], ed. *Recueil des traités, conventions et actes diplomatiques concernant la Pologne, 1762–1862*. Paris: Amyot, 1863.

Sardinia. Federico Curato, ed. *Le relazioni diplomatiche fra il Regno di Sardegna e la Gran Bretagna*. III. serie: 1848–60. 2 vols. Rome: Instituto storico italiano per l'età moderna e contemporanea, 1955.

Sicily. Federico Curato, ed. *Le relazioni diplomatiche fra il Governo provisori siciliano e la Francia*. III. serie: 1848–60. Rome: Instituto storico italiano per l'età moderna e contemporanea, 1971.

United States. Howard R. Marraro, ed. *L'Unificazione italiana vista dai diplomatichi Statunitensi*. vol. II. 1848–52. (Instituto per la storia del Risorgimento italiano. Biblioteca scientifica. serie II. Fonti LI.) Rome: Instituto per la storia del Risorgimento italiano, 1964.

Venice. *La republica Veneta nel 1848–49: Documenti Diplomatici*. 2 vols. Padua: Casa Editrice Dott. A. Milani, 1949–54.

Letters and Memoirs

Apponyi, Rudolf. *De la révolution au coup d'état, 1848–1851*. Geneva: La Palatine, 1948.

Arnim, Heinrich von. *Die politische Denkschrift über die französische Februar-Revolution und ihre Folgen für Deutschland*. Berlin: Wilhelm Herz, 1848.

Bastide, Jules. *La République Française et l'Italie en 1848: récits, notes et documents diplomatiques*. Brussels: Meline, Caus, 1858.

Blanc, Louis. *1848: Historial Revelations inscribed to Lord Normanby*. London: Chapman & Hall, 1858.

Börnstein, Heinrich. *Fünfundsiebzig Jahre in der alten und neuen Welt: Memoiren eines Unbedeutenden*. 2 vols. Leipzig: Otto Wigand, 1884.

Circourt, Adolphe de. *Souvenirs d'une mission à Berlin en 1848*. Georges Bourgin, ed. 2 vols. (Société d'histoire contemporaine, Publications No. 43, 46) Paris: A. Picard, 1908–09.

Gerlach, Ernst Ludwig von. *Von der Revolution zum Norddeutschen Bund: Politik und Ideengut der Preussischen Hochkonservativen, 1848–66: Aus dem Nachlass von Ernst Ludwig von Gerlach*. Hellmut Diwald, ed. 2 vols. (Deutsche Geschichtsquellen des 19. und 20. Jahrhunderts) Göttingen: Vandenhoeck & Ruprecht, 1970.

Gerlach, Leopold von. *Denkwürdigkeiten aus dem Leben Leopold von Gerlachs: General der Infanterie und General-Adjutanten König Friedrich Wilhelms IV, nach seinen Aufzeichnungen hrsg. von seiner Töchter*. 2 vols. Berlin: Hertz: 1891–92.

Hartmann, Moritz. *Revolutionäre Erinnerungen*. H. H. Houben, ed. (Deutsche Revolution. IV) Leipzig: Klinkhardt, 1919.

Heckscher, Johann G. M. *Reden in der Waffenstillstandssache*. Frankfurt/M.: Krebs-Schmidt, 1848.

_____. *Mémoire sur la question du Schleswig*. Frankfurt/M.: Krebs-Schmidt, 1848.

Hübner, Joseph A. *Ein Jahr meines Lebens*. Alexander K. J. Hübner, ed. Leipzig: Brockhaus, 1891.

Lamartine, Alphonse de. *Correspondance de Lamartine*. Publiée par Madame Valentine de Lamartine. 4 vols. 2d. ed. Paris: Hachette, 1881–82.

_____. *La France Parlementaire (1834–1851): Oeuvres Oratoires et Ecrits politiques*, 6 vols. Paris: Librarie Internationale, 1864–65.

_____. *Histoire de la Révolution de 1848*. 2 vols. Paris: Perrotin, 1849.

_____. *Lettre aux dix départements*. Paris: Levy Frères, 1848.

_____. *Oeuvres complètes*. 41 vols. Vol. xxxix: *Mémoires politiques*. Paris: L'Auteur, 1860–66.

_____. *Le passé, le présent et l'avenir de la République*. Brussels: Société typographique belge, 1850.

_____. *Le Piémont et la France en 1848: Lettre de M. de Lamartine à M. Sineo deputé piémontais*. Paris: Imprimerie Cosson, 1859.

_____. *Trois mois au pouvoir*. Paris: Levy Frères, 1848.

Karl Marx and Friedrich Engels. *Briefe*. (February 1842–December 1851) *Werke*. Berlin: Dietz, 1965.

Metternich, Clemens von. *Mémoires, documents et écrits divers laissés par le Prince de Metternich, chancelier de cour et d'état; pub. par son fils la prince Richard de Metternich classés et réunis par M. A. de Klinkowstroem*. Paris: Plon, 1881–86.

Meyendorff, Peter von. *Ein russicher Diplomat an der Höfen von Berlin und Wien: Politischer und privater Briefwechsel, 1826–63*. O. Hötzsch, ed. 3 vols. Berlin: W. de Gruyter, 1923.

Nesselrode, Carl Robert. *Lettres et papiers du Chancelier Comte C. R. de Nesselrode*. Anatol de Nesselrode, ed. 11 vols. Paris: A. Lahure, 1904–12.

Normanby (see Phipps)

Ölsner-Monmerqué, Gustav. *Drei Missionen: Politische Skizzen aus Paris*. Bremen: Schlodtmann, 1850.

Paskevich, Ivan F. *Le feld-maréchal prince Paskevitsch: sa vie politique et militaire d'après des documents inédits*. General Shcherbatov, ed. Vol. VI (1848–49). St. Petersburg: Trenke & Fusnot, 1904.

Pélissier, Amable, Duc de Malakof. *Aspects de la vie politique et militaire en France à travers la correspondance reçue par le Maréchal Pélissier (1828–*

1864). Pierre Guiral and Raoul Brunon, eds. Paris: Bibliothèque Nationale, 1968.

Phipps, Constantine Henry [Normanby, C. H. Lord]. *A Year of Revolution from a Journal kept in Paris in 1848.* 2 vols. London: Longman, Brown, & Green. 1857 (*Une année de révolution d'après un journal tenu à Paris en 1848.* 2 vols. 3 ed. Paris: Plon, 1860).

Raumer, Friedrich von. *Briefe aus Frankfurt und Paris: 1848–49.* 2 vols. Leipzig: Brockhaus, 1849.

Rémusat, Charles de. *Mémoires de ma vie.* Charles H. Pouthas, ed. Vols. II–IV. Paris: Plon, 1959–62.

Szalay, László. *Diplomatische Aktenstücke zur Beleuchtung der ungarischen Gesandtschaft in Deutschland.* Zurich: Orell, Fussli, 1849.

Tocqueville, Alexis de. *Oeuvres complètes: édition définitive. Publiée sous la direction de J. P. Mayer. Introduction par Harold J. Laski.* Paris: Gallimard, 1967ff.

Walter, Friedrich. *Magyarische Rebellenbriefe 1848: Ämtliche und Privat-Correspondenzen der magyarischen Rebellenregierung, ihrer Führer und Anhänger.* Munich: R. Oldenbourg, 1964.

Secondary Sources

Agulhon, Maurice. *The Republican Experiment, 1848–1852.* Janet Lloyd, trans. Cambridge: Cambridge University Press, 1983.

Amann, Peter. *Revolution and Mass Democracy: The Paris Club Movement in 1848.* Princeton: Princeton University Press, 1975.

Andics, Erzsébet. *Die Habsburger und die Frage Zarenhilfe gegen die Revolution: Vom Münchengrätzer Abkommen bis zum Mai 1849.* (Studia Historica, XXXI) Budapest: Akadémiai kiadó, 1960.

——————. *Das Bündnis Habsburg-Romanov: Vorgeschichte der zaristischen Intervention in Ungarn im Jahre 1849.* (Studia Historica, LI) Budapest: Akadémiai kiadó, 1963.

Arneth, Alfred von. *Johann Freiherr von Wessenberg: Ein österreichischer Staatsmann des 19. Jahrhundert.* 2 vols. Vienna and Leipzig: Wilhelm Braumüller, 1898.

Árpád, Károlyi. *Németujvári gróf Batthyány Lajos elsö magyar miniszterelnök förbenjáró pöre.* Budapest: Magyar Történelmi Társulat, 1932.

Ashley, Evelyn. *The Life of Henry John Temple, Viscount Palmerston with selections from his diaries and correspondence.* 2 vols. 2d. ed. London: R. Bentley, 1876.

Averbouch, R. A. *Tarskaia interventsiia v borbe s vengerskoi revolutsiei, 1849–1849.* Moscow: Gosudarstennoe sotsialno-ekonomicheskoe izdaltelstov, 1935.

Bapst, Edmond. *Les Origines de la Guerre de Crimée: La France et la Russie de 1848 à 1854.* Paris: Ch. Delagave, 1912.

Bardoux, Jacques. *Les Origines du malheur européen: l'aide anglo-française à la domination prussienne.* Paris: Hachette, 1948.

Batowski, Henryk. *Legion Mickiewicza w Kampanni Wlosko-Austriackiej 1848 roku.* Warsaw: Wydawn. Ministerstwa obrony Narodowej, 1956.

Becheyras, André. "Lamartine au pouvoir," in *l'Esprit de 1848.* (Cahiers de Sextant, I) Mulhouse: Bader-Dufour, 1948.

Bell, H. C. F. *Lord Palmerston.* 2 vols. London: Longmanns, Green, 1936.

Bertrand, Louis. *Lamartine.* Paris: Arthème Fayard, 1940.

Best, Heinrich. *Interessenpolitik und nationale Integration 1848/49: Handelspolitische Konflikte im frühindustriellen Deutschland.* (Kritische Studien zur Geschichtswissenschaft, 37) Göttingen: Vandenhoeck & Ruprecht, 1980.

Birke, Ernst. *Frankreich und Ostmitteleurope im 19. Jahrhundert: Beiträge zur Politik und Geistesgeschichte.* (Ostmitteleurope in Vergangenheit & Gegenwart, VI) Cologne: Bohlau, 1960.

Bodea, Cornelia. *The Roumanians' Struggle for Unification, 1834–1849.* Liliana Teodoreanu, trans. Bucharest: Publishing House of the Academy of the Socialist Republic of Romania,. 1970.

Böhme, Helmut. *Deutschlands Weg zur Grossmacht: Studien zum Verhältnis von Wirtschaft und Staat während der Reichsgründungszeit: 1848–1881.* Cologne and Berlin: Kiepenheuer, 1966.

Bondi, Gerhard. *Deutschlands Aussenhandel, 1815–1870.* (Schriften des Instituts für Geschichte, Reihe I. Bd. 5) Berlin: Akademie Verlag, 1958.

Bouillon, J. et al. "L'Armée et la Seconde République," in *Etudes.* (Bibliothèque de la Révolution de 1848, XVIII), La Roche-sur-Yon: Imprimerie centrale de l'ouest, 1955.

Boogmann, J. Chr. *Nederland en de Duitse Bond, 1815–1851.* (Historische Studien, V) 2 vols. Groningen: J. B. Wolters, 1955.

Bougin, Georges. *1848.* Paris: Paris Editions, [1948].

Boyer, Ferdinand. *La Seconde République, Charles-Albert et l'Italie du Nord en 1848.* (Bibliothèque de la Revue d'histoire diplomatique, II) Paris: A. Pedone, 1967.

Büchner, Rudolf. *Die deutsch-französische Tragödie, 1848–1864: Politische Beziehungen und psychologisches Verhältnis.* Würzburg: Holzner, 1965.

Calman, Alvin R. *Ledru-Rollin and the Second French Republic.* (Columbia University Studies in History, Economics & Public Law, CIII) New York: Columbia University Press, 1922.

268   *The Liberation of Sovereign Peoples*

Carr, E. H. *Michael Bakunin.* New York: Vintage Books, 1937, 1961.

Carr, W. *Schleswig-Holstein, 1815–48: A Study in National Conflict.* Manchester: Manchester University Press, 1963.

Congrès historique de centenaire de la Révolution de 1848. *Actes du Congrès du centenaire de la Révolution de 1848.* Paris: Presses universitaires de France, [1948].

Croce, Benedetto. *A History of Europe in the Nineteenth Century.* Henry Furst, trans. New York: Harcourt Brace, 1933.

Deak, Istvan. *The Lawful Revolution: Louis Kossuth and the Hungarians, 1848–1849.* New York: Columbia University Press, 1979.

Deme, Laszlo. *The Radical Left in the Hungarian Revolution of 1848.* New York and Boulder, Colorado: Eastern European Quarterly, distributed by Columbia University Press, 1976.

Deschanel, Emil. *Lamartine.* 2 vols. 4th ed. Paris: Calmann Levy, 1901.

Döberl, Michael. *Bayern und Deutschland.* Vol. I. *Bayern und die Deutsche Frage in der Epoche des Frankfurter Parlements.* Munich: R. Oldenbourg, 1922.

Doumic, René. *Lamartine.* 3d. ed. Paris: Hachette, 1922.

Droz, Jacques. *Histoire diplomatique de 1648 à 1919.* Paris: Dalloz, 1951.

_____. *Les Révolutions allemandes de 1848: D'après un manuscript et des notes de E. Tonnelat.* Paris: Presses universitaires de France, 1957.

Duveau, Georges. *1848: The Making of a Revolution.* Anne Carter, trans. New York: Pantheon Books, 1967.

Epting, Karl. *Das Französische Sendungsbewusstsein im 19. und 20. Jahrhundert.* Heidelberg: Kurt Vowinckel, 1952.

Eyck, Frank. *The Frankfurt Parliament, 1848–1849.* New York: St. Martins, 1968.

Fejtö, Francois (ed.) *The Opening of an Era, 1848: An Historical Symposium with an Introduction by A. J. P. Taylor.* London: Allen Wingate, 1949.

Feldman, Józef. *Sprawa Polska w Roku 1848.* Cracow: Nakladem Polskiej Akademji Umiejętności, 1933.

Fortescue, William. *Alphonse de Lamartine: A Political Biography.* New York: St. Martins, 1983.

Gallaher, John. *The Students of Paris and the Revolution of 1848.* Carbondale: Southern Illinois University Press, 1980.

Garnier-Pagès, Louis Antoine. *Histoire de la Révolution de 1848.* 10 vols. Paris: Pagnerre, 1861–72.

Gillissen, Gunther. *Lord Palmerston und die Einigung Deutschlands: Die Englischen-Politik von der Paulskirche bis zu den Dresdener Konferenzen*

(1848–1851). (Historische Studien, vol. 384) Lübeck & Hamburg: Matthiesen, 1961.

Ginsborg, Paul. *Daniele Manin and the Venetian Revolution of 1848–49.* Cambridge: Cambridge University Press, 1979.

Girard, Louis. *La Deuxième République (1848–1851).* (Naissance et Mort) Paris: Calmann-Lévy, 1968.

——————. *La garde nationale, 1814–1871.* (Civilizations d'hier et d'aujourd'hui) Paris: Plon, 1964.

Godart, Justin. *A Lyon en 1848: Les Voraces.* (Collection du centenaire de la Révolution de 1848) Paris: Presses universitaires de France, 1948.

Gooch, Brison D. *Belgium and the February Revolution.* The Hague: Martinus Nijhoff, 1963.

Greenfield, Kent R. *Economics and Liberalism in the Risorgimento: A Study of Nationalism in Lombardy, 1814–1848.* 2d. ed. Baltimore: Johns Hopkins University Press, 1965.

Greer, Donald M. *L'Angletere, la France et la Révolution de 1848: Le 3e ministère de Lord Palmerston au Foreign Office (1846–51).* 2 vols. Paris: F. Reider, 1925.

Griese, William Frederick. "Lamartine: A Portrait," *University of Wisconsin Studies in Language and Literature,* XX (1924), 163–213.

Guichen, Eugene Vicomte de. *Les grandes questions européennes et la diplomatie des puissances sous la Seconde République française.* 2 vols. Paris: Victor Attinger, 1925–29.

Guichonnet, Paul. *L'affaire des "Voraces" en avril 1848: essai de mise au point d'après des documents inédits.* (Miscellanea del centenario, serie I, n. 4) Turin: Museo nazionale del risorgimento, 1949.

Guillemin, Henri. *Lamartine: l'homme et l'oeuvre.* Paris: Bouvin, 1940.

——————. *Lamartine en 1848.* (Collection du centenaire de la Révolution de 1848) Paris: Presses universitaires de France, 1948.

——————. *Lamartine et la question sociale.* Paris: Plon, 1946.

——————. *La première résurrection de la République: 24 février 1848.* (Trente journées qui ont fait la France) Paris: Gallimard, 1967.

Guyard, Marius F. *Alphonse de Lamartine.* Paris: Editions universitaires, 1956.

Hahn, Hans Henning. *Aussenpolitik in der Emigration: Die Exil-Diplomatie Adam Jerzy Czartoryski, 1830–1840.* Munich and Vienna: Oldenbourg, 1978.

Hallgarten. Georg W. F. *Studien über die deutsche Polenfreudschaft in der Periode der Märzrevolution.* Munich: R. Oldenbourg, 1928.

Hajnal, István. *À Batthyány-kórmány külpolitikája.* Budapest: Akademiá, 1957.

Hamerow, Theodore. *Restoration, Revolution, Reaction: Economics and Politics in Germany, 1815–1871*. Princeton: Princeton University Press, 1958.

Hammer, Karl. *Die Französische Diplomatie der Restauration und Deutschland, 1814–1830*. (Pariser historische Studien, II) Stuttgart: Anton Hiersemann, 1963.

Handelsman, Marceli. *Adam Czartoryski*. 3 vols. in 4 (Rozpawy historyczne, 23–25) Warsaw: Nakl. Tow. Naukowego, 1948–50.

_____. *Czartoryski, Nicolas Ier et la question du proche orient*. Paris: Pedone, 1934.

Henry, Paul. *La France devant le monde de 1789 à 1939*. Paris: Aubier, 1945.

_____. *Le Problème des nationalités*. Paris: Armand Colin, 1937.

Hildebrandt, Gunter. *Opposition in der Paulskirche*. Berlin: Akademie Verlag, 1981.

_____. *Parlamentsopposition auf Linkskurs*. Berlin: Akademie Verlag, 1975.

Hjelholt, Holger. *British Mediation in the Danish-German Conflict, 1848–1850*. (Historisk-filosofiske meddelelser udgivet af Det Konglige Danske videnskabernes selskab, Bind 41, nr. 1) Copenhagen: Munksgaard, 1965.

Hofmann, Jürgen. *Das Ministerium Camphausen-Hansemann: Zur Politik der preussischen Bourgeoisie in der Revolution 1848/49*. Berlin: Akademie Verlag, 1981.

Huber, E. R. *Deutsche Verfassungsgeschichte seit 1789*. Vol. II, 2d. ed. Stuttgart: Kohlhammer 1963.

_____. *Dokumente zur Deutsche Verfassungsgeschichte*. Vol. I, 2d. ed. Stuttgart: Kohlhammer, 1961.

Jelavich, Barbara. "The Russian Intervention in Wallachia and Transylvania, September 1848 to March 1849," *Rumanian Studies*, IV (1976–79), 16–74.

Jennings, Lawrence C. *France and Europe in 1848: A Study of French Foreign Affairs in a Time of Crisis*. Oxford: Clarendon Press, 1973.

Kähler, S. A. "Die deutsche Revolution von 1848 und die europäischen Mächte," in *Vorurteilen und Tatsachen*. Hamelin: Seifert, 1949.

Knapowska, Wislawa. "La France, la Prusse, et la question polonaise en 1848," in *La Pologne au VIe Congrès International des Sciences Historiques à Oslo, 1928*. Warsaw: Société Polonaise d'histoire, 1930.

Kovács, Endre. *Szabadságharcunk és a francia közvélemény*. Budapest: Akadémiai Kiadó, 1976.

Kraume, Hans-Georg, *Aussenpolitik 1848: Die hollandische Provinz Limburg in der deutsche Revolution*. Düsseldorf: Droste, 1979.

Kukiel, Marian. *Czartoryski and European Unity, 1770–1861.* Princeton: Princeton University Press, 1955.

Lademacher, Horst. *Die belgische Neutralität als Problem der europäischen Politik, 1830–1914.* (Veröffentlichung des Instituts für geschichtliche Landeskunde der Rheinlande an der Universität Bonn) Bonn: Röhrschied, 1971.

Ley, Francis. *La Révolution romaine et l'intervention française vue par le prince Volkovsky, 1846–1849.* Paris: Fishbacher, 1981.

Luna, Frederick A. De. *The French Republic under Cavaignac, 1848.* Princeton: Princeton University Press, 1969.

Marcks, Erich. *Der Aufsteig des Reiches: Deutsche Geschichte von 1807–1878.* Vol. I. *Die Vorstufen.* Stuttgart: Deutsche Verlags-Anstalt, 1936.

Meinecke, Friedrich. *Cosmopolitanism and the National State.* Robert B. Kimber, trans. Princeton: Princeton University Press, 1970.

Merriman, John M. *The Agony of the Republic: The Repression of the Left in Revolutionary France: 1848–1851.* New Haven: Yale University Press, 1978.

Meyer, Eberhard. *Die Aussenpolitischen Ideen der Achtundvierziger.* (Historische Studien, vol. 337) Berlin: Ebering, 1938.

Moltmann, Guenther. *Deutsch-Amerikanische Beziehungen: Atlantische Blockpolitik im 19. Jahrhundert: Die Vereinigten Staaten und der deutsche Liberalismus während der Revolution von 1848/49.* Düsseldorf: Droste, 1973.

Mommsen, Wilhelm. *Grösse und Versagen des deutschen Bürgertums: Ein Beitrag zur politischen Bewegung des 19. Jahrhunderts, insbesondere zur Revolution 1848–49.* 2d. ed. Munich: R. Oldenbourg, 1964.

Moscati, Ruggerio. *La diplomazia europea e il problema italiano nel 1848.* (Studi storici per la Costituente, XVI) Florence: Sansoni, 1947.

Mosse, W. E. *The European Powers and the German Question, 1848–1871, with special reference to England and Russia.* Cambridge: Cambridge University Press, 1958.

Namier, Lewis. *1848: The Revolution of the Intellectuals.* New York: Anchor Books, 1964.

Nifontow, A. S. *Russland im Jahre 1848.* Berlin: Rütten & Loenig, 1954.

Parmenie, A. and C. Bonnier de la Chapelle. *Histoire d'un éditeur et de ses auteurs, J.-P. Hetzel (Stahl).* Paris: A. Michel, 1953.

Poidevin, Raymond. *Les relations franco-allemandes, 1815–1975.* Paris: A. Colin, 1977.

Pokrovsky, Mikhail. "Lamartine, Cavaignac und Nikolaus I," in *Historische Aufsätze.* Vienna: Verlag für Literatur und Politik, 1929.

Polisensky, Josef. *Aristocrats and the Crowd in the Revolutionary Year 1848:*

A Contribution to the History of Revolution and Counter-Revolution in Austria. Frederick Snider, trans. Albany: State University of New York Press, 1980.

Ponteil, Felix. *1848*. Paris: Colin, 1947.

Pouthas, Charles H. "La politique étrangère de la France sous la Seconde République et le Second empire," in *Cours de la Sorbonne*. Paris: Cours de la Sorbonne, 1949.

Precht, Hans. *Englands Stellung zur deutschen Einheit, 1848–50*. (Historische Zeitschrift Beiheft, III) Munich: R. Oldenbourg, 1925.

Price, Roger. *The French Second Republic: A Social History*. London: B. T. Batsford, 1972.

Quentin-Baucart, Pierre. *Lamartine et la politique étrangère de la Révolution de février (24 février à 24 juin 1848)*. Paris: F. Juven, 1907.

——————. *Lamartine, homme politique: la politique intérieure*. Paris: Plon-Nourrit, 1903.

Rath, R. John. *The Viennese Revolution of 1848*. Austin: University of Texas Press, 1957.

Robertson, Priscilla. *Revolutions of 1848: A Social History*. New York: Harper Torchbooks, 1960.

Salvatorelli, Luigi. *La revoluzione europea, 1848–49*. Milan: Rizzoli, 1949.

Sandiford, Keith A. P. *Great Britain and the Schleswig-Holstein Question, 1848–64: A Study in Diplomacy, Politics and Public Opinion*. Toronto: University of Toronto Press, 1975.

Scharff, Alexander. "Das Erste Londoner Protokoll: Ein Beitrag zur europäischen Problematik der schleswig-holsteinischen Frage," in *Festschrift für Otto Schell: Beiträge zur deutschen und nordischen Geschichte*. Schleswig: Ibbeken, 1952, 314–34.

——————. "Europäische und gesamtdeutsche Zusammenhänge der schleswig-holsteinischen Erhebung," *Festschrift für K. A. von Müller: Stufen und Wandlungen der deutschen Einheit*. Stuttgart: Deutsche Verlags-Anstalt, 1943, 196–223.

——————. *Die europäischen Grossmächte und die deutsche Revolution: Deutsche Einheit und europäische Ordnung, 1848–1851*. (Das Reich und Europa, II) Leipzig: Köhler & Amelang, 1942.

——————. "König Friedrich Wilhelm IV, Deutschland und Europa im Frühjahr 1849," in *Geschichtliche Kraft und Entscheidungen: Festschrift zum 75. Geburtstag von Otto Becker*. Wiesbaden: F. Steiner, 1954, 138–75.

——————. "Revolution und Reichsgründungsversuche, 1848–51," in *Deutsche Geschichte im Überlick: Ein Handbuch*. Peter Rassow (ed.) Stuttgart: Europäischer Buchklub, [n. d.], 430–53.

_____. "Schleswig-Holsteins Erhebung im Spiegel französischer Akten," in *Aus Schleswig-Holsteins Geschichte und Gegenwart: Festschrift für Volquart Pauls*. Neumünster: Wachholtz, 1950, 172–94.

Schiemann, Theodor. *Geschichte Russlands unter Kaiser Nikolaus I*. 4 vols. Berlin: Georg Reimer, 1904–19.

Schwarzenberg, Adolph. *Prince Felix zu Schwarzenberg: Prime Minister of Austria, 1848–1852*. New York: Columbia University Press, 1946.

Sieburg, Heinz-Otto. *Deutschland und Frankreich in der Geschichtsschreibung des neunzehnten Jahrhunderts*. (Veröffentlichungen des Instituts für europäische Geschichte Mainz, vols. II & XVII) 2 vols. Wiesbaden: F. Steiner, 1954–58.

Sked, Alan. *The Survival of the Habsburg Empire: Radetzky, the Imperial Army and Class War 1848*. London and New York: Longmans, 1979.

Sproxton, C. *Palmerston and the Hungarian Revolution*. Cambridge: Cambridge University Press, 1919.

Stadelmann, Rudolph. *Social and Political History of the German 1848 Revolution*. James G. Chastain, trans. Athens, Ohio: Ohio University Press, 1975.

Stewart-McDougall, Mary Lynn. *The Artisan Republic: Revolution, Reaction, and Resistance in Lyon, 1848–1851*. Kingston & Montreal: McGill-Queen's University Press, 1984.

Stroup, Edsel Walter. *Hungary in Early 1848: The Constitutional Struggle Against Absolutism in Contemporary Eyes*. Buffalo, N.Y. and Atlanta, Georgia: Hungarian Cultural Foundation, 1977.

Taylor, A. J. P. *The Italian Problem in European Diplomacy, 1847–1849*. (Publications of the University of Manchester, Historical Series, LXVII) Manchester: Manchester University Press, 1934.

_____. *The Struggle for Mastery in Europe, 1848–1918*. London: Oxford University Press, 1957.

Tersen, E. *Le Gouvernement provisoire et l'Europe (25 février–12 mai 1848)*. (Collection du centenaire de la Révolution de 1848) Paris: Presses universitaires de France, 1948.

Traugott, Mark. *Armies of the Poor: Determinants of Working Class Participation in the Parisian Insurrection of June 1848*. Princeton: Princeton University Press, 1985.

Treitschke, Heinrich von. "Frankreichs Staatsleben und der Bonapartismus," in *Historische und Politische Aufsätze*. Vol. III, 5th ed. Leipzig: Hirzel, 1886.

Trevelyan, G. M. *Manin and the Venetian Revolution of 1848*. London: Longmans, Green, 1923.

Valentin, Veit. *Geschichte der deutschen Revolution von 1848/49*. 2 vols. Aalen: Scientia Verlag, 1930–31, 1968.

Weber, Rolf. *Die Revolution in Sachsen 1848/49: Entwicklung und Analyse ihrer Triebkräfte*. Berlin: Akademie Verlag, 1970.

Weimar Volker. *Der Malmöer Waffenstillstand von 1848*. (Quellen und Forschungen zur Geschichte Schleswig-Holsteins, XL) Neumünster: Wachholtz, 1959.

Whitehouse, H. R. *The Life of Lamartine*. 2 vols. Boston: Houghton Mifflin, 1918.

Wollstein, Günter. *Das "Grossdeutschland" der Paulskirche: Nationale Ziele in der Bürgerliche Revolution 1848/49*. Düsseldorf: Droste, 1977.

Periodical Literature

Albertini, Rudolf von. "Frankreichs Stellungnahme zur deutschen Einigung während des zweiten Kaiserreiches," *Schweizerische Zeitschrift für Geschichte*, V, Heft 3 (1955), 305–68.

Amann, Peter H. "Writings on the Second French Republic," *Journal of Modern History*, XXXIV (1962), 409–29.

Barante, P. de. "Les procédés diplomatiques de Palmerston," *Revue d'histoire diplomatique*, XLV (1931), 413–29.

Black, C. E. "Poznan and Europe in 1848," *Journal of Central European Affairs*, VIII (1948), 191–206.

Boyer, Ferdinand. "Charles-Albert et le IIe République," *Rassegna storica del Risorgimento*, L (1963), 463–512.

⸺⸺⸺⸺. "Comment la France arme le Piémont en 1848," *Rassegna storica del Risorgimento*, XLIX (1962), 485–90.

⸺⸺⸺⸺. "Les entretiens franco-autrichiens de juin 1848," *Revue des Travaux de l'Academie des Sciences morales et politiques*, CVI (1953), 15–24.

⸺⸺⸺⸺. "Le fournitures d'armes faites par le gouvernement français aux patriotes italiens en 1848 et 1849," *Rassegna storica del Risorgimento*, XXXVII (1950), 85–102.

⸺⸺⸺⸺. "Lamartine et le Piémont (24 février–10 mai 1848)," *Revue d'histoire diplomatique*, LXIII (1950), 37–57.

⸺⸺⸺⸺. "La marine de la IIe République et la révolution sicilienne de février à juillet 1848," *Etudes d'histoire moderne et contemporaine*, II (1948), 184–203.

⸺⸺⸺⸺. "Pie IX à Gaète et l'admiral Baudin," *33e Congresso di Storia del Risorgimento italiano* (1954), 56–63.

⸺⸺⸺⸺. "Les premiers contacts entre Lamartine et Brignole de Sale, ambassadeur de Sardaigne à Paris," *Revue d'histoire diplomatique*, LXXIX (1965), 22–35.

_____. "Le problème de l'Italie du Nord dans les relations entre la France et l'Autriche (février–juillet 1848)," *Rassegna storica del Risorgimento*, XLII (1955), 206–17.

_____. "Les rapports entre la France et le Piémont sous le premier ministère de Jules Bastide (11 mai–28 juin)," *Revue d'histoire moderne et contemporaine*, V (1958), 129–36.

[Broglie, Albert de.] "De la politique étrangère de la France depuis la révolution du février," *Revue des deux mondes*, XXIII (August 1, 1848), 293–321.

Carpathinus. "1848 and Roumanian Unification," *Slavic and East European Review*, XXVI (1948), 390–419.

Cataluccio, Francesco. "Piemonte e Prussia nel 1848–49," *Archivo Storico Italiano*, CVI (1948), 62–95.

Chalmin, P. "Les Crises dans l'armée française, 1830–1848," *Revue d'histoire de l'armée*, XVIII (1962), no. 2, 65–82 and no. 4, 45–62.

_____. "La crise morale de l'armée française," *Bulletin de la Société d'Histoire de la Révolution de 1848: Etudes*, XVIII (1955), 28–76.

Chastain, James G. "Bakunin as a French Secret Agent in 1848," *History Today*, XXXI (August, 1981), 5–9.

_____. "France's Proposed Danubian Confederation in 1848," in *The Consortium on Revolutionary Europe 1750–1850: Proceedings 1978*. Robert Holtman, ed. Athens, Georgia: University of Georgia, 1980.

_____. "Iratok Franciaország Magyarországi Politikájának Történetéhez 1848-ban," *Levéltari Közlemények* (Budapest), XVVII (1976) no. 2, 269–94.

_____. "Jules Bastide et l'unité allemande en 1848," *Revue historique*, 511 (juillet–septembre 1974), 51–72.

Curato, Federico. "Il Parlamento di Francoforte e la prima guerra d'indipendenza italiana," *Archivo Storico Italiano*, CX (1952), 254–95; CXI (1953), 109–65, 265–94.

_____. "La Toscana e la mediazione anglo-francese," *Archivo Storico Italiano*, CVI (1948), 96–183.

Deme, Laszlo. "Nationalism and Cosmopolitanism among the Hungarian Radicals," *Austrian History Yearbook*, XII–XIII (1976–77), 36–44.

_____. "The Society for Equality in the Hungarian Revolution of 1848," *Slavic Review*, XXXI (1972), 71–88.

Dziewanowski, M. K. "1848 and the Hotel Lambert," *Slavic and East European Review*, XXVI (1948), 361–73.

Florescu, Radu, "Stratford Canning, Palmerston and the Wallachian Revolution of 1848," *Journal of Modern History*, XXXV (1963), 227–44.

Giradet, Raoul. "Autour de quelques problèmes," *Bulletin de la Société d'Histoire de la Révolution de 1848: Etudes*, XVIII (1955).

Griewank, Karl, "Ursachen und Folgen des Scheiterns der deutschen Revolution von 1848," *Historische Zeitschrift*, CLXX (1950), 495–523.

Guyard, Marius-François. "Les idées politiques de Lamartine," *Revue des Travaux de l'Academie des sciences morales et politiques*, CXIX/pt. 2 (1966), 1–16.

Hamerow, Theodore S. "History and the German Revolution of 1848," *American Historical Review*, LX (1954), 27–44.

Hammen, Oscar. "Free Europe versus Russia 1830–1854," *American Slavic and East European Review*, XI (1952), 27–41.

Handelsman, Marceli, "1848 et la question polonaise," *1848*, XXXIX (1948), 24–38.

_____. "Nicholas I et Czartoryski," *Le monde slav*, N. S. IX (1932), 237–58.

Henry, Paul. "Le gouvernement provisoire et la question polonaise en 1848," *Revue historique*, vol. 178 (1936), 198–240.

_____. "La France et les nationalités en 1848, d'après les correspondances diplomatiques," *Revue historique*, vol. 186 (1939), 48–77; vol. 188 (1940), 234–58.

Hildebrandt, Günter. "Die Stellung der äussersten Linken in der Frankfurter Nationalversammlung zur Polenfrage in Sommer 1848," *Jahrbuch für Geschichte der sozialistischen Länder Europas*, XVII (1973), 87–106.

Hirsch, Helmut. "Karl Ludwig Bernays: Ein Emigrierter Schriftsteller als US-Konsul in der Schweiz," *Jahrbuch des Instituts für Deutsche Geschichte* (Tel-Aviv), IV (1975), 147–65.

_____. "Karl Ludwig Bernays: Heines Kampgefährte aus den vierziger Jahren," *Heine Jahrbuch*, XIII (1974), 85–102.

Jennings, Lawrence C. "French diplomacy and the first Schleswig-Holstein crisis," *French Historical Studies*, VII (1971), 204–25.

_____. "Lamartine's Italian Policy in 1848: A Reexamination," *Journal of Modern History*, XLII (1970), 331–41.

Knieniewicz, Stefan. "L'histoire polonaise de l'année 1848," *1848*, XLII (1950), 167–73.

Knight, Jean. "Lamartine: ministre des affaires étrangères," *Revue d'histoire diplomatique*, XX (1906), 260–84.

Lefevre, Andre. "La reconnaissance de la Seconde République par l'Angleterre," *Revue d'histoire diplomatique*, LXXXII (1968), 213–31.

Lengyel, Thomas. "La mission parisienne du Comte Ladislas Teleki," *Nouvelle Revue de Hongrie*, February, 1941, 100–17.

Ley, Friedrich. "Frankreich und die deutsche Revolution von 1848–49," *Preussische Jahrbücher*, CCXIII (1928), 199–216.

Lucet, Charles. "Lamartine, Tocqueville, Gobineau . . . les Ministres des Affaires Etrangères de la Seconde République et leurs cabinets," *Revue d'histoire diplomatique*, XCIII (1979), no. 3–4, 247–78.

Marcks, Erich. "Die europäischen Mächte und die 48er Revolution," *Historische Zeitschrift*, CXLII (1930), 73–87.

Mattheisen, Donald J. "Review Essay: History as Current Events: Recent Works on the German Revolution of 1848," *American Historical Review*, LXXXVIII (1983), 1219–37.

Obermann, Karl. "Die Rolle der zaristischen Hilfs- und Interventionspläne gegen die Revolution in der ersten Häfte des Jahres 1848," *Jahrbuch für Geschichte der U.d.S.S.R. und den volksdemokratischen Länder Europas*, VIII (1964), 179–212.

Orr, William J. Jr. "La France et la révolution allemande de 1848–49," *Revue d'histoire diplomatique*, XCIII (1979), 300–30.

Pascal, Roy. "The Frankfurt Parliament 1848 and the *Drang nach Osten*," *Journal of Modern History*, XVIII (1946), 108–22.

Pfitzner, Josef. "Michael Bakunin und Preussen im Jahre 1848," *Jahrbücher für Kultur und Geschichte der Slaven*, n. s. VIII (1931), 231–84.

Rath, R. John. "The Viennese liberals of 1848 and the nationality problem," *Journal of Central European Affairs*, XV (1955), 227–39.

Schieder, Theodor. "Das Italienbild der deutschen Einheitsbewegung," *Studi Italiana*, III (1959), 141–62.

——————. "Nationalstaat und Nationalitätenproblem," *Zeitschrift für Ostforschung*, I (1952), 161–81.

Urbán, Aladár. "Zehn kritische Tage aus der Geschichte der Batthyány-Regierung (10–20 Mai 1848)," *Annales Universitatis Scientiarium Budapestitenis . . . Sectio Historica*, (1960), II, 91–124.

Vidal, Caesar. "La IIe République et le Royaume de Sardaigne en 1849," *Rassegna Storica del Risorgimento*, XXXVIII (1950), 505–30.

——————. "La France et la question italienne en 1848," *Etudes d'histoire moderne et contemporaine*, II (1948), 162–83.

——————. "La Toscane et la France au lendemain de la chute de Louis-Philippe, mars–septembre 1848," *Bullettino senese di storica patria*, 3e serie 58–59 (1951/52), 19–27.

Weber, Frank G. "Palmerston and Prussian Liberalism, 1848," *Journal of Modern History*, XXXV (1963), 125–36.

Weber, Rolf. "Das Verhältnis der kleinbürgerlicher Demokratie in Sachsen zur polnischen Frage 1848," *Zeitschrift für Geschichtswissenschaft*, XVI (1968), nr. 7, 855–73.

Zaniewicki, W. "L'armée au lendemain de la révolution de février 1848," *Cahiers d'histoire*, XIV (1969), 393–419.

Unpublished Doctoral Dissertations

Bader, E. "Lamartine Stellung zur Februar Revolution 1848." Thun, Switzerland, 1923.

Bernstein, Paul. "The Rhine Problem during the Second Republic and the Second Empire." University of Pennsylvania, 1955.

Berry, Robert Allen. "Czartoryski and Balkan Policies of the Hotel Lambert." University of Indiana, 1974.

Castelli, Helen Johnson. "Alphonse de Lamartine: A Re-evaluation of his Role in Nineteenth Century French Political Life." University of Colorado, 1975.

Droz, H. "Lamartine und die Revolution von 1848." Zurich: J. Ruegg, 1919.

Flaad, P. "England und die Schweiz: 1848–52." Zurich: Baretswil, 1935.

Hahn, Robert John. "The Attitude of the French Revolutionary Government toward German Unification in 1848." Ohio State University, 1955.

Hawgood, John A. "Political and Economic Relations between the United States of America and the German Provisional Central Government at Frankfurt am Main in 1848–49." Heidelberg, 1928.

House, Jonathan Mallory. "Public Force in Paris: February 22 to June 26, 1848." University of Michigan, 1975.

Jennings, Lawrence. "The Conduct of French Foreign Affairs in 1848: The Diplomacy of a Republic divided within itself." Wayne State University, 1967.

Kunde, Günther. "Die deutsche Revolution von 1848 und die italienische Frage." Königsberg dissertation 1937, excerpt published Saalfeld (East Prussia), 1938.

Lange, Ernst-Georg. "Frankreichs Preussenpolitik in den Jahren 1848 bis 1850." University of Berlin, 1930.

Ley, Friedrich. "Frankreich und die deutsche Revolution 1848–49." Kiel, 1923.

Martin, Kenneth Robert. "British and French Diplomacy and the Sardinian War, 1848–1849." University of Pennsylvania, 1965.

Mertes, Alois. "Frankreichs Stellungnahme zur deutschen Revolution im Jahre 1848," Bonn, 1951.

Pfisterer, Otto. "Preussen und Frankreich im Jahre 1848." Tübingen, 1921.

Poesponegoro, R. A. Marwati Djoened. "La France devant le problème polonais en 1848–1849." University of Paris, 1968.

Renzing, Rudiger. "Die Handelsbeziehungen zwischen Frankreich und Deutschland von der Gründung des Zollvereins bis zur Reichsgründung." Frankfurt/Main, 1959.

Roth, Hans. "Die Linke in der Paulskirche und der Nationalismus." Freiburg, 1950.

Scherer, Paul H. "British Policy with respect to the Unification of Germany, 1848–1871." University of Wisconsin, 1964.

Tannewitz, Hans-Karl. "M. A. Bakunins publizistische Persönlichkeit dargestellt an seiner politisch-journalistischen Arbeit 1849 in Dresden." Free University of Berlin, 1962.

Telle, H. G. "Das österreichische Problem im Frankfurter Parlament in Sommer und Herbst 1848." Marburg, 1933.

Williams, Harvey R. "British Policy and Attitudes towards France, February 22 to June 23, 1848." University of Chicago, 1962.

Zaniewicki, Witold. "L'Armée française en 1848, introduction à une étude militaire de la Deuxième République (22 février–20 décembre 1848)." 2 vols. Thèse de 3e cycle. University of Paris, 1966.

INDEX

In the sequence of entries, diacritics have been disregarded.